Japanese American
Celebration and Conflict

AMERICAN CROSSROADS

Edited by Earl Lewis, George Lipsitz, Peggy Pascoe,
George Sánchez, and Dana Takagi

Japanese American Celebration and Conflict

A History of Ethnic Identity and Festival, 1934–1990

Lon Kurashige

University of California Press
Berkeley · Los Angeles · London

Cover: Japanese American youth in 1972 burning a
Japanese World War II "war flag" in protest of
Japan's participation in the Vietnam War and the
rising influence of Japanese multinational
corporations in Little Tokyo. *Courtesy Visual
Communications.*

University of California Press
Berkeley and Los Angeles, California

University of California Press, Ltd.
London, England

Library of Congress Cataloging-in-Publication Data

Kurashige, Lon
  Japanese American celebration and conflict : a
history of ethnic identity and festival, 1934–1990 /
Lon Kurashige.
     p.   cm.—(American crossroads ; 8)
  Includes bibliographical references (p.) and index.
  ISBN 0-520-22472-5 (alk. paper)—
  ISBN 0-520-22743-3 (pbk. : alk. paper)
  1. Japanese Americans—California—Los
Angeles—Social life and customs—20th century.
2. Japanese Americans—California—Los
Angeles—Social conditions—20th century.
3. Japanese Americans—Ethnic identity—
California—Los Angeles.   4. Ethnic festivals—
California—Los Angeles—History—20th century.
5. Citizens' associations—California—Los
Angeles—History—20th century.   6. Los Angeles
(Calif.)—Ethnic relations.   7. Los Angeles
(Calif.)—Social life and customs—20th century.
8. Los Angeles (Calif.)—Social conditions—
20th century.   I. Title.   II. Series.

F869.L89 J338   2002
979.4'94004956—dc21   2001006510

Manufactured in the United States of America
10   09   08   07   06   05   04   03   02
10   9   8   7   6   5   4   3   2   1

The paper used in this publication meets the
minimum requirements of ANSI/NISO Z39.48–1992
(R 1997) (*Permanence of Paper*).⊗

To my parents
Nori and Mil Kurashige
for teaching me about my ethnicity
and then letting me figure it out for myself

Contents

Illustrations

Tables

Preface

American history shows that immigrant groups eventually become incorporated into the mainstream society and adopt the nation's social norms, values, culture, and sense of peoplehood. But it is also clear that newcomers and their descendants retain a sense of ethnic group identity rooted in an affective connection to the old world as well as to hardships and advantages experienced in the United States. The historian offers a compromise between these seemingly divergent patterns by approaching ethnic identity as a historical proposition, whose meaning and significance change over time. This perspective nicely captures the chameleon-like nature of identity, which is a historical creation contingent upon the structural and symbolic systems of a society at a given point in time. But recognizing identity as a situational affinity still leaves open the question of how immigrants and ethnics have recognized group ties in the first place. The question is not simply what identity has meant, but how its meaning has been inculcated, socialized, imposed, or, more generically, created at specific historical moments.

How this *process* of identity formation played out in the experience of Japanese Americans in Los Angeles reveals the false dichotomy between assimilation and ethnic retention. What is needed is a new framework for understanding ethnic identity that sees it as more than the antitheses of assimilation. It is my contention that conceptions of Japanese American identity operated like laws and statutes. While prompted by historical circumstances, these conceptions were not determined by them alone. Ideas of group and group membership were always mediated through an unstable, unpredictable, and uneven process of political conflict. Because there were no legislatures through which ethnic identity could be created nor any sanctioned body that could enforce such a disposition, Japanese Americans engaged in informal means of promoting and policing group boundaries. One of the most effective of these was ethnic tradition, which communicated intensive meanings about who belonged to the group and on what terms. If we are to comprehend the formation of Japanese American identity, we must be made aware of the political significance of the rituals, commemorations, folk histories, and other community dramas of the group. To gain this awareness, there is no better place to start than Los Angeles's annual Japanese celebration, the Nisei Week festival.[1]

The title of this book, *Japanese American Celebration and Conflict*, underscores the politics behind Nisei Week festivities. Always lurking in the *celebration* was the fact—and fear—of racial *conflict*. Conflict continued to occur even after the dramatic decline in unabashed anti-Japanese hostility and discrimination since World War II. The main concern among generations of Nisei Week leaders was the public image of Japanese Americans, which consistently managed to put the group at risk in American society. In this sense, the festival was the ethnic leadership's attempt to defuse threatening images of the group, a process race theorists Michael Omi and Howard Winant call "racial rearticulation." But in rearticulating racial sentiments, the celebration also re-created other conflicts internal to the Japanese American community. These were indigenous orchestrations of authority conveyed through differences in generation, culture, and nationality, but they were also rooted in less-acknowledged and less-understood distinctions of gender and class within the ethnic community. In this way, a range of overlapping social hierarchies internal to Japanese America was legitimized and maintained by the response to anti-Japanese racism at Nisei Week.

To recognize, let alone make sense of, these inner conflicts requires a second look at the terms used to describe Japanese American history. The cornerstone of almost all studies of Japanese Americans is the delineation of generations, known as Issei, Nisei, Sansei, etc. I have maintained these distinctions because they have become unavoidable vehicles of Japanese American self-identification. But I have expanded the definition of generation to also mean historical and age cohorts (e.g., the 1960s generation and the older Nisei). I have done so in order to capture the affinities (and conflicts) within and between the conventionally marked generational groupings. Thus the word *generation* refers to both a demographic-historical formation and a revealing interpretive stance.

Ethnic leadership and *ethnic community* also signify a range of objective positions and subjective understandings of them. Instead of limiting leadership solely to officers of ethnic associations, such as Nisei Week's board of directors or official staff, I have expanded the notion of group leadership to include journalists, businesspersons, and others who were able to sway or represent group opinion, whether or not they were involved with Nisei Week. *Ethnic community* connotes a nested geography of populations, from all Japanese Americans in the United States to those in southern California (where the largest concentration remains in the city of Los Angeles) to the historic downtown neighborhood of Little Tokyo. (*Ethnic enclave* has the same meaning but is reserved for business and economic relations.) *Community* also takes on a political designation as the constituency from which ethnic leaders have sought to manufacture consent.

The principal term in this book, *identity*, is hardest to pin down. Perhaps historian David A. Hollinger is right in suggesting that *identity* carries too much psychological (I would add ideological) baggage to convey the social process and contingencies in formulating conceptions of one's ethnic or racial group(s). But his alternative, *affiliation*, seems to tip the balance too far to the voluntary side of being Japanese American. There was, and still is, an inescapable degree of "fixity and giveness" of being a racial minority like Japanese Americans.[2] So instead of deleting *identity*, I have distinguished different types of identities (Nisei identity, cosmopolitan identity, student radical identity, etc.) and placed them within an arena of competition by contrasting identities of internal legitimation (ethnic orthodoxies) with identities of illegitimized contestation (ethnic options or heterodoxy). Such a perspective structures the fluidity and multiplicity of identity along a coherent, though hardly simple, grid of intragroup relations.

I have sought to capture the indigenous process of Japanese American identity by tracing the transformation of Nisei Week since it was first observed in 1934. This task has required the reconstruction of parades, folk dances, beauty pageants, talent shows, essay contests, and cultural exhibits and a wide variety of other planned and spontaneous performances. There are no specific archival records to help the historian in this task. To understand what happened at Nisei Week, as well as the objectives and motivations of its leaders, I relied considerably upon selective, and sometimes frustratingly sparse, information contained in

Japanese American newspapers. The two main sources—*Rafu Shimpo* and *Kashu Mainichi*—were published daily and, by the time Nisei Week began, had nearly independent sections written in both English and Japanese. Another important source was Nisei Week's souvenir booklet, which was created for every celebration since 1940.

To supplement written records, I conducted more than fifty interviews with former Nisei Week officials and participants, who, as a whole, comprised a cast of thousands, since the festival sought to embrace the entire ethnic community, and its leadership, which was always extensive, changed nearly every year. These interviews, then, were not a random sample. They highlighted the recollections of men (and a few women) in positions of authority and those who had reigned as festival beauty queens. The results confirmed the strengths and weaknesses of oral history: Some informants provided invaluable insights, while others, although friendly and cooperative, had less reliable recollections.

If the historical record does not permit one to piece together the complete history of Nisei Week, it is more than adequate for observing the process of identity formation embedded within this festival. In examining Nisei Week, I have assumed that this event has been crucial for learning what it means to be Japanese American. To the ethnographer, Nisei Week may be an important ritual in which Japanese Americans "reveal themselves to themselves" and, in the process, reenact their deepest values, norms, and social practices. But to the social historian, the festival is a window to understanding the inner history of a subordinated racial minority group. More than a cultural affair, Nisei Week has been a means for Japanese Americans to craft group identity from, and against, a lexicon of racial images and discourse in American public life. From this perspective, Nisei Week becomes a critical site of political conflict and a means of social transformation.

The setting in which these power relations were worked out is important. More than two decades before the first Nisei Week, southern California was dotted with Japanese farms feeding the development of coethnic retail and wholesale markets in the budding metropolis of Los Angeles. By 1930, there were more than twenty-one thousand Japanese Americans in the city of Los Angeles. This was, and after World War II remained, the largest urban concentration of its kind in continental North America. Indeed, the case can be made that the significance of Los Angeles grew after World War II. As farmers migrated to cities and residents in Hawaii increasingly moved to the mainland, the urban pattern of Los Angeles became the unquestioned norm of Japanese American life. To understand Nisei Week, then, is to grasp the changing face of Japanese American settlement in Los Angeles. John Modell's *Economics and Politics of Racial Accommodation: The Japanese of Los Angeles* is particularly helpful in mapping the social structures prompting the creation and early growth of Nisei Week. There is, however, no comparable account of the long period since 1941. This book offers a beginning. Woven into the analysis of Nisei Week texts, symbols, and performances is a narrative about the development of the ethnic community from 1934 to 1990 that has been culled from internment camp records, city reports, oral interviews, the ethnic press, census and other statistical data, and a wealth of unpublished studies, particularly from the Japanese American Relocation and Resettlement Study collection at the Bancroft Library, University of California, Berkeley.

The focus on Los Angeles is not meant to deny the fact that every Japanese American community in the United States has had its own version of Nisei Week. The most obvious examples were *obon*, the Buddhist celebrations honoring dead ancestors.[3] While some of these *obon* festivals have been observed as long or longer than Nisei Week, as a rule, they were private affairs for temple members and their circle of family, friends, and fellow Buddhists. Organizers of Nisei Week, on the other hand, reached out to Japanese Americans irrespective of religion or neighborhood, and especially welcomed civic leaders and the general public. As a decidedly public event, Nisei Week stood at the crossroads between a wide variety of constituencies within and outside the Japanese American community. Consequently, only a few Japanese American festivals rivaled its attendance and scale of production, and none of these matched Nisei Week's longevity. In this sense, the Nisei Week festival is the most appropriate place to search for the political significance of Japanese American traditions.

Acknowledgments

One of the greatest rewards in pursuing this study was discovering, over and over again, the rich diversity within the Japanese American community. I want to thank the following individuals, many of whom I relied upon for information: Yaye Aihara, Kenji Arai, Misusa Bando, Judy Sugita de Querioz, Gerald Fukui, Warren Furutani, Frances Hashimoto, Robert Hayamizu, Faith Higarashi Ono, Edwin Hiroto, Wimp Hiroto, Harry Honda, Roy Hoshizaki, Yuji Ichioka, Carol Itatani, Candice Ito, Fujima Kansuma, Taro Kawa, Margaret Kawaichi, Hiromichi Kume, Katsumi Kunitsugu, the late John Maeno, Archie Miyatake, the late Katsuma Mukaeda, Chris Naito, Brian Nakagiri, Mike Nakayama, Sue Okabe, James Okazaki, Sandra Posey, Kevin Quock, Masami Sam Seno, Victor Shibata, Louise Suski, Yo Takagaki, Arthur Takei, Togo Tanaka, Sandra Toshiyuki, Henry Tsurutani, Ron Wakabayashi, Emiko Yamada, Harry Yamamoto, Mike Yamamoto, Joanne Yamashiro, George Yoshinaga, and Riye Yoshizawa.

This project began as a Ph.D. dissertation at the University of Wisconsin, Madison, where Tom Archdeacon introduced to me the historiography of American immigration and ethnicity. This was also where John Fiske introduced to me the significance of popular culture. Other professors who directly or indirectly shaped my initial thoughts about race, identity, and American history include Allan Bogue, Linda Gordon, Gerda Lerner, Herbert Hill, Suzanne Desan, Richard Flores, Michael Thornton, and Elizabeth Ellsworth. Tom Archdeacon, Allan Bogue,

Laura Guy, Halliman Winsborough, Yuko Mizuno oriented me to the world of statistics. Amy Ling, Mary Rouse, and Suzanne Jones graciously enabled me to get paid for raising my own awareness of Asian American history and U.S. race relations. Most of all, my peers and friends in seminars and political struggle challenged me to approach history as a vehicle for social change. I owe my greatest debts to Peter Chen, Joan Varney, Victor Jew, Jennifer Frost, Paul Taillon, Laura McEnaney, Susan Traverso, Gunther Peck, Steve Casanova, Alejandra Elenas, Fong Hermes, Wendy Ho, Jan Miyasaki, Peggy Choy, and Marc Goulden.

Another invaluable resource for this book was the University of California. My debt to the UC system began at UC Santa Barbara, where Laura Kalman and the late Robert Kelley began my interest in U.S. history as an undergraduate, and, where, from 1993 to 1994, Sucheng Chan welcomed me back to complete my dissertation on fellowship in the department of Asian American Studies. The Asian American Studies Center at the University of California, Los Angeles, provided me with a Rockefeller fellowship in 1992–93, which enabled me to tap the school's rich archives in Japanese American history. Being at UCLA also allowed me to forge ties to an outstanding group of researchers and thinkers including Brian Hayashi, Brian Niiya, David Yoo, Valerie Matsumoto, Yuji Ichioka, Eiichiro Azuma, and Russell Leong.

The third university that figures prominently in the writing of this book is the University of Southern California, where I have taught history and American Studies and Ethnicity since 1995. At USC I have benefited from discussions with George Sanchez, Steve Ross, Lois Banner, Mauricio Mazon, Charlotte Furth, Jack Willis, Vince Cheng, Judith Jackson-Fossett, Dorrine Kondo, Mary Dudziak, and Soo-young Chin. Special mention must be reserved for Philippa Levine for reading many drafts of my work and training me in the game of academia. Also at USC, I was fortunate to receive a junior faculty stipend for the completion of my book through the Southern California Studies Center.

This book has benefitted as well from a generous grant from the Civil Liberties Public Education Fund. I have also been honored to receive funding from the National Endowment for the Humanities and the John Randolf and Dora Haynes Foundation. The Japanese American National Museum, through Akemi Kikumura, was instrumental in helping me locate and interview my informants. Cameron Trowbridge, JANM's Hirasaki national resource center manager, has been extremely gracious in allowing me to reproduce images in this book from the museum's extensive photographic archives. Likewise, I want to thank the *Journal of*

American History and the *Pacific Historical Review* for permitting me to reproduce major parts of my articles "The Problem of Biculturalism: Japanese American Identity and Festival before World War II," *JAH* 86, no. 4 (March 2000): 1632–54 and "Resistance, Collaboration, and Manzanar Protest," *PHR* 70, no. 3 (August 2001): 387–417. As *JAH*'s former editors, David Thelen and David Nord offered intelligent feedback on this article that ended up sharpening my ideas about the relationship between internal and external orchestrations of Japanese American identity. At an earlier stage in this research, Alice Yang-Murray pointed out valuable sources regarding the criticism of Japanese American beauty pageants. Dean Toji generously loaned to me a wealth of materials about Little Tokyo redevelopment. And the Los Angeles History Research Group, through the graces of Clark Davis, Father Michael Engh, and the Huntington Library, provided a welcome forum to reflect upon the early history of Nisei Week.

My "American Crossroads" editors at the University of California Press in many ways served as a dream dissertation committee. George Sanchez, Dana Takagi, and especially Peggy Pascoe gave me more and better criticism than I could hope for, while always being upbeat and complimentary. I am happy to say that I have incorporated virtually all of their suggestions, as well as many of those from two anonymous reviewers. At UC press, I also want to thank my editor, Monica McCormick, and Suzanne Knott, Ellen G. Browning, and Diana Feinberg for facilitating the publication process.

My biggest intellectual debt is to Asian American Studies, which early on in my studies had a transformative impact on my sense of self, ethnic community, race relations, and American history. The writings of Roger Daniels, Ronald Takaki, and many others opened my eyes to the profound significance of anti-Asia racism and inspired me to insert Asian American history into multicultural struggles within and beyond the academy. The most lasting impact of my thinking came from those scholars with whom I have had a personal connection. I met Michael Omi not long after the publication of his and Howard Winant's *Racial Formation in the United States,* and ever since then I have been pleased to know that such a brilliant thinker can also be accessible, genuine, and downright fun. The importance of his and Winant's theory of racial formation is everywhere apparent in this work. Dana Takagi influenced me in different ways. In 1985, she taught the first course I took in Asian American Studies and has continued to teach me about the ironies and contradictions of race in American society. Finally, Brian Hayashi took me under his wing and showed me, mostly through his own example, how to do archival research. He has taken time away from his pathbreaking studies of Japanese American history to send me sources and to read my entire book manuscript in two different versions. His pages of learned comments have saved me from many intellectual missteps and factual errors. Those that remain, of course, are neither his nor anyone else's fault—they are, as convention dictates, mine alone.

Here, it seems, is perhaps the greatest occupational hazard for the historian: the solitary nature of our work. While it may be cliché to thank one's spouse and children for simply being there with love and encouragement and laughter, I cannot think of another way to acknowledge the deepest source of my support. Anne Cherian Kurashige, in addition to editing repeated drafts of the manuscript, has talked with me about it almost every day of our married life; in this capacity she did more than anyone to facilitate its completion. In contrast, our sons, Cole and Reid, were born in the midst of this project and, in their own way, impeded its fruition. Nothing, however, has pleased me more. My ultimate hope is that they and their generation will approach ethnic identity as neither a thing to embrace nor reject but as an opportunity to understand and recast systems of power, privilege, and subordination among Japanese Americans, within American society, and even beyond the nation's borders.

Introduction

The Problem of Racial Rearticulation

This study was born of the conviction, held even more firmly now at the study's conclusion, that our perception of American history is misserved by the image of Japanese Americans as a successful "model minority" group. The Issei and their descendants are certainly worthy of appreciation for having overcome intense and prolonged bouts of racial persecution, including the forced internment of 120,000 American citizens and permanent residents. But the many "unsuccessful" peoples (e.g., blacks, Native Americans, Latinos) also command our deepest admiration for having broken through formidable barriers of subjugation—sometimes merely by surviving and passing down glimpses of what they had endured. To speak of a model minority is to ignore the range of ways in which American racism has been experienced, engaged, and resisted. In such a discourse, the historian's craft is reduced to judging "success" or "failure" rather than the more enlightening challenge of understanding the past with all its contradictions and complexity.[1]

Antimodel–minority literature is plagued by a similar reductionism. Critics of the model majority idea turn the image of Japanese Americans as a successful minority on its head. Rather than applauding Japanese Americans for gaining mainstream acceptance, these critics condemn American society for failing to provide a truly level playing field for all races. Their argument underscores the persistence of anti-Japanese racism by contending that the radical decline in overt, institutionalized prejudice since World War II is a smokescreen, concealing clandestine hatreds and discrimination in white America.[2] Japanese Americans, it has been observed, have continued to be victimized by racism and thus share a common experience with America's less-advantaged racial minority— "Yellow," one proponent asserts, "is a shade of black and black a shade of yellow."[3]

The critique of the model minority thesis is not wrong, but in blurring the distinction between Japanese Americans and blacks, it reproduces the narrow vision of Japanese American history as a process of success or failure. What explains this duality within the model minority critique, anthropologist Sylvia Yanagisako maintains, is the "tension between the desire of the founders of Asian American Studies to stand in solidarity with other people of color and the fact that in socioeconomic terms Asians Americans are more like White Americans."[4] That Japanese Americans confronted overt and entrenched racist institutions and structures before World War II makes it tempting to understand their response to racism within the theoretical framework of slave resistance. Doing so, however, risks relying upon notions of resistance made to explain power relations in vastly different social contexts.

The historical conditions for Japanese Americans on the West Coast were not the same as for blacks in the American South. The Issei and Nisei operated in racial situations in which they had a range of cultural, economic, and political resources at hand to contest and deflect domination. As both free immigrants and American citizens, Japanese Americans were able to challenge hegemonic assumptions about their racial characteristics through print media, public events (including Nisei Week), litigation, and formal conferences with government and military officials, even while they were interned during World War II. They also had the advantage (which of course was also a terrible burden during World War II) of representing a powerful nation. Through its consulates in the United States, the Japanese government guided and protected its overseas population, giving the Japanese American community in Los Angeles the imprimatur of diplomatic significance.

How, then, did Japanese Americans contest their racial predicament before, during, and after their World War II internment? What has been written about Japanese American responses to power falls into two schools of thought. The dominant perspective portrays Japanese Americans as trapped between the insularity of old-world traditions and hypermodern realities of American life. Its advocates maintain that as "marginal men," the second generation felt compelled to resolve their identity dilemma by rejecting Japanese traditions (often epitomized by their parents' generation) in order to root the ethnic group more firmly in the white American mainstream.[5] The narrative is a familiar one in immigration history: the American-born children of immigrants gradually and willfully liberate the ethnic group from the language and traditions that have kept the immigrant generation at the bottom of society. Thus Roger Daniels, a leading historian of Japanese Americans, insists that Japanese Americans were an ethnic group not intrinsically different from white ethnics. The twist for Japanese Americans was that racism delayed entrance into the American melting pot that already included European immigrants.[6]

A more recent but less-developed revisionism sees a promise, not a problem, in biculturalism. Focusing on U.S.-Japan relations before World War II, its proponents portray immigrant leaders as cultural diplomats seeking to reduce misunderstanding and conflict by creating a bridge between the cultures of Japan and America. The revisionists argue that most Nisei accepted assimilation only because the repression during World War II made alternative identities untenable. In short, not all Nisei were assimilationists in the 1930s. Brian Masaru Hayashi finds a deep ambivalence among second-generation Protestants about choosing between American or Japanese culture and deciding whether to join their parents' support for Japan's aggressions in East Asia. Jere Takahashi pins this ambivalence to different political perspectives among the second generation: assimilationists, notably the Japanese American Citizens League (JACL), a group of well-educated, second-generation businessmen and professionals, identified squarely with the United States and American culture, while other Nisei and *Kibei* (American citizens raised primarily in Japan) were either less interested in blending into the American mainstream or placed labor politics above one's cultural orientation. Finally, Yuji Ichioka contends that the JACLers' identity was more complex than their unquestioned allegiance to the United States suggested, for their assimilationism did not preclude support for Japanese imperialism.[7]

The differences between these two schools of thought are predicated on one of the central debates in the historiography of American immigration and ethnicity: whether newcomers choose to assimilate into the cultural mainstream or retain ethnic identities. The debate between "assimilationists" (the dominant perspective on Japanese Americans) and "retentionists" (the revisionist stance) has been reflected in the questions asked: When has ethnic or national identity been strong or weak? What factors in American history have made it this way? And, what role has racism in particular played in this process? Answering these questions, however, has forced the acceptance of a narrow range of choices that overlooks the commonalities between the assimilationist and retentionist positions. One of these similarities is that both sides more often than not have viewed race and ethnicity as artifacts of culture, as something to possess or of which to be dispossessed. As a result, they have approached identity as a thing to be discovered and measured rather than as a jumble of social texts to be sorted out and interpreted.[8] With respect to a similar problem in Chicano historiography, George J. Sánchez maintains that the emphasis on "bi-polar models that have stressed either cultural continuity [retentionists] or gradual acculturation [assimilationists] has short-circuited a full exploration of the complex process of cultural adaptation." In his study of Mexican Americans in Los Angeles, Sánchez contends that group identity was actually "betwixt and between" the poles of assimilation and retention; it was fluid, ambiguous, and contingent upon historical experience.[9]

In the past twenty years, students of American race and ethnicity have jettisoned the notion of assimilation, signaling the ultimate triumph of retentionism. But in so doing, a new debate has arisen within the retentionist camp. Writings from literary criticism, cultural studies, race theory, and sociology have changed the question from *whether* ethnic and racial identities are desirable to *how* they have been constructed. "Constructionists" see identity not as an inherent, social fact but as a transitive action predicated on attaining and maintaining authority.[10] To Michael Omi and Howard Winant, for example, race is a dialectic of contested racial meanings in which options compete for authenticity within a broad range of political struggles and everyday situations. By enacting "racism" in explicit and implicit ways, dominating groups have set the stage for those they have subordinated to advance their cause by reinterpreting racist discourse—thereby rearticulating it into an empowering racial identity.[11]

Omi and Winant ground their definition of racial rearticulation in the emergence of the Civil Rights Movement. They argue that the "greatest triumph" of civil rights leaders was not their legislative victories. Rather, it was the ability to infuse black folk culture with the teachings of Mahatma Gandhi and other students of colonial resistance: in other words, the creation of a "home-grown liberation theology." It was only by tapping into the cultural and religious language of black life that Dr. Martin Luther King Jr. and his colleagues were able to mobilize the black masses to support something entirely new to them and to American history: a direct, sustained, and collective confrontation with racist policies and practices. The Civil Rights Movement, Omi and Winant conclude, rearticulated black identity by offering its "adherents a different view of themselves and their world; different, that is, from the world-view and self-concepts offered by the established social order."[12]

The significance of racial rearticulation as conceptual device is its ability to explain more than the emergence of the Civil Rights Movement. If the movement's direct action politics were new, its transformation of racist discourse into grounds for black dignity and empowerment were, as Lawrence W. Levine explained more than two decades ago, part of a cultural lineage rooted in slavery. Levine reveals that slave work songs and spirituals, folktales, and understanding of Christianity were each reformulated from the master culture to sustain the slaves' self-esteem and nourish their souls.[13] In a more recent analysis, Evelyn Brooks Higginbotham also asserts that blacks and whites have interpreted race differently, evidencing a "double-voiced discourse" that has long served the "voice of black oppression and the voice of black liberation."[14] Yet she complicates the understanding of racial rearticulation by asserting that the voice of black liberation has concealed other voices within black America. She maintains that race is not simply a passive result of social pathologies and jaundiced assumptions about physical and cultural difference. Rather it is a vibrant and constantly changing creature that "impregnates the simplest meanings we take for granted" by subsuming "other sets of social relations, namely, gender and class." What makes race even more difficult to apprehend, Higginbotham adds, is that it "blurs and disguises, suppresses and negates its own complex interplay with the very social relations it envelops."[15] In other words, racial rhetoric contains hidden assumptions that establish gender and class hierarchies within, as well as outside, the black community.

This book addresses the problem of racial rearticulation for Japanese Americans as a response to pressures from white America and as a strategy for engineering consent within the ethnic community. In important ways, the formation of ethnic identity within the Los Angeles community was a process of turning the dominant language of race against itself. The overwhelming majority of Japanese Americans did not, as proponents of ethnic retention would have us believe, reject American institutions and ideals of democracy, patriotism, economic opportunity, and cultural adaptation. But this did not mean, as assimilationists would be quick to assert, that Japanese Americans got beyond race by forging color-blind affinities and perceptions of social reality. The main challenge to anti-Japanese sentiments and practices was rooted in neither the preservation nor the abandonment of ethnic traditions. It was Japanese Americans' fighting back by rewiring racism to serve their own collective needs and interests. Ethnic traditions, like those practiced during Nisei Week, may have been both preserved and abandoned, but more often they were rearticulated on the basis of perceived opportunities to gain broad-based acceptance, legitimacy, and class status—an American dream for any subjugated minority.

But racial rearticulation had boundaries of its own. In defining their identity, most Japanese Americans were constrained by their own desire to succeed in American society. Like folk heroes in black America, they sought to defeat white society on its own terms and by its own rules. They would triumph, as Levine says of legendary railroad worker John Henry and prizefighter Joe Louis, "not by breaking laws of the larger society but by smashing its expectations and stereotypes, by insisting that their lives transcend the traditional models and roles established for them and their people by the white majority." [16] For Japanese Americans this meant giving credence to social distinctions and hierarchies at the core of American culture: Men and masculinity were privileged over women and femininity; middle-class lifestyles and sensibilities were valued over those of the subordinate classes; and a Whiggish faith in the ultimate fairness of American government subsumed more critical and pessimistic concerns about state authority. Such preferences, of course, were not difficult for many Japanese Americans to accept, given the patriarchal and caste structures they had known in Japan. But once in the United States, this cultural inheritance fused with the new social circumstances to become distinctly Japanese American.

The imperative of group mobility also gave rise to a metalanguage of Japanese American identity that opposed external impositions of race by imposing a fictive sense of group solidarity within the ethnic community. The challenge for successive incarnations of the Japanese American leadership was to persuade, prod, or cajole their constituents to accept (or at least not to openly contradict) its particular version of collective identity. This *ethnic orthodoxy* concealed the opinions and experiences of those who did not (or could not) conform to the leadership's sanguine image of Japanese Americans. And more than this, they disciplined, punished, and stigmatized a shifting set of social groups (including generations, women, workers, radicals, and juvenile delinquents) whose very existence jeopardized group orthodoxy. Highlighting these sorts of *internal others* became an indispensable mechanism for teaching by example.

To point out the disobedient and disorderly was to underscore the cultural and political orientations befitting "proper" Japanese Americans.

But these internal others, too, were more than victims. They opposed ethnic orthodoxies, especially during times of severe crisis, such as the internment, through acts of criticism, aversion, disorder, and protest. And so it was that at the Manzanar, California, internment camp, where a large part of the Los Angeles Japanese American community was held, the ethnic leadership was unable, even with government coercion, to persuade the majority of their fellow internees to surrender their ethnic affiliations. In this sense, the rearticulation of Japanese American identity was a struggle not only for the ethnic group's self-determination but also for who within the group would determine the ethnic self.

The relationship between the community's leadership and its internal others was typically seen as a conflict between generations (such as Issei versus Nisei), but it was also rooted in a deep, historically precedented class cleavage within the ethnic community. By class, I do not mean a relationship to the means of production, for in this sense the overwhelming majority of Japanese Americans have belonged to the same class. I refer instead to different degrees of what Pierre Bourdieu calls economic and cultural capital (i.e., one's income, educational level, occupational prestige, family pedigree, aesthetic competence, moral authority, and gender consciousness). Social identities, according to Bourdieu, are rooted in the unconscious habits of mind and behavior (or *habitus*) that emerge with a given combination of economic and cultural capital.[17] Throughout the Japanese American experience, it was common for ethnic leaders, who possessed the highest forms of economic and cultural capital, to embrace a flexible identity that transcended racial and ethnic boundaries. On the other hand, those with the lowest degrees of economic and cultural capital were more likely to be viewed as internal others at odds with the leadership's ethnic prescriptions.

For example, *Meiji* intellectuals, Japan's great advocates of immigration to the West in the late nineteenth and early twentieth centuries, blamed the formation of anti-Japanese laws and immigration restrictions on the "backwardness" and parochialism of Japanese immigrants, who descended largely from the farming classes. As community leaders, the Meiji championed a sense of "cosmopolitanism" that upheld Western society as the highest standard of civilization and thus urged Japanese immigrants to adapt felicitously to American values, norms, and institutions. As a ruling orthodoxy, cosmopolitanism was an inherently gendered construct. It emphasized the importance of the public sphere as the crucial site where different races (and nations) engaged in a masculine struggle for power, resources, and respect. On the contrary, the ethnic community, given its perceived inferiority to white America, was seen as a feminine space in need of protection and governance. And so cosmopolitanism rested on a fictive opposition between courageous, intelligent, and cultured ethnic leaders and the childlike, clannish, and emotionally driven masses of Japanese Americans.

This class conflict among Japanese Americans should not be surprising; Harry H. L. Kitano, in an influential study of Japanese American identity, identified significant economic strata within the group. Based on sociologist Milton M. Gordon's conclusions about the primacy of class divisions within American ethnic groups, Kitano argued that Japanese Americans identified most closely with ethnic kin who shared their class and generational status. Hence a wealthy Nisei's first allegiance would be to other wealthy Nisei, and only secondarily to poorer Nisei, wealthy Issei, and other members of the ethnic group. Such class factions are also highlighted in more recent work in the social sciences. William Julius Wilson, for example, analyzes the economic and political forces after World War II that strained and severed ties between middle-class and working-class black Americans. And Peter Kwong points to a similar polarization occurring between Chinese Americans as a result of post-1965 immigration policies that attracted both highly skilled professionals and unskilled service and industrial workers.[18]

Still, despite the significance of class (and generational and gender) divisions, Japanese Americans retained a strong cohesiveness. This is the main question about Japanese American identity: How has the ethnic group maintained a sense of commonality given its internal diversity and unequal distribution of power? The notion of racial rearticulation suggests that Japanese Americans developed a sense of identity out of duress, having come together, despite their differences, for the greater purpose of fighting outside racial pressures. But understanding the racial stakes of group ties does not explain how Japanese Americans have come to recognize ethnic bonds. How did they know what it meant to be Japanese American as opposed to another ethnic group? Where were these group boundaries learned?

The burden of my argument is to show that the Nisei Week festival was a critical event at which Japanese American identity was promoted and enacted. In the past two decades, a growing number of historians have come to recognize that group identities are not the spontaneous products of social conditions (structures) but are mediated through the repetition of cultural experiences and practices. Eric Hobsbawn calls these mediations "invented traditions" since they fabricate a sense of group norms and values by disguising them as historical, primordial truths.[19] In this sense, festivals are among the most effective and universal mechanisms for inculcating fictive identities. Anthropologist and folklorists have long known that festivals are more than a mere moment of fun and celebration and more than a temporary escape from everyday life. "They are occasions," John J. MacAloon explains, "in which as a culture or society we reflect upon and define ourselves, dramatize our collective myths and history, present ourselves with alternatives, and eventually change in some ways while remaining the same in others."[20]

The historical study of festivals is predicated on this broad conception of such events as producers of social change and continuity. Mona Ozouf has shown that celebrations during the French Revolution instilled cultural orientations that were instrumental to the new regime. Takashi Fujitani maintains that Japan's modernization in the late nineteenth and early twentieth centuries was indebted to invented celebrations of the nation's emperor, while John Bodnar, in focusing on the festivals of American immigrant ethnics during the era of heightened nativism and xenophobia, also sees celebrations as a means of transforming local identities into a national consciousness. Robert Anthony Orsi focuses on the significance of ethnic festivals within the same period. His examination of an Italian American celebration reveals the evolution of an ethnic community as it comes to terms with rapidly changing gender roles, generational orientations, and religious perspectives and rituals.[21] It is within this body of work that I have come to investigate the Nisei Week festival. What studies there are about Japanese American festivals see the events as evincing a decline in authentic Japanese traditions or look at them for insight into contemporary social issues. There has never been an examination of Nisei Week that seeks to understand its historical significance for Japanese Americans and American immigration, ethnicity, and race relations.

The narrative of Nisei Week in this book reveals the articulation and rearticulation of Japanese American identity across six historical and social contexts. Chapter 1 traces the origins of Nisei Week in the Great Depression and within mounting tensions between the United States and Japan in the early 1930s. To bridge this international divide, the Los Angeles chapter of the JACL cooperated with the Issei leadership in sponsoring and planning Nisei Week. How these JACLers sought to use the festival to stimulate the depression-weary ethnic enclave is the subject of chapter 2. To drum up business, the Nisei were told that buying in Little

Tokyo was a litmus test of an authentic Japanese American, while, at the same time, whites were informed that shopping in the ethnic enclave offered them a true-to-life Japanese adventure. Yet outsiders were assured that underneath the exotic image of Japanese Americans was a safe community committed to the nation and its moral and cultural norms. As relations between the United States and Japan collapsed in the late 1930s and early 1940s, the connection of Nisei identity to ethnic consumption (through the medium of "biculturalism") was abandoned in an attempt to prevent the second generation from appearing anything less than 100 percent American.

In the absence of Nisei Week and other ethnic traditions during World War II, the enactment of Japanese American identity relied heavily upon the use of force and naked aggression. Chapter 3 follows many of Nisei Week's JACL leaders to Manzanar, where, with government backing, they championed a strong commitment to Americanization. Confronted with intense, and at times violent, resistance from their fellow internees, most of the leading JACLers left Manzanar as soon as they could and resettled away from the West Coast. The vast majority of the ethnic community, however, returned to Los Angeles and salvaged what they could of the ethnic enclave.

Chapter 4 examines the revival of Nisei Week within the re-creation of southern California Japanese America. With the removal of racist restrictions to employment within a decade of being released from the internment camps, Japanese Americans were much less constrained from pursuing social, economic, and educational opportunities in mainstream society. Yet how far to pursue integration was an open question. The principal division was between hard-line integrationists, typically JACLers who opposed any sort of ethnic community or mandatory solidarity, and most Japanese Americans, who were committed to a less radical integrationism that encouraged the voluntary retention of ethnic identity and affiliation.

By the late 1960s, America's involvement in Vietnam and the heightening criminalization of blacks generated a new tension among Japanese Americans that would explode at Nisei Week. Chapter 5 addresses the rise of a new generation of Japanese American intellectuals and activists who challenged the ideal of integration with a new, radical version of cosmopolitanism. These student activists, many of whom participated in a social movement among Asian Americans, clashed with the Nisei "old guard," but the two sides eventually managed to come together in their attempts to resuscitate the ethnic community. In the 1970s and 1980s,

Nisei Week rearticulated the radicalism of the Asian American movement in crafting a notion of identity politics that eschewed its utopian vision yet appropriated its more pragmatic calls for ethnic pride, political assertiveness, charitable mutual aid, and liberalization of women's roles.

Finally, the tremendous expansion of Japan's economy set the stage for a new conflict within Little Tokyo. Chapter 6 examines the division between a diverse group of Japanese Americans and multinational corporations from Japan. The influence of these corporations grew in the 1960s as the city of Los Angeles used the redevelopment of Little Tokyo to attract Japanese capital and tourism to southern California. By the 1980s, these corporate interests sought to change Nisei Week's name to "Japanese festival." The proposition galvanized a cross section of Japanese Americans (Nisei, Issei, conservatives, and radicals) to defend the festival's original name and to resist, as one Nisei put it, the "Jap invasion" in Little Tokyo.

In this way, the Nisei Week festival embodied the themes and identities of three large historical periods, characterized by the prewar ethnic enclave, the Manzanar internment camp, and postwar communities of professional, radical, and international identities. The festival was established to bolster Little Tokyo businesses and protect them from the goals of the anti-Japanese movement. During World War II, the festival's leadership became the internee leaders at Manzanar, and after the war, the festival symbolized the social mobility and increasing political power of Japanese Americans. In the 1970s, it was a repeated site of protest by student activists and, through this and the next decade, became increasingly Japanized, reflecting the growing amount of funds it received from Japanese multinational corporations. This trajectory of Nisei Week, as the following narrative will reveal, is, to a great extent, the trajectory of urban Japanese American history.

PART I

Enclave

ONE

Succeeding Immigrants

Ethnic Leadership and
the Origins of Nisei Week

Little Tokyo's weeklong celebration of ethnic pride, racial harmony, and international friendship emerged from very basic motivations. During the most severe depression the United States had ever seen, the immigrant leadership hoped that a Nisei festival, which included a parade, talent and fashion shows, cultural exhibits, and an essay contest, would entice patronage from Japanese American youth. The depression had compelled owners and managers of Japantown stores to look beyond the reliable base of Issei customers, whose rising incomes had transformed the ethnic enclave from an immigrant way station to a thriving business district. Indeed, the burgeoning of California agriculture and the increasing balance of power between the United States and Japan continually opened limited opportunities for the Issei that the anti-Japanese movement sought to deny. But the global crisis of 1929 changed all this. The depression did more than still abacuses in Little Tokyo; it undermined the entrepreneurial and diplomatic foundations of Issei settlement.

The origins of Nisei Week stemmed from this increasing domestic and international uncertainty. Although born of economic motivation, it was never simply a marketing gimmick. From the beginning, festival leaders realized that getting the Nisei to "buy in Lil' Tokio" (a prewar slogan) meant giving them a greater stake in the future of the ethnic enclave. In order to do this, the Issei had to inculcate the younger generation, beginning with its elite leaders, with the Issei's ethnic orthodoxy, which centered on protecting Little Tokyo from threats both external and indigenous to the Japanese American community.

PARADOX OF ANTI-JAPANESE PREJUDICE

When the Americans forced Japan into the world of commerce and diplomacy, they also forced the Japanese to wrestle with the status of their race, which in this new world put them at a disadvantage. In the later nineteenth century, officials of the Meiji court were convinced that the West's military and technological superiority, which enabled European powers to control much of Asia, was somehow tied to whiteness. The only hope for Japan, they believed, was for their feudal nation to become totally Westernized. Soon enough, the nation's breakneck pace of modernization enabled the Japanese themselves to become an imperial power. But neither the defeat of China in 1895 nor Japan's more impressive victory over Russia a decade later managed to bridge the racial gap with the West. An American correspondent to the Russo-Japanese War revealed the depths of this divide by supporting the Russians because they were white, and, as he reported, "that means much." "For no particular reason, with no real cause for complaint," he wrote, "I now find myself hating the Japanese more than anything in the world. It is due I presume to the constant strain of having to be polite and seek favors from the yellow people."[1] For the Japanese, imitation of the West's colonial enterprises only heightened racial tensions with the white world.

This was especially true for the immigrants who ventured to the Pacific Coast of the United States. Convinced of the "unassimilability" of the Japanese, American labor unions, interest groups, and politicians feared that the steady, though relatively small, influx of Japanese laborers signaled an impending Asian invasion. At the start of the twentieth century, such groups rekindled racial fears that had fueled the earlier exclusion of Chinese immigrants. Pushed by the resounding West Coast cry for Japanese exclusion, President Theodore Roosevelt in 1907 convinced Japanese officials to stop the flow of laborers to the United States. This "Gentlemen's Agreement" between American and Japanese officials seemed to have achieved its objective. The agreement, however, placed no restrictions on the wives and children of those Japanese already in the United States, who, along with other "nonlaborers," contributed to the flow of immigrants in the decade following the Gentlemen's Agreement. Western states sought to discourage Japanese settlement by preventing them from owning land. Without such safeguards, anti-Japanese forces predicted, the Issei's "phenomenal fecundity" would cause Japanese Americans to outnumber California's Anglo population within three decades.[2]

These racial fears stood in stark contrast to census records of the day. While the number of Japanese Americans in California more than doubled between 1910 and 1930 (growing from 41,356 to 97,456), so too did the state's total population (increasing from 2,377,549 to 5,677,251). Even though they were California's largest racial minority group during this period, Japanese Americans never consisted of more than 2 percent of the state's residents. Their low numbers vis-à-vis the overwhelming majority of white Californians were also true in Los Angeles, despite a fivefold increase in the city's Japanese American community between 1910 and 1930.[3] For the anti-Japanese pundits, the real issue was not Japanese fertility but their own fear. They assumed that the cheap labor of Japanese immigrants would undermine the standard of living of white workers, propelling American society into a downward spiral of economic, moral, and racial degeneration. The rhetoric, and the resulting anti-Japanese policies, embodied the worst sort of paranoia in American politics, as even states with few Japanese or any other residents of color took pains to secure the future of their white populations.

In the early 1920s, anti-Japanese forces won another series of victories. California strengthened the enforcement of the Alien Land Law, which enterprising Japanese immigrants had evaded, and the Supreme Court in *U.S. v. Ozawa* confirmed that the Issei were barred from American citizenship because of their race. The time was ripe for the protectors of white America to press on for the ultimate goal of immigration exclusion. Theirs was a common nativism in the "tribal twenties" when a broad array of American groups sought to close the door to immigration from both Europe and Asia. This isolationism culminated in the Immigration Act of 1924, which established the most restrictive immigration policy in American history. But while the new policy severely limited newcomers from Europe, it excluded Asians altogether, and it was no secret that the real target of "oriental exclusion" were the Japanese.[4] The new law had an immediate impact on Japanese immigration. The stream from Japan became a trickle, declining from roughly eight thousand immigrants a year in the early 1920s to 723 in 1925. The exclusionists' victory was sweetened even more by the windfall of remigration. It was not unusual for Japanese immigrants to uproot themselves from the United States—indeed, one out of four had left between 1908 and 1924. But after exclusion, the thousands who left the United States each year were no longer offset by a greater number of new arrivals.[5] Table 1.1 indicates

TABLE 1.1   JAPANESE AMERICAN POPULATION
IN THE UNITED STATES BY NATIVITY
(1900–40)

	1900	1910	1920	1930	1940
	Number (%)	Number (%)	Number (%)	Number (%)	Number (%)
Immigrant	24,057 (99)	67,655 (94)	81,338 (73)	70,477 (51)	47,305 (37)
Native born	269 (1)	4,502 (6)	29,672 (27)	68,357 (49)	79,642 (63)
Total	24,326 (100)	72,157 (100)	111,010 (100)	138,834 (100)	126,947 (100)

SOURCES: "Color or Race, Nativity, and Parentage," General Reports and Statistics by Subject, *Characteristics of the Population* (vol. 2), Fifteenth Census of the United States (1930), t. 8.34; and *Characteristics of the Population* (vol. 2), Sixteenth Census of the United States (1940), t. 6.21.

that the Issei population declined 42 percent from 81,338 in 1920 to 47,305 two decades later. By 1940, six out of ten Japanese in the United States were American-born. In this way, the Immigration Act succeeded where the Gentlemen's Agreement and alien land acts had failed: It diminished the presence of Japanese immigrants in the United States. This legislation, according to Yuji Ichioka, confirmed the Issei's inability to become American and caused them no longer to see "any future for themselves in this country."[6]

While it is clear that Issei leaders, and especially Tokyo officials, were upset and offended by the exclusion of Japanese immigrants, it is misleading to think that the Issei simply gave up the fight. There is strong evidence indicating that the Immigration Act did not thwart the Issei's entrepreneurial spirit, most likely because exclusion failed to severely damage their ethnic economy. If the Gentlemen's Agreement had been the barrier the exclusionists had planned, then Japanese America might not have taken root in southern California. But by 1924 the Issei already had established a firm foothold in the region's agriculture. Between 1910 and 1920, the number of Japanese-controlled farms tripled, and the total acres managed within the enclave increased more than seven times. The Japanese presence was particularly powerful in the near monopolies they maintained in the markets for lettuce, berries, celery, and tomatoes. The growth of Japanese farming in Los Angeles, John Modell asserts, "was fully as spectacular as the group's opponents would have wished to portray it in arguing for the Alien Land Law."[7] But did not this law, especially after it was strengthened in 1920, dampen Issei enterprise? Modell believes not, because to him there were simply too many American citizens (both Nisei and white) who enabled Japanese immigrants to get around it. He disagrees with those who blame the land act for the sharp decline in farm acreage controlled by the Japanese in the 1920s. The falling numbers are misleading because, as he reveals, they reflect an overall decline in farm acreage throughout Los Angeles County. The proportion of Issei land holdings compared to the overall number of farms remained relatively constant from 1920 to 1930, while the value of their property rose fourfold.[8]

The Issei success in agriculture benefited other sectors in the immigrant economy. The expansion of farming enabled the creation of wholesale and retail networks that brought each step of crop production under Japanese control. Issei growers sold goods to Japanese American wholesalers who, in turn, sold to enclave retailers. These kinship bonds enabled the Japanese to dominate the Los Angeles City Market, the region's largest produce distribution center. A similar pattern of collective endeavor was evident in the Issei's involvement in floriculture, fishing, domestic service, and contract gardening. What resulted was a thriving niche economy based on certain products and services that were not otherwise being offered to the people of southern California.

The only part of the enclave that looked inward for its clientele was Little Tokyo. While certainly welcoming outsiders, the restaurants, dry goods and grocery stores, confectioneries, hotels and boarding houses, barber shops, pool halls, bathhouses, and medical and professional services that made up the heart of Japantown catered primarily to Issei customers. Such establishments mushroomed along with agricultural growth. The number of these establishments, Richard Nishimoto reported in an unpublished study, increased dramatically, from 160 in 1904 to 495 in just five years.[9] Nishimoto grouped commercial activity in Little Tokyo into three categories: (1) shops, such as art curio shops, that imported Japanese merchandise and catered mainly to white Americans; (2) restaurants, laundries, and domestic services that also catered to those outside the ethnic group; and (3) grocery stores, boarding houses, barbers, and other businesses that provided goods and services almost exclusively for Japanese Americans. This last category, Nishimoto maintained, had expanded at a greater rate than the other two, because the "rapid influx of new Japanese immigrants and vigorous anti-Japanese agitation" had given rise to "segregated communities . . . designed to meet the wants of fellow countrymen."[10]

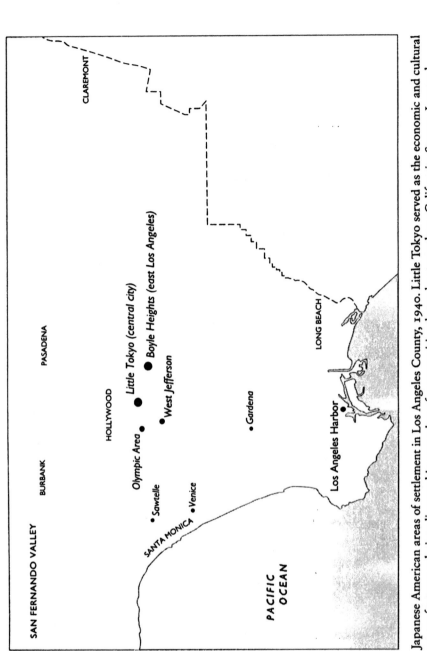

Japanese American areas of settlement in Los Angeles County, 1940. Little Tokyo served as the economic and cultural center for a population dispersed in a number of communities throughout southern California. Source: Leonard Broom and Ruth Riemer, *Removal and Return: The Socio-Economic Effects of the War on Japanese Americans.*

That most Japanese immigrants rose quickly and decisively from the ranks of "cheap labor" presents a curious paradox regarding the impact of anti-Japanese prejudice in Los Angeles. It is true that Japanese immigrants were victimized by structures of white supremacy and that this in turn distinguished their experience from most of the nation's immigrants. But the system of racial prejudice that the Issei confronted prevented neither the accumulation of wealth nor the rising class status that normally denotes social mobility. Clearly, anti-Japanese racism never reached the level of the institutions that had enslaved blacks or colonized Native Americans. Instead, Japanese immigrants faced what sociologist Stanford Lyman calls "modern racism," in which they possessed some enumerated rights and maintained autonomy within racially segregated spheres in mainstream society.[11] Such spaces were especially prevalent and lucrative in regions experiencing a rapid commercial and population growth, like southern California. The booming Los Angeles economy could easily accommodate Japanese immigrants, whose success, it should be remembered, also benefited many whites who helped Japanese farmers own and lease land and who otherwise profited from the farmers' enterprise. Thus the spaces within West Coast racism that Japanese immigrants so deftly exploited were made possible by economic opportunities.[12]

The frontiers of U.S.-Japan relations also managed to protect the Issei's business niches. The American government took Japan very seriously as the leading power in Asia and sought repeatedly to calm anti-Japanese sentiment in California so as not to offend the island nation. To Theodore Roosevelt, the Gentlemen's Agreement, in which the Japanese government imposed its own restrictions on emigration to the United States, was an alternative to the humiliation of an outright exclusion. That Japanese officials were allowed to save face in the eyes of the international community was of little consolation to the Issei, who always bore the brunt of anti-Japanese hostility. But at least restriction did not doom them to bachelorhood in the same way it did Chinese immigrants. In permitting, though certainly not encouraging, Issei family reunification, the Gentlemen's Agreement enabled the expansion and reproduction of the ethnic labor force, which contributed significantly to the growth of the enclave.[13]

Washington, however, did not come to the defense of Japanese immigrants without being nudged by Tokyo. Concerned about their nation's image in the West, policy makers in Japan (including the nation's leading journalists, intellectuals, and government officials) called on the

American government to protect Japanese immigrants, occasionally lacing their protests with veiled threats of warfare. Yet the upper classes in Japan held the overseas community equally culpable for the discrimination it suffered on the West Coast. Japanese officials imposed strict guidelines for the nation's emigrants and, once they were abroad, sought to groom and control them through the Japanese consulate. This micromanaging of immigration, historian Akira Iriye notes, was designed to do more than preserve the good name of the Japanese emperor. Japan's policy community saw immigration as a peaceful process of colonization, seeking to establish "New Japans," particularly in capital-rich nations like the United States, that would foster the economic development of the home country. Keeping opportunities open to Japanese immigrants and encouraging their social mobility were key parts of the colonial design.[14]

So it was that the frontiers of California settlement and international diplomacy set the parameters of anti-Japanese racism. Although discriminatory statutes were enacted, white businessmen, American and Japanese officials, and a favorable physical and economic environment enabled Japanese immigrants to establish a robust agricultural economy. This is to say nothing of the immigrants' dogged determination and hard work, which was so prevalent that some students of Japanese American history have attributed the success of the Issei to these personal motivations and cultural values alone. But the idea that mobility was somehow culturally programmed ignores the historic configuration of racism that allowed Japanese immigrants to exploit viable windows of entrepreneurship. John Modell goes so far as to suggest that racial discrimination proved to be a hidden element of Issei success. Legally enforced segregation, he argues, reinforced in-group solidarity that in turn became the basis of ethnic enterprise. In his reading, bonds of ethnicity gave the Issei underdog a competitive advantage in a competitive marketplace because it ensured cooperation between labor and management, allowed shared resources and pricing schemes among firms, and regulated enclave ties through "a kind of ethnic-based welfare capitalism." These ethnic-business ties, Modell concludes, were "quite compatible with (and indeed, sustained by) racial separation."[15]

But the future success of the immigrant enclave was no sure thing. While the exclusion of Japanese immigrants in 1924 did not damage Issei agriculture, it did cause growers to rely increasingly on a non-Japanese labor force. This sowed seeds of interethnic friction between Japanese growers and Filipino and Mexican workers that grew into contentious labor relations.[16] The heightening of U.S.-Japan tension had even more dire consequences for the ethnic community. Japanese statesmen and policy makers denounced the way its immigrants were excluded, urging their government to avenge the Immigration Act's blatant discrimination. The immediate crisis passed when the foreign minister remained steadfast to the commitment of global cooperation and peace emerging from the Washington, D.C., naval conference in 1922, but such racial insults nonetheless convinced many Japanese military leaders that war with the United States was inevitable. They bided their time until the global economic crisis of the 1930s undermined the international order.

In the meantime, the onset of the depression slowed, and in some cases stalled, the impressive growth of the Issei economy. Modell estimates that the value of Japanese farms was at its peak in 1930 and that the emergence of florists-nurseries and retail food outlets, the growth industries of the 1920s, tapered off after the stock market crash.[17] He contends that hard times made Issei entrepreneurs "essentially defensive," consumed with maintaining what they had while "sharing the conventional enemies of white petty businessmen: innovation and labor." [18] On the political front, the depression encouraged the introduction of new legislation designed to doom the ethnic enclave. Although State Department officials tried to prevent Congress from excluding Japanese immigrants, after the collapse of the Washington naval accords in the late 1920s, neither American nor Japanese diplomats were able to shelter the ethnic community from racial assault. The global crisis diminished U.S.-Japan trade and therefore pushed each nation to protect its beleaguered economy.[19]

These rising nationalisms had their analogue in Little Tokyo as Issei merchants began to preach the gospel of self-sufficiency. Their main target was the second generation. Given their ability to speak English and their American lifestyle, the Nisei were less inclined to shop exclusively in Japanese stores. "The majority of the second generation," said one of the Issei founders of Nisei Week, "mistakenly believe that goods procured outside Little Tokyo are of better quality and less expensive [sic] than goods of the same type found in Japanese stores." Even worse, some merchants claimed that the Nisei were developing consumption tastes that left them unsatisfied by the enclave's "oriental" flavor. Newspaper publisher Sei Fujii argued that lower prices were not the only reason the Nisei avoided Japanese stores. The youngsters, he bemoaned, were embarrassed to wear clothes with Japanese labels.[20] This is not hard to believe since even urban youth in Japan idealized Western fashions and lifestyles. The Nisei grew up in an era of mass culture and consumption in which all of the role models and marketing ploys encouraged them to desire Western aesthetics.

But avoiding Little Tokyo stores was more than a cultural matter. The exclusion of Japanese immigrants had caused Little Tokyo merchants to look to the Nisei as their future customer base. By 1930 the ethnic community was composed of as many American-born youths as immigrant adults, and within a few years, the majority of Nisei would come of age as consumers. Issei merchants fantasized about a loyal bloc of second-generation shoppers spending half a million dollars a year in Little Tokyo. But how could they ensure that successive generations of Japanese Americans would "buy in Lil' Tokio"? This was the burning question that sparked the formation of the Nisei Week festival.[21]

SECOND CHANCES

In spring 1934 a group of Little Tokyo merchants pitched the idea of a second-generation festival to the Los Angeles chapter of the JACL, a promising ethnic welfare organization that linked Nisei throughout the West Coast region. The merchants took it upon themselves to do something about the depression-weary enclave, but to their chagrin, they were not the only ones to stand up for Little Tokyo businesses. Three other Issei groups vied for the sponsorship of Nisei Week, each courting the young JACLers. In the process, preparations for the summer celebration were held hostage to politics internal to the ethnic community.[22]

Like children caught between feuding parents, the JACLers withheld support from all parties. "Nisei Week," they stated, "will be in cooperation with, and not under the jurisdiction of any organization in Lil' Tokio" (*Rafu Shimpo*, July 3, 1934). In an earlier editorial, the young leaders insisted that neutrality was the only way to avoid soiling what they called their own "pure" and "altruistic" motives. They condemned the "factionalism" and "selfishness" of the competing Issei groups, asserting that the Nisei "cannot afford to risk being the political football of petty strife among the elders" (*Rafu Shimpo*, July 1, 1934). Yet what the JACLers feared most were political forces *outside* Little Tokyo, since after the successful exclusion of Japanese immigrants, the second generation had become the major target of the anti-Japanese movement. The Nisei press warned that the JACL should keep out of the battle for Nisei Week because close public ties with what columnist Larry Tajiri called

"Japanese nationalistic groups" would ruin its chances of gaining critical acceptance in American society (*Kashu Mainichi,* June 10, 1934. For the pressure of anti-Japanese groups, see also June 24, 1934).

While the details are not entirely clear, it is apparent that the prospect of losing this chance to calm anti-Japanese hostility eventually freed Nisei Week from the political gridlock among the Issei leadership. Despite their differences over the sponsorship of Nisei Week, Issei leaders agreed that such a celebration would be an important opportunity to present the second generation as the basis for racial harmony and international friendship. The inaugural festival opened in August 1934 with financial backing from Little Tokyo businesses and an ostensibly independent JACL at its helm.[23]

In postexclusion Little Tokyo, the Nisei's public image was a primary concern. Because the Immigration Act had made clear that the American public was not convinced by the Issei's assurances that they were assimilating and loyal to American society, the immigrant leadership looked to their children's generation to defuse anti-Japanese tension. Kyutaro Abiko, newspaper publisher and respected Issei leader, maintained that "oriental exclusion" resulted primarily from racial misunderstanding, which the Nisei, given their ability to communicate with both Americans and Japanese, could best resolve. To him, the second generation embodied a new biculturalism that reflected the changing international landscape. Japan's foreign policy experts had long heralded the birth of the "Pacific Century," a new era in which the Pacific Basin would be the center of world affairs. In this scenario, Abiko believed that the Nisei were to occupy a special position as a "bridge of understanding" linking the two dominant powers in the region, the United States and Japan.[24] Nisei biculturalism offered a second chance for expansionists in Japan and ethnic leaders in the United States to challenge the discrimination against Japanese immigrants.

Issei leaders like Abiko understood the significance of biculturalism firsthand. Stifled by the lack of opportunities in Japan, Abiko migrated to San Francisco in 1885. By working at a number of menial jobs, he paid for his schooling at the University of California, Berkeley, where he became fluent in English. He left college to take advantage of business opportunities catering to the growing community of Japanese immigrants in the San Francisco Bay Area. He opened a restaurant and a laundry and began publishing what would become the leading newspaper for Japanese immigrants in the United States, *Nichibei Mainichi (Japanese American News).* But it was his bilingual capabilities that enabled Abiko to earn a good living. As many Japanese students would discover, their ability to speak English put them in high demand as mediators between Japanese laborers and American firms. Abiko himself become one the founding members of the largest labor contracting agencies in California.[25]

Education and bilingual ability also proved to be the foundations of immigrant leadership in southern California. Katsuma Mukaeda, who at different times presided over the two leading Issei organizations in southern California, the Japanese Association and the Japanese Chamber of Commerce, came to America just before the Gentlemen's Agreement barred Japanese laborers. But unlike most Issei, he became proficient in English and earned a bachelor's degree in law. His language skills and command of American law secured him a position as an interpreter for the Los Angeles Superior Court. As a community leader, he backed Nisei Week because he saw it as a means of encouraging reluctant Japanese Americans to build better relations with whites.[26] Another supporter of the festival was the outspoken newspaper publisher Sei Fujii. A graduate of Compton High School and the University of Southern California, he went on to serve as the president of the Japanese Association.[27] Through the English section of his paper, the *Kashu Mainichi,* the avuncular Sei Fujii instructed the second generation in its opportunities and obligations to their parents' generation. Nisei Week, he challenged, was their best chance to prove to the immigrant old guard that they were now an "asset" rather than a "burden."[28]

The Nisei response was overwhelming. For all their reluctance to be closely associated with Issei groups, the JACLers welcomed the opportunity to lead Nisei Week, since the festival was billed as the "greatest civic project undertaken by a second-generation group."[29] Their enthusiasm, however, stemmed as much from self-interest as community service. Despite their American citizenship and acculturation, the Nisei faced the same social barriers as Japanese immigrants: In the American imagination both generations were reduced to the common denominator of race. Neither could find much work in the mainstream labor market, where employers discriminated against them and major labor unions denied them membership. Racial discrimination was especially galling to the Nisei, socialized as they were with American mores and customs. They had been taught that the "American way" was to reward intelligence, hard work, and "fair play," but before World War II, none of their achievements opened the doors to white America—not their negligible crime rate, their model records in school, or even their quiet, don't-make-waves industriousness. If anything, these characteristics reinforced widespread fears of Japanese cunning, the sine qua non of the "yellow peril." [30]

Most Nisei were fortunate simply to achieve their parents' economic position. Even college graduates faced racial restrictions that derailed their career fulfillment and forced them back to the humble world of the ethnic enclave. In the late 1920s and the 1930s, the immigrant press was replete with warnings against the value of higher education. Sei Fujii, for instance, warned of college-educated Nisei working as janitors and gardeners and concluded that schooling offered no employment advantages for the second generation. "These being the facts," he asserted, "I cannot see any reason why most of our Nisei should be encouraged to attend college and permit their aged and already worn-out parents to continue doing all sorts of hard work in order to provide their college expenses." Nisei Joseph Shinoda, himself a university graduate, quipped sarcastically about his peers' job prospects, "They go to college, learn a heterogeneous body of facts relating to anything from art to architecture and end their days in a fruit stand." [31]

Indeed, the fruit stand worker typified the Nisei's occupational frustrations. While the immigrant enclave offered a safety net for high school and college graduates, the jobs they found available rarely met their expectations or educational backgrounds. "I am a fruit stand worker," said one Los Angeles Nisei about his plight. "It is not a very attractive or distinguished occupation. . . . I would much rather it were a doctor or lawyer . . . but my aspiration of developing into such [was] frustrated long ago. . . . I am only what I am, a professional carrot washer." [32] In a study of Japanese American employment conducted during the World War II internment, Richard Nishimoto documented a grim pattern of Nisei frustration. One of his informants explained that "it just wasn't conceived that a Nisei could get a decent job working with a Caucasian company." As a result, Nishimoto concludes that they "took on the prevailing Nisei attitude of hopelessness because they had to cling to any kind of job they could get." [33]

For most Nisei, this meant relinquishing hopes of getting beyond the ethnic economy. In the early 1930s Edward Strong and his Stanford University colleagues asked 9,416 California Nisei about their job preferences and found that 40 percent favored professional occupations, 20 percent indicated business careers, and only 15 percent chose farming. Such aspirations placed many Nisei in a predicament: They could not work outside the enclave but could not be fulfilled within it. This prompted Joseph Shinoda's report that his generation was reluctant to

Although the wholesale produce market was a boon to many Issei businesses, it was often a dead end for Nisei with white-collar ambitions. *Courtesy Japanese American National Museum, gift of Theresa Aki Sasaki Hayakawa (98.158.2).*

follow the career path of Issei fishermen because this was "at best an ill-smelling, wet, and dismal calling." But deferred professional fulfillment was not the only reason to resent being shipwrecked in Little Tokyo. Even within the enclave, the Nisei were disproportionately positioned in the lower levels of the immigrant economy. In 1941 the second generation made up 80 percent of the enclave's salesclerks but only 40 percent of its retail managers. On the farms Nisei were half of all laborers but only 30 percent of the farmers.[34]

The overwhelming majority of the second generation were forced to work in the same industries as their parents' generation—they even went into commercial fishing. Table 1.2 reveals the similarities between the most common Issei and Nisei occupations in 1941. While it was more likely for each generation to enter certain occupations (such as sale clerking and chauffeuring for the Nisei or gardening and restaurant cooking for the Issei), most immigrant and native-born Japanese Amer-

TABLE 1.2   MOST COMMON OCCUPATIONS
OF EMPLOYED JAPANESE AMERICAN MEN
IN LOS ANGELES COUNTY BY NATIVITY
(1941)

Japan-born (N = 6812)	American-born (N = 5881)
Occupation	Occupation
1. Gardener	1. Salesclerk
2. Retail manager	2. Retail manager
3. Truck farmer	3. Farmhand
4. Hotel and restaurant manager	4. Gardener
5. Restaurant cook	5. Truck farmer
6. Nursery operator	6. Chauffeur
7. Farmhand	7. Nursery laborer
8. Wholesale manager	8. Nursery operator
9. Salesclerk	9. Commercial fishing
10. Commercial fishing	10. Wholesale manager

SOURCE: "WRA Form 26: Evacuee Summary Data ('Locator Index')," electronic dataset, 1942, U.S. Department of the Interior, War Relocation Authority, RG 210 (Washington, D.C.: National Archives). NOTE: Occupations listed comprised 65.5 percent of the Japan-born workforce and 61.2 percent of the American-born workforce.

icans found themselves in the same types of jobs in the ethnic enclave's primary sectors: agricultural production, retail and wholesale enterprises, and domestic service (including gardening). The younger generation could not afford to ignore the immigrant generation, nor could they by themselves mount a substantial challenge to the racial restrictions that kept them in Little Tokyo. Even with the advantage of American citizenship, the Nisei did not have the experience or material base to launch a strong opposition against anti-Japanese critics. The pressures of American racism and the dictates of the ethnic economy created symbiotic ties between the two generations.

Nothing illustrated the significance of Issei-Nisei relations better than the emergence of the JACL. As early as 1918, older Nisei in San Francisco and Seattle had started groups to improve their generation's political and economic position. But none of these groups grew beyond their respective communities or received strong support from the Issei leadership until the emergence of JACL. Founded in 1930, the JACL gained support from Japanese American communities throughout the West Coast and with strong Issei backing grew from eight original chapters to thirty-eight in just six years. Respectful of their benefactors, JACLers fought for causes benefiting both immigrants and native born, such as efforts to have the government fulfill its promise to grant American citizenship to

TABLE 1.3   DISTRIBUTION OF MAJOR OCCUPATIONS
FOR JACLers COMPARED WITH POPULATION
OF EMPLOYED NISEI MALES IN LOS ANGELES
(1941)

Occupation	JACLers (N = 183)	Nisei (N = 4105)
Professional	26.3	8.4
Salesclerk	20.8	19.4
Retail manager	13.7	10.3
Bookkeeper/cashier	6.6	1.1
Wholesale manager	4.4	2.2
Farmhand	2.7	4.1
Gardener	1.1	8.4

SOURCES: "WRA Form 26: Evacuee Summary Data ('Locator Index')," electronic dataset, 1942, U.S. Department of the Interior, War Relocation Authority, RG 210 (Washington, D.C.: National Archives). Data are for the Los Angeles JACL and are based on a sample derived from the organization's membership list published in the *Pacific Citizen*, May 1941. The sample comprises 183 members (78 percent male), out of the 371 names on this list, for whom biographical information was contained in the WRA Form 26 records.

those Issei who served in World War I and the campaign to amend legislation that caused Nisei women to lose their American citizenship upon marrying a Japanese immigrant. In the end, the early JACL merely provided a new vessel for the Issei's attempt to protect Japanese American communities through vigorous public relations. "The early devices of the rising Nisei organization," claimed Togo Tanaka, in an unpublished history of the JACL, "were in many instances mild imitations of the Issei." [35]

The social profiles of the JACL's Nisei leaders also resembled the immigrant old guard. The typical JACLer was born in 1913, about a decade before the Nisei "baby boom" of the early 1920s. This age difference had enabled the JACLers to achieve a greater degree of occupational mobility in the ethnic enclave than most of their generation. Table 1.3 is based on a comparison of half of the Los Angeles JACL membership in 1941 to the total population of employed Nisei males in Los Angeles. The results indicate that the JACLers were slightly more likely than the rest of their generation to be retail managers (14 percent of JACLers, 10 percent of all Nisei) and twice as likely to work as wholesale managers (4 percent of JACLers, 2 percent of all Nisei). But what really distinguished the JACLers was that they were over three times more likely to be professionals than their generation as a whole. The flip side of this was the almost total absence of JACLers from one of the mainstays of Nisei employment, gardening (1 percent of JACLers, 8 percent of Nisei).

TABLE 1.4   DISTRIBUTION OF SOCIAL CHARACTERISTICS
FOR JACLers COMPARED WITH POPULATION
OF OLDER NISEI IN LOS ANGELES
(1941)

Social Characteristic	JACLers	Nisei Born before 1920 (N = 7242)
Sex ratio (men:women)	78:22	51:49
Religion ratio (Buddhist:Christian)	38:45	42:20
College education	28 percent	19 percent

SOURCES: "WRA Form 26: Evacuee Summary Data ('Locator Index'),'' electronic dataset, 1942, U.S. Department of the Interior, War Relocation Authority, RG 210 (Washington, D.C.: National Archives). Data are for the Los Angeles JACL and are based on a sample derived from the organization's membership list published in the *Pacific Citizen*, May 1941. The sample comprises 183 members, out of the 371 names on this list, for whom biographical information was contained in the WRA Form 26 records.

As lawyers, dentists, medical doctors, and entrepreneurs, the JACL leaders, however, still relied on the ethnic enclave for their incomes. Known as the "businessmen's group," the Los Angeles JACL had a vested interest in enhancing and protecting Little Tokyo.

A second comparison between JACLers and other older Nisei in southern California suggests three other differences that distinguished them from their generational peers. Table 1.4 reveals that more than three quarters of JACL members were men, despite a balanced sex ratio among those Nisei born before the baby boom of the 1920s. JACLers were about as likely as their peers to identify as Buddhists (38 percent of JACLers, 42 percent older Nisei), but they were more than twice as likely as the larger group to be Christian (Protestant or Catholic). Further, members of the organization were much better educated than their peers. Twenty-eight percent of JACLers had attended college (either in the United States or in Japan) compared to only 19 percent of their peer group. Thus taken together, tables 1.3 and 1.4 paint a picture of the JACL as a select group of Nisei men. These were not frustrated "carrot washers" trapped at the bottom of the immigrant economy. They were young, educated, urban professionals who had climbed the ranks of the ethnic enclave and sought to become community leaders. Though hardly an average Nisei himself, Joseph Shinoda expressed a kernel of truth when he criticized the JACL as a "perpetual committee" excluding the "average-man." [36]

This elite status was doubly true for JACL leaders, who were seen as role models for Japanese American youth. Consider the success story of

Kay (Keiichi) Sugahara, the first president of the Los Angeles chapter. Born in 1909, Sugahara was thirteen when he and his younger siblings were orphaned. "I was saved from total despair," he remembered in a 1983 interview, "by a university student from Japan who encouraged me to read Tolstoy, Dostoevsky, and other classic Russian writers." To help provide for his brother and sister, Sugahara worked at a fruit stand from junior high through his years at the University of California, Los Angeles. But unlike most Nisei, Sugahara considered produce retailing merely one step on the ladder of economic success. In 1932, as a senior at UCLA, he teamed with white partners to launch the first customs brokerage firm in Little Tokyo, capitalizing on his ability to bridge American and Japanese cultures and to link Japanese imports with American firms. The success of his venture, he claimed, made him a millionaire well before World War II.[37]

A college roommate of Sugahara, Patrick (Kiyoshi) Okura also symbolized the type of Nisei who became active in the Los Angeles JACL. Okura graduated with a master's degree in psychology, but the difficulty of finding suitable employment in a racially restrictive labor market turned him into an "angry young man." In 1936 he became the JACL's first executive director and worked to support the ethnic enclave by forging ties with local politicians and businessmen outside Little Tokyo. But he refused to be denied a job commensurate with his education and left JACL employment, eventually to become one of the first Japanese American civil servants in Los Angeles.[38]

Togo Tanaka graduated from UCLA a few years after Sugahara and Okura. Born in 1916, he moved as an infant with his parents from Portland, Oregon, to Los Angeles. He recalled that his mother was friendly toward white Americans, while his father, whom he called a "racial chauvinist," kept his distance. As he grew up, Tanaka himself had no illusions about racial prejudice but nurtured many dreams of moving beyond it. Before he was to graduate Phi Beta Kappa from UCLA, Tanaka became the associate editor of the English section of the *Kashu Mainichi,* a bilingual Japanese newspaper, but left in a short time to become English editor of the *Rafu Shimpo,* the leading Japanese daily in southern California. Through his regular column, Tanaka provided the Nisei with a perspective on the political events of the day. As both editor and JACL's publicity director, he sought to communicate the views of Japanese Americans to the broader public. His grasp of Little Tokyo affairs made him a perceptive social analyst, a skill he would later put to great use as a historian of the ethnic community.[39]

One of the main subjects of Tanaka's later studies was Fred (Masaru) Tayama, JACL's president in 1941. Tayama was born in 1905 and, according to Tanaka, moved from Hawaii to central California when he was in high school. Tayama earned a bachelor's degree from an engineering school in Illinois and first got involved with the Los Angeles JACL in the late 1930s. In southern California he controlled a series of business ventures (including a chain of restaurants and an insurance franchise) and was known to be a successful entrepreneur. He was Christian, married with a daughter, and a home owner. As a JACL leader, Tayama maintained good connections with the Japanese consulate (he kept a regular golf date with the consul general). But he was no Japanese nationalist. He sought repeatedly to establish the Nisei's undivided loyalty to the United States and even worked with American intelligence agents to root out potential subversives in Little Tokyo. Tanaka maintained that Tayama pushed Americanism more than any other JACL president.[40]

JACLers like Sugahara, Okura, Tanaka, and Tayama seemed to fit the classic mold of American ethnic leadership: Their achievements brought them acclaim within the group but, more importantly, made them acceptable outside it. In this way, most Nisei leaders were chosen with white America in mind, thus narrowing the choices to high achievers, who by definition were outside the norm of their generation. Such persons, social psychologist Kurt Lewin has argued, might well have fled the ethnic community. In his study of Jewish Americans, Lewin found that ethnic leaders, especially from the second generation, were preoccupied with being accepted by mainstream society. They avoided "too close a contact with those sections of the underprivileged group which are not acceptable to the majority" and approached leadership roles as both a "substitute for gaining status in the majority" and as a stepping stone to assimilation.[41]

What has been written about the JACL's history confirms Lewin's observations. Roger Daniels, for example, describes the organization in the 1930s as "America-oriented" and "on a collision course with the organizations of the older generation." He contends that JACL's "Americanized ideology" revealed that its members' true loyalties lay outside Little Tokyo and not with the Issei leadership.[42] But the emergence of Nisei Week suggests that while Daniels's claims might hold for the national organization, they do not fit local chapters well, since the JACLers in Los Angeles did not have the luxury of sustaining an entrenched generation gap. They may have wanted to leave the immigrant community, but until the opportunity arose, they did not separate themselves from it or contest seriously the authority of the Issei leadership. Rhetoric about distancing themselves from "nationalistic" groups did not prevent the Nisei from cooperating with the Issei leadership, for theirs was a relationship sealed by common political and economic interests.

THE ENEMY WITHIN

The final thread that bound the two generations of leaders was a fear of common enemies *within* the ethnic community. Each believed that the future of the Japanese American community rested upon the group's willingness and ability to embrace core American values, ideals, and lifestyles. As the founders of modern Japan knew well, the Japanese were scrutinized more than most foreigners entering the United States, and Americans used signs of cultural incompetence to confirm perceptions of racial inferiority. Economic mobility, on the other hand, sparked fears of an Asian takeover. Ethnic leaders had to navigate the treacherous waters between the Scylla of white supremacy and the Charybdis of yellow-peril paranoia. As a result, the path to acceptance in American society required Herculean efforts of self-control, discipline, and community solidarity, while the failings of mere mortals put the entire race in jeopardy.

In negotiating the racial currents in American society, the Issei leadership was convinced that the worst enemies of Japanese American settlement were the settlers themselves. This was what the upper classes in Japan had feared all along in sending its people abroad. One of the original reasons for permitting Japanese citizens to go overseas was to show the world how Westernized they had become, since even after Japan's defeat of Russia, the nation's people were still considered inferior to Americans and other Westerners. Yet deep down Japan's elite classes worried that the Japanese people were incapable of catching up with the West, and they bemoaned the intellectual and physical "shortcomings" of the Japanese people.[43] The ideal for many Japanese intellectuals was to live in the United States so that they could shed the trappings of what would be seen today as a third-world culture. "Before you know it," one writer observed, "your mind will be opened up, your horizon broadened, and your narrow provincialism will melt like a block of ice placed under the sun."[44]

The proposition of developing a cosmopolitan sensibility, however, was an entirely different matter when it came to the discussion of Japanese immigrants. If the elites in Tokyo believed the immigrants were no match for the West, they saw the farming classes that made up the bulk of the overseas community as a national disgrace. Socialist leader Katayama Sen, who had studied in the United States in the 1880s and had become a principal spokesman for going abroad, chastised the Issei for wearing village clothing and continuing the ways of rural life. In his criticism, Katayama gave voice to descriptions of the overseas population written by fellow students abroad. "The Japanese here," wrote one of them, "are all mediocre types, unable to breathe the air of civilization even though they are in America." Another was more brutal, noting that 80 percent of California Issei "are simply idlers with whom it is below my dignity to deal."[45]

The combination of adulation of the West and class antagonism made it difficult for Japanese elites to see the rise of racism on the West Coast as anything but an appropriate response to the wretchedness of Japanese immigrants. It was common for the upper echelons in Tokyo to blame the racial crisis leading to the Gentlemen's Agreement on the behavior of the Issei. The consul general in San Francisco himself recommended that the labor migration from Japan be halted. "Among our emigrant laborers," he wrote, "are many lacking in intelligence and education. Few are capable of any judgment and of looking after themselves. . . . In fact they are rather to be pitied for their stupidity and lack of propriety."[46] After visiting the United States, a researcher for a Japanese journal of economics concurred and sympathized with the consul general. He blamed anti-Japanese antagonism on the Issei, whom he regarded as unworthy representatives of the "real Japanese people."[47]

The immigrant leadership was equally critical of its brethren. Kyutaro Abiko constantly berated his fellow immigrants in the pages of *Nichibei Mainichi*. He encouraged marriage and land ownership as means to counter the get-rich-quick mentality that he saw at the root of gambling, prostitution, and crime in immigrant society. The *Nichibei*'s rival, the *Shinsekai (New World)*, criticized the Issei by filling its pages with stories about crimes, robberies, rapes, and breeches of contract within the immigrant community. "To speak very frankly," one editorial read, "there are too many Japanese who come to America [who] are barbaric. . . . Unless some improvement is made, the reputation of Japanese will fall, and the hatred of the white community will increase."[48] Even those Issei bitterly critical of American racism were convinced that Japanese immigrants were not beyond culpability for acts of discrimination. Kayahara Kazen, a leading journalist who had urged Japanese immigrants to "[s]truggle, endeavor, and overwhelm the white race" during the immigration crisis leading to the Gentlemen's Agreement, softened his belligerence when it came to the character of the Issei generation. Kayahara left the United States in 1907 nearly convinced that the overseas Japanese were incapable of sustaining good relations with the West.[49]

Nisei leaders inherited this negative image of their parents' generation. Joseph Shinoda complained that the peripatetic nature of agricultural work made Japanese immigrants a "discredit to the community." "Like agricultural gypsies, they roam the country squatting here for a spell, there for a spell, then moving out en masse to some other district." This rootlessness, he maintained, prevented them from understanding and contributing to the American way of life. A graduate of Stanford University and prosperous nursery owner in southern California, Shinoda shared an outlook more in common with the educated classes in Japan (and America) than most Japanese immigrants. He believed that the best and brightest of the Issei returned to Japan, while the "unsuccessful, the lazy, the unenterprising, the improvident continue forever from one hitching post to the next—dragging their children constantly through new regions and giving them the general upbringing of a wandering harvest crew's rabble."[50]

Other Nisei were less critical of the Issei than of their own generation. In a submission to the Nisei Week's essay contest, Taishi Matsumoto accepted that the exclusion of Japanese immigrants stemmed mostly from "the Issei's low standard of living." This, however, was no excuse for the Nisei who "grew up with a better standard of living and a better understanding of whites." The problem was that the Nisei were too reserved to open "our hearts" to white Americans and "accept them as one of us."[51] A *Rafu Shimpo* editorial also implored the second generation to reach out beyond their familiar. "They have a tendency," the paper concluded, "to resign themselves within the[ir] own group and peer out into the American community and say: 'It can't be done. They won't treat you right—they're prejudiced.'"[52]

The image of the Nisei as an overly insular and frightened generation was a recurring theme in Los Angeles Japanese American newspapers. A *Kashu Mainichi* editorial in 1936 blamed the Nisei for assuming "(very foolishly) that their old American school chums" are not receptive to their friendship. While acknowledging the significance of the very real "stone walls" of racism, the editorial concluded that the "greatest tragedy of the Nisei" was that generation's "clannishness."[53] A letter to the editor was both sympathetic and critical of Nisei inhibitions. Although he acknowledged the pitfalls of clannishness, the author insisted that the young Nisei needed more time and stronger leadership to grow out of their shell. "The psychology of the Nisei," the letter read, "is at one and the same time both remarkable and pitiful. Remarkable because of its perseverance, industry, frugality, simplicity, and relatively high moral standards. Pitiful because of its lack of initiative, independence[,] leadership . . . and grossly exaggerated 'inferiority complex'!"[54] Such psychologizing harkened back to the earlier critique of Japanese provincialism and underscored the nagging question of whether Japanese Americans could ever become truly American.

As with the Issei, the Nisei's attempt to embrace the modernity of American life was rooted in class oppositions. Community leader Masao Satow's view of his generation was reminiscent of the Tokyo elite's disdain for Japanese immigrants. The Nisei, he wrote, are a "shallow generation" because their American dress, mannerisms, speech, and attitude are only skin deep. While appearing "American on the outside, they lack the culture, refinement, and class background of Americans," thus making it painfully clear that "[w]e are still the sons and daughters of immigrants." After graduating from college, Satow worked with the Young Men's Christian Association (YMCA) to cultivate in the Nisei an appreciation for high art and society, which he insisted was more productive than his generation's preoccupation with sports and dance crazes. "We are so one-sided," he concluded, and yet "we naively wonder why Americans won't accept us as equals!"[55]

To the Nisei leaders, women posed particular problems to the cultivation of cosmopolitanism. Joseph Shinoda, for example, viewed Nisei coeds at the University of California, Berkeley, as "mentally deficient" because of their allegedly poor academic performances. These women, he asserted, made a mockery of higher education and thus were undeserving of their parents' sacrifices to send them there. At the same time, Shinoda blamed parents for turning college into a holding pen for their unfortunate daughters who had difficulty getting married. For these women, the university was a "marriage mart," which enabled them to "snag a husband" while "dancing through a college education." The mere idea of abusing the "luxury" of going to college was enough for Shinoda to conclude that higher education for Nisei women (and a handful of men whom he also characterized as intellectually deficient) was a waste of time.[56] WRA statistics suggest that he was not alone in opposing the value of educating daughters, since Nisei women were less likely than their male counterparts to go to college and rarely studied for four or more years. The percentage of Issei women who had earned college credits was much smaller than that of Nisei women, reflecting ever greater prohibitions against women's education in turn-of-the-century Japan.[57]

As ruling orthodoxies, Issei and Nisei cosmopolitanisms legitimized status and social hierarchies internal to the Japanese American community. Both generations of community leaders considered Westernized values, norms, cultural competencies, and bodies to be the highest standards of civilization. From this perspective, they defined as internal others those who purportedly did not embody the Protestant work ethic but were mere "idlers" engaging in morally questionable practices (such as gambling, prostitution, crime) and the powerful materialism that fueled a get-rich-quick mentality. An appreciation of Western high culture and assessments of physical and mental capabilities (based on the aesthetic and intellectual ideal of white America) were other litmus tests for distinguishing the best and the brightest within the ethnic community. In these determinations, women, men who did not meet the social standards for "manliness," and the least economically and culturally advantaged routinely found themselves at the bottom of the social ladder and thus were especially vulnerable to being blamed for formulations of anti-Japanese prejudice that not even the most Westernized Japanese American community could prevent.

At any point in time, a large proportion of the ethnic community could be cast as a threat to the group's public image. Most of the Issei, after all, were not part of the educated classes at the forefront of Westernizing Japan. For instance, more than 93 percent of the ethnic community's immigrant population in 1942 had not attended college, let alone graduated with a bachelor's degree.[58] These were people of the soil, raised with the pragmatic manners, dress, and customs of village life. In the United States, they continued their rural lives—or, if concentrated in cities, resided in immigrant enclaves—that afforded few opportunities for higher education, leisure time, or refinement. This was indeed true for the 20 percent of the ethnic community in 1940 who lived in Little Tokyo. John Modell found that at this time Little Tokyo was one of Los Angeles's poorest neighborhoods, containing a large population of non-Japanese—low-income whites, blacks, Mexicans, and Filipinos. Even the more upwardly mobile who fled to nearby suburbs, Modell reports, were still far more likely than the average person in Los Angeles to rent rather than own property and when doing so to live in cheaper quarters with family members and boarders.[59]

The Nisei had more freedom to embrace the urbane style of life outside the ethnic community. Although saddled with work and domestic responsibilities, the second generation was encouraged to perform well in school and, indeed, was recognized for academic excellence. But only

20 percent of Nisei adults in 1942 had attended at least one year of college, while the vast majority of these people did not earn bachelor's degrees.[60] While higher education was not an option for most Nisei, they were still expected to take on the mannerisms and customs of respectable white Americans. To this end, the Issei established Boy Scout troops, youth organizations, and athletic leagues and strongly supported a white kindergarten teacher's efforts to create after-school programs to occupy Japanese American children and adolescents. Nellie Oliver was so beloved by the Issei for starting Little Tokyo's first youth organization in 1917, which would grow to become a second home for hundreds of Nisei, that they raised money to send her on a "dream trip" to Japan. At the Oliver clubhouse, the children practiced Robert's Rules of parliamentary procedure, engaged in community sing-alongs, learned to dance and use correct grammar, planned fund-raising events and sports competitions, and ate warm meals and snacks.[61]

But the "Olivers" also reflected a darker side of Nisei youth. Much to the chagrin of its founder, some of its members devolved eventually from athletic competition to gang fighting. One Nisei recalled that "Miss Oliver cried many a time because of the battles we used to get into." She would insist that "her boys" behave like "nice gentlemen," but her admonishments had little or no effect.[62] Nellie Oliver simply could not change the realities of life in Little Tokyo. It was common for Nisei to join a gang as protection against other groups who preyed upon unsuspecting Japanese Americans. "The colored had gang fights, the Mexicans had gang fighting," explained one Nisei, and so in a ghetto community, "you have to . . . form a gang to protect yourself."[63] James Sakoda saw Nisei gangsters, whom he referred to as "rowdies," as more than a defense mechanism against racial hostility. In an unpublished study of Nisei personality types, he noted that rowdies failed "to maintain the social codes of the Nisei group"; they spurned work, marriage, and community responsibilities and identified with people of "lower social status" such as blacks and Filipinos.[64]

Yet the ethnic community's dirty laundry was not nearly as problematic as its leaders and the elites in Japan portrayed it. The immigrants, although unpolished and foreign to polite company (either American or Japanese), nevertheless were representative of most of the Japanese population. These people by and large did not herald from the lowest classes in Japan, and many of their so-called vices were hardly the sign of inferior breeding or intelligence. Gambling, for one, was a common practice in the Meiji era, so it should not have been surprising that the immigrants transplanted it to America. Nor should it have come as a surprise that the immigrants fumbled with appropriate dress, for despite the idealization of the West, very few Japanese, even in Tokyo where the Western influence was most pervasive, were familiar with Western clothing.[65] The discourse of cultural incompetency also obscured the immigrants' positive values and behaviors, such as the ability to save money and remit it to Japan. This was no small amount since it impressed Tokyo officials so much that they often saw such remittances as a rationale for Western colonization.[66] Most importantly, while rowdies were a great concern in Little Tokyo, youth delinquency was never the problem that it was in other ghetto communities. A study conducted in the early 1930s found that the percentage of juvenile delinquents among Japanese and Chinese Americans in Los Angeles was considerably less than in any other ethnic or racial population, including native-born whites.[67]

Self-criticism within the ethnic community, therefore, was not an exercise in objectivity. Ethnic leaders exaggerated the failings of Japanese Americans in ways that highlighted their own values as a ruling class. Since their education, language skills, and familiarity with American customs gave them more cultural capital than the rest of the group, they believed that it was their responsibility to mold the community in their image. This was a familiar paternalism that elites in all societies have long used to convince themselves of the burdens of their privilege. But among Japanese Americans, such class relations were overlaid with the common experience of racial persecution. Ethnic leaders, no matter how much they disdained their own kind, could not distance themselves from the group in the eyes of white America. They knew that in American society their abilities were tied inextricably to the weight of the Japanese American masses, and so they worked as hard to improve the masses as they did to elevate their own social status. From their perspective, self-interest and group interest were two sides of the same coin of racial uplift.[68]

If critical condemnation was the direct means to discipline the ethnic community, then celebrations like the Nisei Week festival were indirect ways to condition the thoughts and behaviors of Japanese Americans. The importance of such events is that they use fun and games to disguise the inculcation of group norms, values, and standards. Socialization becomes an integral part of the spectacle. Yet this is not to say that Nisei Week leaders easily scripted or consciously orchestrated the socialization process. Festivals work best as sites of cultural reproduction and change when audiences are not merely being told how to enjoy themselves—when they, as literary critic Mikhail Bakhtin put it, live in the spectacle, "and everyone participates because its very idea embraces all the people. While carnival lasts, there is no other life outside it." In his famous reading of medieval festivities in the Europe of the novelist François Rabelais, Bakhtin highlights the notion of "carnival time" as a self-contained reality in which "life is subject only to the laws of its own freedom." [69]

Thus explains the immediate success of Nisei Week and its lasting significance for the ethnic community. Although economically inclined, this festival was not just a device to spur consumption in Little Tokyo, nor was it merely an excuse to improve public relations for a racially marked minority or even to groom and discipline the ethnic community. Nisei Week, to be sure, was all of these things, but at heart it began as an open text for members of the second generation to understand themselves and their role as the progeny of a historic admixture of Japanese and American civilizations.

TWO

Rise and Fall of Biculturalism

Consumption, Socialization, and Americanism

"Chaplin is here . . . Chaplin is here!" The message spread through the crowd gathered in Los Angeles's Japanese quarter to watch the finale of the first Nisei Week festival. On that August night in 1934, a thousand kimono-clad youth halted their *ondo,* or Japanese folk dance, to get a glimpse of the screen idol. Urged to address the gathering, Chaplin praised Nisei Week for its dancing, its food, and especially its "beautiful Japanese girls." "I'm very happy to see all of you enjoying yourselves in the ondo," he announced. "It reminds me of my delightful days when I visited Japan." [1]

The Japanese in Japan and their overseas community were no strangers to Chaplin, who surrounded himself with Issei servants and maintained a reverence for Japanese traditions. As his autobiography reveals, the actor viewed Japan as a fleeting refuge from the pitfalls of modernity. "Her people's appreciation of those simple moments in life so characteristic of their culture—a lingering look at a moonbeam, a pilgrimage to view cherry blossoms, the quiet meditation of the tea ceremony—seems destined to disappear in the smog of Western enterprise." [2] Aghast at the signs of industrialization he witnessed in Japan, Chaplin cherished rituals like Nisei Week as treasured artifacts of an endangered culture.

Yet, in actuality, the festival was never an attempt to replicate Japanese folk traditions. Its leaders initially had envisioned the celebration as a Mardi Gras–type of event, partly because of their Western orientation, but also because they had no real conception of Japanese festivities. They had to be taught the basic steps of the ondo, the type of line dancing that most villagers in Japan inherited as part of their local culture, and schooled in the customs, folklore, and history of their ancestral homeland. Nisei Week was an educational experience they sought to share with the entire second generation, the majority of whom, like the JACLers, had not grasped the economic and political significance of their dual heritage. Through spectacles, performances, contests, speeches, essays, advertisements, street decorations, and costumes, the festival heralded the Nisei as a new breed of American citizen who was at home in both Japan and the United States. But as relations between the two nations degenerated in the late 1930s, Nisei Week leaders retreated from the notion of biculturalism. Mounting anti-Japanese belligerency on the West Coast caused them to use the same rituals that once celebrated Nisei ties to Japan, this time to highlight their exclusive loyalty to the United States.

It was this regenerative process of Nisei Week that Chaplin failed to understand. Rather than quaintly imitating Japanese and American traditions, the festival repeatedly inculcated them with new strains of ethnic identity so that time-honored rituals and memories were reprogrammed to meet changing historical circumstances. In this way, the rise and fall of biculturalism revealed the fluidity and contingency of identity within the ethnic community. Defining the Nisei was never an issue of articulating primordial dispositions or remaining true to a fixed strategy of adaptation or resistance. The form of ethnicity (be it biculturalism or Americanism) was less important at Nisei Week than the goal of resolving the three concerns from which the festival emerged: the slumping Little Tokyo economy, troubled U.S.-Japan relations, and feared disorderliness within the ethnic group.

BUY CULTURAL

The first sign of Nisei Week was a barrage of advertising. Little Tokyo merchants flooded the vernacular press with sales announcements and redesigned display windows to appeal to the second generation. In 1934 one retailer assured that such preparations were "All for the Satisfaction of the Nisei!" That same year Roku Sugahara, brother of JACL president Kay Sugahara, promised his generation that Little Tokyo stores were stocked with merchandise that was as fashionable and as low priced as any carried by "American" department stores.

In case these assurances were not enough, the JACLers linked enclave purchases with Nisei Week participation. Admission to festival events required receipts from Little Tokyo stores, and by the late 1930s, buying merchandise enabled shoppers to cast votes for their favorite beauty contestants. About a month before the festival, the vernacular newspapers began reporting tallies of the top vote getters, turning the Nisei Week Queen race into a weekly drama. The papers provided photographs and brief biographies of each of the candidates so that voters were able to choose their favorites. All this served to hype the competition, as the shoppers backed their preferences by purchasing an extra bottle of soy sauce, bag of rice, or tin of rice crackers. It was not uncommon for enthusiasts to wait until the festival to buy expensive items like refrigerators to increase their say in choosing the festival queen.[3]

But JACLers knew that even the most successful gimmick ended with Nisei Week. In order to secure year-round patronage, they strove to give the second generation a larger stake in the future of the immigrant enclave. The logic was straightforward: If the Nisei benefited materially from Little Tokyo, they would have more reason to shop there. The most compelling incentive that could be offered to the younger generation was employment. While free to patronize white-owned businesses, Nisei usually could not work for them, and Little Tokyo retailers made matters worse by refusing to hire many Nisei because of their inability to meet the needs of Japanese-speaking clientele. Festival organizers established an employment bureau to persuade the enclave merchants that Nisei salespersons would boost their businesses by attracting second-generation shoppers. In 1934 the bureau claimed to have placed thirty-five workers in just three days, but their jobs, like the special sales and beauty pageant, ended with Nisei Week.[4] Such positions were only temporary, one Issei merchant suggested, because the Nisei's language skills were "badly lacking." If they were to take over Little Tokyo, he concluded, the youngsters needed to be fluent in Japanese.[5]

The strongest appeals for Nisei patronage invoked bonds of ethnicity. According to Roku Sugahara, Little Tokyo offered a more pleasant shopping experience than the stores outside its protective borders. It makes for "a better understanding, a feeling of freedom and congeniality, and friendliness" because the "seller knows the background and characteristics of the buyer much better."[6] The winner of Nisei Week's essay contest in 1938 portrayed Little Tokyo as an ethnic sanctuary by listing the enclave's unique benefits for Nisei customers. Answering the question, "Why should I buy in Little Tokio," Warren Tsuneishi wrote, "Japanese can serve Japanese people with good taste. They know what type of clothing or merchandise would be best suited, whereas an American firm naturally would not. And, too, they are inclined to be more personal and understanding, as there are no barriers of speech or race. This results in friendly, sociable business tactics, and not cold ruthless negotiations." [7]

Supporters of the "buy in Lil' Tokio" campaign also insisted that shopping in the enclave benefited the entire community, not just the individual consumer. Buying from Japanese, Tsuneishi contended, "would greatly aid Issei and Nisei merchants who might not be able to cope with keen competition and racial discrimination should they have to establish themselves elsewhere." "The final result of this extensive trading," concluded his award-winning essay, "will be a closer union of our race— drawn together by the cohesive force of economic and social dependency." [8] Another essay contestant in 1938 celebrated Nisei patronage as a means to achieving economic self-sufficiency. If the enclave could rely upon Nisei customers, George Yamada argued, then they "will not need to depend upon the banks of Japan nor . . . the financial houses of our American brethren." [9] What buying in Little Tokyo boiled down to, Roku Sugahara explained, was that the ethnic community had a "common interest." "Money spent in the community and at Japanese stores means a greater degree of prosperity within our own circle," whereas money "spent outside of our community does not return to us" and thus "weakens the financial structure of the Japanese as a whole." [10]

Festival leaders used ethnicity as a carrot and stick to attract Nisei shoppers. While they played up the "natural" affinities among Japanese Americans, they also stressed the obligations that such ties entailed. "If the Nisei expect to see Lil' Tokio exist and rise out of its present depression," the *Rafu Shimpo* urged, "they must cooperate and help build Lil' Tokio by putting some funds into the businesses" and "buy all necessities at Japanese stores and only buy those things which are not carried in Lil' Tokio at American stores." Perhaps Roku Sugahara's do-or-die scenario best characterized the invocation of group obligation: "It all depends on the [N]isei, whether they will aid in strengthening our economic foundation or will stand idly by while it crumbles into oblivion." [11]

Not everyone at Nisei Week bought into the obligations of ethnic consumption. Carl Kondo, the runner-up in the Nisei Week essay contest in 1935, criticized the "buy in Lil' Tokio" campaign, warning that Little Tokyo should not rely on Nisei consumption because its mom-and-pop establishments could not compete with the department stores in nearby downtown Los Angeles. Moreover, Kondo argued that the Nisei were too influenced by American culture to be interested in Japanese merchandise or to be swayed by invocations of racial responsibilities. An editorial in the *Kashu Mainichi* added that this form of ethnic insularity was not only unfeasible but also "un-American." Isami Suzukawa insisted that buying only within the ethnic community would both curtail the Nisei's assimilation and betray the Roosevelt administration's attempts to end the depression. Japanese Americans, he wrote, needed to put the needs of America before the interests of Little Tokyo businesses by pumping money into the broader economy rather than hoarding it among themselves.[12]

Opposing the "buy in Lil' Tokio" plan, however, did not mean that one was unsympathetic to Issei merchants. The essayist Carl Kondo suggested that Japanese businesses cultivate interest from outside the ethnic community. Given white Americans' increasing curiosity about Japan, he believed that marketing Japanese culture and artifacts to them offered the best hope for Little Tokyo's economic stability. Suzukawa also championed the benefits of white consumption, proposing that the enclave serve as both tourist attraction to outsiders and a "cultural and spiritual center of the second generation."[13] Los Angeles's Chinese and Mexican American communities, the *Kashu Mainichi* advised, already were reaping the profits of ethnic tourism. The lesson the paper learned from China City, Chinatown's tourist center featuring a faux reproduction of the Forbidden City, and Olvera Street, a commercially oriented restoration of pueblo Los Angeles, was that the Nisei "should strive to make our section of town entirely different from the rest of the great metropolis. As it is, one cannot immediately feel the foreign atmosphere or distinction upon entering Lil' Tokyo."[14]

The "buy in Lil' Tokio" criticism had merit. According to one Nisei leader, most of the community's young consumers were more interested in the bottom line than the color line. They were not enticed or pressured to remain within the ethnic enclave, remembered Sam Hohri, because they simply shopped where it was most convenient and affordable or where they could receive the best service—which usually meant leaving Little Tokyo.[15] Conversely, it was apparent from the construction of China City and Olvera Street that white consumers were willing to cross the color line in the other direction. While the middle-class whites in New York City packed the nightclubs and cabarets in Harlem, their Los Angeles counterparts escaped the humdrum of mainstream America by adventuring into their own racial minority communities. The privileged few, like Charlie Chaplin, left the country altogether, seeking the "authentic" exotic in Tahiti, the Philippines, and Japan, while generating a boon in travel writing to whet the appetite of the rest of America.

Even in the best of times, Little Tokyo merchants would be hard-pressed to ignore this growing clientele. By 1936, a second fashion show was added to Nisei Week that was designed to attract outside interest in the Japanese kimono. The festival's souvenir booklet billed the event as "an exhibition of Japanese pajamas and lounging clothes" with refreshments served by "petite Japanese maidens in picturesque kimonos." The JACLers invited hundreds of "leading women in Los Angeles society" and selected fashions that would "appeal particularly to American women." [16]

Enclave merchants proposed that Nisei women wear kimonos while serving as tour guides who provided a "night of adventure to Americans in Little Tokyo." The hostesses were to greet tourists as they entered the enclave, answer questions about Japanese culture, including flower arrangements and tea ceremonies, and assist them in purchasing merchandise. Nisei Week's souvenir booklet was redesigned in 1940 to increase the enclave's tourist appeal. A glossy full-page advertisement was especially addressed to white Americans. "WELCOME TO LITTLE TOKYO" appeared in orientalized script inserted within a photograph of the community's main thoroughfare. The night scene featured a group of well-groomed, entertainment-seeking white Americans chaperoned by four smiling, kimono-clad women. Shining Little Tokyo storefronts, particularly the Fuji theater's elaborate neon marquee, in front of which the group stood, radiated an energy and enthusiasm that seemed to overwhelm the tourists. The smiling Japanese women reflected the enclave's warmth and hospitality, while the flood of bright lights and signs symbolized its entrepreneurial vigor—a shopper's paradise. [17]

It was, and was not, surprising that eventually Little Tokyo merchants sought to capitalize on the tourist market. They could point to the allure of Chinese and Mexican tourist sites and to the fact that curio shops, diners, and other Little Tokyo businesses always had relied on the patronage of non-Japanese. But it was not clear if they embraced tourism on their own or were driven to it by the inadequacy of Nisei consumption. Catering to whites seemed to be a dramatic turnaround from the self-help position that initiated Nisei Week. Yet upon closer inspection the appeals to an outside clientele and an internal solidarity were not seen as mutually exclusive. The "buy in Lil' Tokio" campaign continued at Nisei Week, as the festival's orientalized street displays, decorations, music, dance, and fashions assumed double meanings. What stood as symbols of ethnic pride for Japanese Americans were also exotic enticements for white America. Through their Nisei interpreters, white shoppers

A 1938 Nisei Week's tea ceremony embodied the "bridge of understanding" that Issei and Nisei leaders envisioned between Japan and the United States. *Courtesy Japanese American National Museum, gift of Jack and Peggy Iwata (98.102.273), photo by Jack Iwata.*

could develop an appreciation for the enclave as a place of both enchanting mystery and comforting familiarity.

Catering to the tourist market did not require Nisei Week leaders to abandon their notion of biculturalism, for this identity was important for attracting both Nisei and white customers. Gaining an equal admiration for Japanese and American cultures meant that the Nisei might become more loyal to enclave merchandise and services and yet also serve as crucial brokers between Little Tokyo and outside consumers. Either way, festival leaders still saw them as the "sole salvation for the preservation of Japanese town."[18] But they knew that they could not win the loyalty of the Nisei simply by tempting them with prizes, gimmicks, merchandise, or the possibility of long-term employment. Nor was it enough to place them in community leadership positions. In their minds, changing Little Tokyo for the Nisei was not nearly as important as changing the Nisei for Little Tokyo.

Tourists visiting Los Angeles's Little Tokyo in 1941 were treated to a night of adventure and consumer pleasures, while being assured that Japanese Americans were law-abiding residents and citizens of the United States. *Courtesy Nisei Week Japanese American Festival, Inc.*

RITE TO BE JAPANESE

Before the Nisei could be relied upon as consumers and cultural ambassadors, festival leaders sought to create a Nisei "community consciousness" centered on appreciation for Japanese traditions. Folk dancing, which had deep religious and cultural meanings in Japan, would become Nisei Week's pièce de résistance. While outsiders like Chaplin saw these dances as a mirror of Japanese culture, festival leaders considered them the epitome of Issei-Nisei cooperation. The publisher Sei Fujii was struck by the communal spirit exhibited at the ondo practice sessions because the different generations of dancers felt "just like one family." He expressed these same sentiments at the ondo finale, where he gazed with delight at the young Nisei girls dancing with hoary Issei men.[19]

The columnist Joseph Shinoda also commented on the bonds between the generations at the Nisei Week ondo. The Issei's enthusiasm for dancing, he wrote, enabled the Nisei to "see a very amusing side to this older generation." "It is no wonder that they try to keep a stiff upper lip with all the traditions of Japan to live up to . . . , [b]ut down deep they are apparently the same rhythm-loving frivolous bunch of individuals that we much-deplored second generation are." Shinoda went on to expose the mystique of Issei authority. He told his fellow Nisei that, given the opportunity, "these respected elders of ours . . . can make better monkeys and spectacles of themselves than we." His ultimate message underscored not only the Issei's humanity (placing them on a par with their children) but also their vulnerability as aliens in a foreign land.[20]

The ondo finale relied upon the talents of Nisei like Yoshiko Mori, who was more interested in Japanese traditions than Western entertainment. Born in Sacramento in 1920, Mori, in her early teens, convinced her parents to move to Los Angeles where she would be better able to pursue Japanese dance. After graduating from high school, she studied Kabuki dancing in Japan and then returned to the ethnic community, where she taught a large number of volunteers to perform the ondo at the Nisei Week finale. Mori agreed to the task not only to share her love of Japanese dance but also to encourage her generation to learn about their ancestral culture. She maintained that Japanese dancing counteracted the Nisei's Americanization by teaching them to be more graceful, considerate of others, and respectful to their "higher-ups."[21]

The Nisei Week leaders also hoped that ondo dancing would increase the younger generation's awareness of their parents' hardships. Chiye Nagano, another professional dancer and the choreographer of the Nisei

Week ondo, selected routines with themes that centered upon issues of hard labor and martial strife. The idea of the ondo, Nagano explained, was to encourage the community to laugh at the realities of immigrant life and, thus, to release the stresses of its work-a-day world. Nagano's own life mirrored her art. Trained at a revered classical dance school in Japan, she returned to Los Angeles where, to her dismay, the traditions of Noh and Kabuki were far from worshipped. With her mother's guidance, she became one of the first Nisei to teach Japanese dance in Los Angeles. But not even her earnings from teaching were enough to please her father, who bemoaned the fact that she had no brothers. Nisei Week was a chance to show him that she could be as good as a son, and to make this unmistakably clear, she dressed in men's clothes and pretended to be his missing heir. Nagano believed that it was imperative for her generation to relieve the tensions between parents and children. To bridge this generation gap, she designed the ondo to attract as many Issei and Nisei participants as possible; she simplified the dance steps, held practices after work hours, and paid no attention to the performers' humble dress. The goal was to unite Japanese Americans in the celebration of the old world.[22]

In addition to the ondo, Nisei Week leaders sought to unite the generations in the knowledge of Japanese history. The festival's parade in 1935 featured children in various costumes that characterized Japan's historical periods, from its mythic creation in 600 B.C. to the present era of the Taisho emperor. But Nisei Week's most pronounced construction of memory focused on the Issei as pioneers in the United States. The JACLers originated Nisei Week's Pioneer Night as a way of highlighting the experiences of the earliest Japanese immigrants to the United States. In 1935 the Issei were feted with an afternoon tea followed by a banquet in their honor at a local Japanese restaurant. The Nisei were urged to be thankful to their parents because they had traveled so far "to create a future for their children in the land of the free."[23] Pioneer Night reminded them that the Issei, too, were Americans and deserved respect for their heroic efforts to achieve the "American dream." The event welcomed members from white immigrant societies in the spirit of celebrating the nation's diversity of immigration experiences.[24]

The image of the Issei as rugged pioneers, struggling against all odds to claim America as their home filled the pages of the Nisei press. Tsuyoshi Matsumoto noted that the "Issei has refused to become a symbol of man's injustice toward his fellow human being, and instead . . . has become a symbol of man's eternal victory over circumstances." The Issei,

Participants in Nisei Week's parade educated the Americanized second generation about the periods and dress of premodern Japan. *Courtesy Japanese American National Museum, gift of K. Patrick and Lily A. Okura (96.321.8).*

Matsumoto continued, "has refused to give up when the going was tough, and instead . . . has built a home for himself and his children, a happy American home from which new generations of American citizens will come still in the future." [25] Another Nisei praised his pioneer father thus: "We know the struggles and the difficulties that he has to encounter. We have often heard time and again of his hardships in meeting oppression from the *hakujin* [white people] and the depression of the times." The conclusion revealed the Nisei's begrudging respect. "Our gratitude is manifold no matter how queer he may seem to us at times." [26]

The legitimacy of the notion of Issei pioneers was such that Nisei appropriated the term for themselves. In 1940 the Nisei Week booklet described the meaning of the Issei pioneer event for the second generation: "The true significance of Pioneer Night must not be lost upon the Nisei. . . . Although the occasion is primarily dedicated to our pioneering parents, it concerns, in a deeper sense, our own realization and acknowledgment of their courage and perseverance. This realization can better be brought to bear when we perceive that we too are pioneers. With the stirring of unkind prejudices which tread upon the heels of complex affairs, the fact is obvious that the Nisei are destined to undergo similar experiences. Upon these premises, the Nisei and their parents will gather about the festive board in a *spirit of mutual understanding and affection*" (emphasis added). [27]

Yet in celebrating intergenerational unity, little consideration was given to those Issei who returned to Japan, sometimes having fulfilled a successful "sojourn" or sometimes having suffered a bitter defeat. Nor did the pioneer event acknowledge the nagging racism that continued to cripple the first generation. The leftist newspaper *Doho* took issue with the romanticized construction of Issei history. Instead of glorifying Japanese immigrants, columnist John Kitahara placed them within working-class history and appraised their heroism as that of an exploited proletariat. He waited for the day when "a chronicle of the [I]ssei may be written, not about the handful who succeeded and made their 'mark' in this world, not about those who become leaders in their small circles, but those who have given the best years of their lives in the struggle in a new land, and found nothing at the end of the trail but failure and disillusion." [28]

Kitahara's critique hinted at the larger working-class experiences and perspectives that were absent at Nisei Week. It was common for the Nisei to carry on the probusiness ideology of the Issei old guard and to portray labor organizers and other left-leaning activists as anathema to the group's social prestige and respectability. In a published study of social groupings among Japanese Americans, James Sakoda reported that even a slight interest in trade unionism was sufficient for a person to be branded an *aka* ("red," or communist). According to him, these so-called radicals and communists, who did not maintain the middle-class ideology, were considered "unacceptables" and hence "ostracized by the community." So too were the Issei migrant workers who "lived in hotels, boarding houses, and labor camps and usually did not participate in the activities of the community." [29]

Nisei Week hid these "unacceptables" behind a facade of entrepreneurial success. Its leaders totally ignored *Doho*'s insistence that the festival address troubling issues "of Nisei labor, of dual citizenship, of anti-alien legislation, of vocational problems, [and] of unity of [N]isei organizations." [30] *Doho* editors labeled Sei Fujii, the publisher of the *Kashu Mainichi*, a "jingoist" because of his support for Japan's military leadership and branded Fred Tayama, the 1940 JACL president, a "labor-baiter." Tayama, reportedly one of the most successful Nisei entrepreneurs in Little Tokyo, owned a chain of restaurants ("U.S. Cafes") that *Doho* accused of subjecting workers to "sweatshop conditions." The newspaper backed labor organizers who set up picket lines in front of Tayama's businesses. But the JACL president prevailed in court by winning an injunction against the picketers; he opposed labor unions and dismissed *Doho* as a communist rag: "Just the fact that it singles you out for attack," he said, "means you're all right."[31]

The JACLer's middle-class values were also apparent at the ceremony to crown the Nisei Week queen. Its formal dress code, luxurious setting, and full orchestra legitimized the Coronation Ball as a highbrow affair that often landed Nisei on the *Los Angeles Times's* society pages. Props and costumes—like a tiara, cape, and gown—distinguished the queen as the figurehead of Little Tokyo. Since its beginning in 1935, the ball increased in popularity, grandeur, and mystique. Festival leaders eventually moved it from Little Tokyo's all-purpose auditorium to the Biltmore Hotel, a prestigious Los Angeles landmark. Issei merchants complained bitterly that removing the ball from Little Tokyo defeated Nisei Week's original purpose of boosting enclave business. Yet the JACLers claimed that the event not only had outgrown its previous venue but also that many Nisei "look forward to and attend the ball because it is held in an atmosphere such as the Biltmore Hotel."[32]

Nisei Week's screen of success was best captured by the parade floats in 1936 that revealed different parts of the enclave's agricultural economy. A gargantuan celery stalk symbolized the bountiful harvests in Venice, California; horticulturists from the San Gabriel Valley adorned their float with bouquets of flowers; Orange County farmers decorated their tractors and other farm implements, while the wholesalers at Los Angeles's central produce market displayed a huge mural showing a thriving business environment. Yet, revealingly, the entrepreneurial spirit of the floats ignored the significance of labor to the ethnic enclave. There was no credit given to those who worked the celery fields in Venice or picked flowers in San Gabriel. Likewise, there was no mention of those who loaded the produce at the central market or lost their jobs in Orange County to innovations in farm vehicles. The workers, or their advocates, in the ethnic enclave played no official role in Nisei Week.[33]

The same could not be said for women in Little Tokyo. During Nisei Week they were encouraged to leave the domestic sphere to participate in the community's public life. The festival leaders depended upon women to organize the ondo and fashion shows, and the beauty pageant contestants were relied upon not only to attract shoppers to Little Tokyo through merchandise voting but also to represent the community at official receptions. The criteria for the queen in 1939 was that she be able to serve as goodwill ambassador among groups of Issei, Nisei, and white Americans.[34] The opportunity to "bring the Japanese people together" was what motivated one admittedly shy nineteen-year-old to enter the

Coronation of the 1938 Nisei Week queen, held at the Biltmore Hotel in Los Angeles, revealed the second generation's bourgeois and Americanized aspirations. *Courtesy Japanese American National Museum, gift of Jack and Peggy Iwata (93.102.239), photo by Jack Iwata.*

A float in the Nisei Week parade displays that prominence of Japanese Americans in southern California's wholesale produce industry. *Courtesy Japanese American National Museum, gift of Dick Hirasuna (96.110.5E).*

beauty contest. She and her parents, who were merchants in Little Tokyo, saw the contest not as a beauty pageant but as a way for young women to get involved in issues of great concern to the ethnic community.[35]

The role of the beauty contestants was to reflect a bicultural identity that instilled ethnic solidarity in Japanese Americans, even while communicating ethnic fantasies to the outside world. The JACL president in 1938 declared that the ideal candidate blended "the quiet charm of the Japanese wom[a]n with the more lively personality of the American girl." The *Rafu Shimpo* expounded that "[s]he must be able to wear a kimono and walk with zori [slippers] on as well as look radiant in a white evening gown." The Nisei Week queen in 1940 reportedly epitomized the hybrid of East and West and, according to the *Kashu Mainichi*, "represented the best of [N]isei womanhood." The newspaper reported that she went to sewing school three nights a week, took *koto* lessons two nights, studied Japanese language one night, and worked a full-time job as a secretary for a Japanese doctor. The queen "knows her Japanese manners as well as American etiquette." Industrious, cultured, and community-minded, she was, more importantly, humble. "Her winning modesty doesn't permit her to talk very much about herself. She would rather listen to you." [36]

Nisei Week glorified women's reproductive labor through the addition of a baby contest. A panel of medical doctors and dentists judged the contestants on the basis of their overall health, personality, and appearance. Like the beauty queen, the winners were celebrated as embodiments of biculturalism. The "prince and princess" were said to reflect the increasing stature, improving personality, and abilities of each successive generation in the United States.

Yet the experiences of one beauty contestant suggest that the roles for women at Nisei Week were primarily symbolic. Sandra Sakai wanted to be more than a pretty symbol. She was born and raised in Los Angeles and had attended UCLA briefly before her father decided that college was unnecessary for women. Like many in her generation, she found job opportunities only within the ethnic community and even there had to beat out hundreds of applicants for a secretarial position. Sakai entered the beauty contest with the encouragement of a JACL member and was enthusiastic about promoting "goodwill between different types of Japanese." Yet her delight at being named "Queen of the Nisei" soon turned to frustration because she resented taking orders from the festival leaders and regretted the lack of opportunity to voice her own opinions. "They ordered us," she remembered, "and we just followed." [37]

For one *Rafu Shimpo* columnist, domesticated roles for women in Nisei Week were better then none at all. Martha Kaihatsu suggested the introduction of a cake- and pie-baking contest to increase women's involvement in the festival and pointed out the need for more leadership roles for women in both Nisei Week and the concurrent JACL convention that took place in 1938. But well aware of the sexual division of labor within the Japanese American community, the writer predicted that women's participation in both Nisei Week and the JACL convention "will be overshadowed by male domination." [38] Her cynicism was not unfounded. Although women were crucial to Nisei Week as volunteers, performers, and bait for consumers, they were excluded from the higher levels of decision making. [39]

The participation of women in Nisei Week reproduced the sexual division of labor within the ethnic community. In her study of kinship patterns among Japanese Americans, anthropologist Sylvia Yanagisako observed that gender roles placed women in charge of "things inside the home" *(uchi no koto),* while the men tended to "things outdoors" *(soto no koto).* This, of course, did not mean that wives and daughters did not work outside the home. Many of them earned wages tending the houses of Los Angeles's expanding upper class. They also could be found typing letters and taking phone calls in the less-distinguished environs of Little Tokyo. But mostly they were counted upon as unpaid workers, helping out on the family farm or small business. *Doho* blamed traditional gender distinctions for relegating women to the "lowest and hardest work." [40]

The inclusion of women in Nisei Week also embodied the second generation's racial anxieties. One Nisei suggested that the beauty contestants refrain from wearing Western fashions, because "kimonos look best on Japanese girls." "The costume," he said, "makes them look taller" and conceals the "elementary short-comings [sic] of the typical Nisei girl." [41] The *Kashu Mainichi's* beauty expert cautioned Nisei against dyeing their hair to appear more like white Americans. "To try to change the color to blond or red," she advised, "is idiotic, since it would throw the whole face off balance." The challenge for Nisei women was to be imaginative in compensating for the "definite handicap [of] . . . their short figures" and their "inevitable black hair." [42]

One of the funnier moments at an early Nisei Week revealed that the symbolic subordination of women occurred even in their absence. The festival's talent revue in 1936 featured a routine when the JACL's leading men dressed as women. They appeared as "anvil-footed, muscle-bound Romeos in women's garb" in a skit, known as the "flora-dora sextet,"

which parodied a scene from an 1890s Broadway hit famous for its idealization of feminine beauty.[43] Patrick Okura, one of the flora-dora members, explained that the JACLers initially recruited women for the routine but thought that an all-male cast would prove more entertaining.
A graduate of UCLA and one of the first Nisei to successfully challenge
the segregationist hiring practices by the city of Los Angeles, Okura was
somewhat of a star in his own right. The flora-dora act, he noted, was a
"big hit" that the JACLers would remember as a trial by humiliation
that bonded the Nisei leaders. But the cross-dressing revealed more than
the JACLers' sense of humor and status as the Nisei elite. The success of
the performance, Okura confirmed, was founded upon the community's
understanding of gender difference: men in Little Tokyo were not supposed to be erotic objects unless in the realm of play.[44]

THE INVERTED WORLD

While the flora-dora routine reenacted a traditional sense of gender
roles, Nisei Week was not simply a filial commitment to Little Tokyo's social order. Indeed, the JACLers interpreted the premise of Nisei Week—
children leading parents—as an opportunity to change the ethnic community by creating a vision of its Americanization. While they could
appreciate the Issei experience and learn Japanese rituals, their cultural
orientation remained decidedly American. Neither racial segregation
nor the animosity that perpetuated it discouraged their attachment to
Western norms of behavior.

The instability of U.S.-Japan relations only increased the JACL's commitment to Americanization. During the 1930s, Western nations became
alarmed as Japan expanded its empire into Korea and then northern
China. The League of Nations, with the support of the United States,
condemned Japanese aggression in Manchuria in 1931, causing the Asian
power to pull out of the international organization and to grow increasingly defensive about its territorial claims. The United States was particularly concerned about the threat Japanese colonialism posed to its markets and trade throughout Asia. This conflict between the two nations
generated new anti-Japanese fears that had direct repercussions for Japanese Americans. An ardent foe of the ethnic community in Los Angeles
was Lail Thomas Kane, the self-proclaimed leader of a crusade to exclude Japanese Americans from commercial fishing. Kane testified to the
House Special Committee on Un-American Activities in 1934 that Japa-

nese American fishermen were prepared to lay mines and torpedo American vessels should U.S.-Japan relations disintegrate into war. He gained support from the American Legion and drafted state legislation to support his cause. Although his antifishing bills never left committee, Kane's campaign placed the ethnic community in the limelight of suspicion.[45]

In stark contrast to these fears, the JACLers used Nisei Week to underscore the community's adaptation to American culture. The 1936 talent show displayed Nisei Week's American influences by featuring—in addition to the flora-dora routine—a waltz ensemble, tap and Spanish dances, songs from the current hit parade, and "for the first time in Little Tokyo," a chorus line of Nisei women. The festival's carnival also would have been familiar to white Americans, notwithstanding the smell of teriyaki and the sea of Japanese faces. Scores of Nisei social, athletic, and religious organizations raised money for a community center where they all could gather and coordinate their activities. They sold snacks, hosted games, and emulated the festivities found at county fairs and church bazaars held across America.[46]

But the appropriation of American rituals, Nisei Week leaders realized, did not mean that the majority of the Nisei wanted to blend indiscriminately with mainstream society. James Sakoda, in an unpublished study of Japanese American "patterns of adjustment," identified what he called the "Nisei world." Sakoda claimed that before World War II many Nisei, especially those who took part in ethnic organizations, athletic teams, and community events, preferred to "keep to themselves" and to avoid both the Issei and those outside Little Tokyo. They built their own social universe—complete with styles of dancing, dating, dressing, and language—that paralleled, yet rarely intersected with, white America. "The identification," Sakoda clarified, "was with American ways, but not with Caucasians."[47]

The JACLers sought to break up this ethnic exclusiveness since their idea of biculturalism was to connect Little Tokyo with the American mainstream. The Nisei Week leaders maintained that the second generation's "clannishness" hurt the festival's appeal. One leader complained that despite the glamour of Nisei Week "it may still appear to be a 'private affair' of the [N]isei in Lil' Tokio."[48] Another leader assured the Nisei that the exemplary behavior of whites at Nisei Week proved that they were willing to accept Japanese Americans as equals. "Their good-natured mingling and joshing with the crowds and their genuine admiration for the Japanese arts showed their capacity for tolerance and appreciation. Many came to see what they could see; some went back with a deeper understanding of the Japanese as human beings rather than as a 'peril.'"[49]

Even more troubling than the Nisei's inability to get along with whites was their inability to get along with each other. Nisei Week, as a designated place of play, encouraged excessive and exaggerated forms of behavior that resulted in violent clashes between groups within the ethnic community. This permissiveness, folklorist Roger Abrahams maintains, is what makes festivals potentially subversive: They "bring us together in celebration but let each of us 'do our own thing,' write our script of progress within the events," and thus these "mad moments in the margins of time continue to provide us with models of revolution. . . ."[50] The strongest evidence of this sort of subversiveness at Nisei Week were the disturbances caused by groups of delinquent youth.

According to some observers, the festival's street dance in 1938 seemed the same as it had always been. There were the socialites mingling freely, looking and acting important, and there were the "rowdies," the streetwise young men (and women) whose very appearance threatened to disrupt order. But that night the rowdies did more than look tough. Word on the street said that "a bunch of thugs" from Orange County were coming to Nisei Week; they were coming to look for the "tough L.A. bunch," and they were bringing along "big hakujin fellows."[51] Like hundreds of other Japanese Americans, these Orange County Nisei (and their white buddies) drove miles of dusty roads to reach Little Tokyo and to take part in Nisei Week festivities. In Little Tokyo they were out of place. To be sure, as Japanese Americans they belonged in the ethnic community, but the crowded grid of downtown Los Angeles with its Chicano, African American, Chinese, Filipino, Japanese, and Eastern European neighborhoods was a far cry from Orange County's spacious tracks of land. Little Tokyo was not their home; it was not their turf. Of course, what brought these farmers' sons to the big city was not just the annual Japanese festival. Nisei Week was merely the occasion, the pretext, the license to work out their aggressions against Little Tokyo "rowdies," namely the gang known as the Cougars.

The local boys, for their part, returned the animosity against the *inakamono* (country hicks). Little Tokyo was their town; it was their manly duty to defend it. The fight that erupted became legendary; perhaps it was the origin of Nisei Week's reputation for street fighting. Yet, according to one source, the scuffle proved better as folklore than spectacle. "I remember when people told me about it—when Jake hit this guy, he just flew—he hit him so hard. To make a long story short, . . . [the Orange County Nisei] ran from Central Avenue, they ran clear up Main Street, and these guys chased them. And that was the end of the fight. That's it. I mean, they talked about that thing for the longest time, saying it was a big bloody mess, but it wasn't really that bad." According to the same source, the results of this Little Tokyo showdown underscored the local boys' reputed fighting skill. The Orange County guys, he boasted, were "crazy to do this, to come into town with big hakujin guys to fight because it wasn't just the Cougars, but the Olivers are there, and the Spartans are there. There's a bunch of tough guys." [52]

Street fights occurred throughout the year, usually at dances or other social events. To one informant, rowdies were so ubiquitous that "you couldn't plan a social event without taking them into consideration—gee, suppose they come and crash the party. They were preying upon their own people. . . . if they crash the party, what are you going to do?" [53] An increase in "rowdyism" seemed to be correlated with the emergence of a vast network of Nisei social clubs. Isami Arufuku Waugh found that by 1938 there were four hundred of these clubs in Los Angeles alone. One source commented on the connection between clubs and deviance. He noted that "in those days, there were so many clubs, there was always one group fighting against another group, the Olivers, the Oliver Tigers, Cubs, Mustangs, Broncos, they had about five different clubs. They were always playing basketball with Terminal Island, and they would fight, and some of the Harbor City guys would come up for Nisei Week and they'd fight." [54]

In the early 1940s, the ethnic press reported a spate of incidents: June 1940 "drunken [N]isei boys" brawled after a southern California Retail Produce Workers dance; February 1941, the Pasadena police broke up the beating of a Pasadena Junior College student; meanwhile an incident erupted at a private party on the west side involving "a fistfight, window-smashing, screen door ripping, milk bottle hurling, vandalism, flight in retreat, apprehension by the Police"; September 1941 witnessed a fight in the heart of Little Tokyo and an "ugly spectacle" at the Ocean Park pier in Santa Monica. [55]

The Nisei Week leaders acknowledged their inability to control "rowdyism." One publicly regretted the fact that "past Nisei Weeks have had the undeserved blotch of not being prepared to control those infantile groups whose malicious boisterousness have been of much annoyance." In 1940 the rowdies were instructed that the "girls will respect you for being gentlemanly," because Nisei Week "is the time to have FUN but not for hell-raising, picking fights and drunkenness." A year later in 1941 the Nisei Week leaders warned "rowdy individuals or purported gangs" that twenty police officers accompanied by a "squad of a hundred judo experts would be patrolling the grounds" and anyone caught fighting "will be taken into custody and prosecuted." But the rowdies were not to be stopped; that year the *Kashu Mainichi* reported that Nisei Week claimed four fights, two visitors injured, six Nisei on police suspect lists, and arrests of peace disturbers.[56]

The most serious crime committed by the rowdies was jeopardizing the JACLers' public relations campaign. In her criticism of "gate crashers" in Little Tokyo, *Rafu Shimpo* editor Louise Suski warned that rowdies "have become so bold that they even attend without invitation a social held in a private home" and would curse and yell at a white American "who refused to admit them to a particular hall because their names weren't on the list." The idea of youngsters getting their way through threats and intimidation was anathema to Suski's model of the "self-made man." Her immigrant father, after all, had suffered devastating hardships, including losing the family possessions in the San Francisco earthquake of 1906, to earn a medical degree and become a leading figure in Little Tokyo. The younger Suski herself was no less of an autodidact, having taught herself the craft of print journalism as the first editor of the ethnic community's newly established Nisei press. She was presumably embarrassed by the rowdies' behavior, but her mentioning that the ticket taker was white exposed the broader racial stakes of community delinquency. The main significance of the "gate crashers," Suski maintained, "was that they reflected poorly on all Japanese Americans" and that "any good that the other [N]isei have built up, these youths are knocking down and tearing away by their actions and language."[57]

To Nisei Week leaders, the rowdies symbolized everything that was wrong with Japanese America. JACL's national publication, the *Pacific Citizen*, revealed the leadership's concern: "Crime and immorality are increasing among the Japanese in the United States at a rate such as to render active repressive efforts an urgent necessity. Murder, banditry, issuance of false checks, peeping toms and the like. The most deplorable feature of the whole situation is that this tide of crime is in great part due to the youth—boys and often girls of the bobbed-hair type."[58] The construction of the rowdies stood in opposition to the Nisei leadership's core values. "If the Japanese people are to become members of this nation," the *Pacific Citizen* editorial continued, "they must be *better and more respectable citizens than their Caucasian brethren. Legally speak-*

ing they are Americans by birth. But socially, they are still Japanese. It is just as important to be accepted socially, since in America, society comes before law. If the second-generation Japanese are to become an integral part of American society, they must be more law-abiding, more educated, more decent and in every way above others" (emphasis added).[59] The strategy of Japanese American superiority left no room for mediocrity or, even worse, inferiority. All of them had to be "better" than the average white American or else the possibility of complete Japanese American inclusion in the American mainstream would be squandered.

The JACLers' response to the rowdies was to disassociate them from the ethnic community. The Nisei leaders described the disaffected youth not only as abominations but also aberrations in an otherwise upstanding community. The gang fight at the Nisei Week street dance in 1938 so upset the current JACL president that he warned those involved that "unless you boys change your ways" he would have them "blackballed" from jobs in the Japanese enclave. The ethnic press applied additional pressure. After the street dance incident, the *Rafu Shimpo* did something it had rarely done: It named the individuals and groups involved in the fracas. The newspaper stood firmly behind its action, insisting that "the good name of the Japanese Americans must be preserved."[60]

AMERICAN FRONT

The economic and cultural motives that began Nisei Week and the concerns about the group's Americanization were inextricably tied to the demonstration of the second generation's civic virtue and political allegiance. "Through the medium of this festival," John Maeno declared in 1936, "the JACL hopes to present, acquaint, and contact you directly with the young Japanese American citizen, his life and environment." Maeno, the organization's second president, was one of the few Nisei lawyers in Little Tokyo. A graduate of the University of Southern California, he used his college ties to make inroads into Los Angeles political circles. He explained that as a "new American" the Nisei was a "true and loyal citizen of the United States" who sought to take "part in civic development and community progress."[61] This theme was echoed in the early 1940s by then–JACL president Eiji Tanabe, who noted that as "new Americans, we earnestly strive to foster, develop and encourage active interest in our community and government."[62]

The JACLers used the Nisei's citizenship to gain advantages in the political arena. They, like the leaders of African Americans and many

Nisei Week queen Margaret Nishikawa rides in festival parade with Los
Angeles Mayor Frank Shaw in 1938. The pairing of young, attractive Nisei
women with political leaders was intended to symbolize trust and goodwill
between the ethnic community's male leadership and city hall. *Courtesy
Japanese American National Museum, gift of Jack and Peggy Iwata
(93.102.315), photo by Jack Iwata.*

urban immigrant groups, attempted to gain electoral power by combin-
ing Japanese American votes into one large ethnic bloc. They hoped that
as the number of Nisei came of age, they could expand their impact on
local elections. A group of white office seekers took the Nisei vote seriously and showed up at the festival's inauguration in 1934. There were so
many that their numbers raised concerns in Little Tokyo that the festivities would turn into a "political rally." [63] Nisei Week also had always been
an occasion to pay respects to the highest elected official in Los Angeles.
In the opening ceremony in 1936, a colorful procession moved through
the streets of Little Tokyo on its way to Los Angeles's City Hall two blocks
away. The ethnic community's "leading citizens" accompanied the Nisei
Week queen and "her pretty and charming attendants" as they were carried along in Japanese rickshaws. The ceremony concluded with these
"kimono-clad, dark-eyed beauties" presenting the mayor of Los Angeles "with an official invitation to attend this gala event in Lil' Tokyo." [64]

Such visible displays of goodwill toward the Los Angeles community illustrated the type of citizenship that the JACLers espoused. To them, being American meant not just possessing legal entitlements but also performing a wide range of civic duties. Isamu Masuda, the winner of the JACL's oratorical contest in 1938, placed the responsibility of improving "our race problem" on the Nisei's shoulders. He encouraged the Nisei to engage in "active citizenship" by voting and involving themselves in public affairs. Civic involvement, he asserted, would prove that the Nisei are a "racial group worthy of being accepted on an equal plane" because "it will show to the white citizenry that we are not a culturally or mentally inferior race . . . , that we are beneficial to America's social and economic welfare, and that we desire to cooperate with the white race in solving our community and national problems." The ultimate significance of active citizenship, the orator explained, was that eventually it would compel "the white race, themselves, to take down the racial barriers that have been erected against us." [65]

At the heart of the JACLers' "active citizenship" was a profound love of country. A typical expression of this was articulated by an essayist in the *Pacific Citizen*. Asayo Kuraya vented his outrage at racist groups that viewed the Nisei as disloyal to the United States. "If I were stoic like the true Oriental and wise, perhaps I would . . . ignore such a remark. But instead my blood boils and I crave action against persons making derogatory remarks. . . . The color of my skin maybe different but I'm willing to wager that my loyalty and love for country is on the par with any of you. . . . And last but not least, I'll always be proud of my citizenship even if I am not a white American." [66]

But the faith that JACLers placed in American society was not entirely blind. Throughout the 1930s the Nisei often pondered the consequences of warfare between the United States and Japan. One fictionalized account predicted that eventually the two nations would go to the brink of war, causing the Nisei to flee to Mexico to escape the threat of their imprisonment in concentration camps. With war being averted, the author claimed that the Nisei would return to Los Angeles and confront "no more trouble." Joseph Shinoda was characteristically less sanguine as he pondered the consequences of a Pacific war. "This is our country but if its people, our fellow citizens, will not permit us to be Americans, Hell would be a picnic by comparison for us who are American but whose faces are as Japanese as the face of the emperor himself." [67]

While they emphasized Americanism, the JACLers did not equate loyalty to the United States with severing ties to Japan. Despite America's opposition to Japanese imperialism, they sided with their parents, who, like most expatriates, reveled in the military victories of their homeland. The formal declaration of the second Sino-Japanese War in 1937 heightened these ties to the motherland, as both generations sent money, supplies, and good wishes to Japanese soldiers. Issei leaders called upon the JACLers to counteract the American public's overwhelming support for the Chinese (President Franklin Roosevelt, in fact, disobeyed his own policy of neutrality in foreign wars by sending American arms to Chinese troops). The older generation, with assistance from the Japanese consulate, briefed the young leaders on the necessity and righteousness of Japan's foreign policies and helped to establish a Nisei "speakers bureau" to inform Americans about Japan's side of the story. Togo Tanaka confirmed that the English section of his newspaper, *Rafu Shimpo,* based its editorials and coverage of the Sino-Japanese War on information provided by Issei who blamed Japan's negative image on Chinese propaganda. The staff of the paper's Japanese section prepared pamphlets for their Nisei colleagues about Japan's plight in the West—the subtitle of one of these read, "How about Giving Japan a Break?"[68] Thus Tanaka concluded that the JACLers, despite their strong commitment to American political institutions, were mindful "not to disparage the cultural values of Japan, nor to antagonize Issei feelings in the latter's sympathies for Japan. JACL leaders even rationalized their Americanism as being rooted in Japanese culture."[69]

But the public's opposition only grew when Japanese troops captured Beijing and pressed on to victory. In 1939 Roosevelt abrogated the treaty that had safeguarded U.S.-Japan trade and a year later, in response to Japan's Tripartite Alliance with Germany and Italy and its apparent movement into Southeast Asia, threatened to cut off the shipment of about 80 percent of the island nation's war supplies. The growing opposition to Japan's war advances buoyed antagonism against Japanese Americans. By 1938 Lail Thomas Kane was in the habit of sharing his opinions with *Rafu Shimpo* editor Togo Tanaka, who duly noted them as an alarming indication of popular sentiment. "By this time," Tanaka later noted, "Kane's attitude toward the Nisei as 'Jap-stooges' appears to have crystallized." This was evident in Kane's telling Tanaka that "I'm rapidly being convinced that the JACL, which represents the Nisei leadership, is nothing more than an instrument of the Issei. You really take your orders from Japan."

Still backed by the American Legion, Kane continued to lobby for legislation against Japanese American fishermen. He told Tanaka that if the

JACLers, whom he referred to as "jackals," were really loyal, "you would support this fishing bill which is a national defense, patriotic proposal," and "you should know that the security of the United States is menaced by the presence of fishing boats manned by naval reserve officers of the Imperial Japanese Navy." These fears reached a national audience through Kane's various publications, including an article in the *Saturday Evening Post,* and spread beyond the issue of Japanese American fishermen. The immediate problem for Little Tokyo was that increasing anti-Japanese sentiment gave rise to boycotts against Japanese businesses that placed the depression-weary enclave in even further jeopardy.[70]

"A direct correlation exists," wrote Tanaka, "between the growing intensity of America-Japan friction and the increasing frequency of Nisei and even Issei loyalty pledges."[71] The Issei old guard responded to anti-Japanese affronts as they had done before: They had the Nisei reassure Americans that their support for Japan was in no way at odds with their commitment to living and raising their children in the United States. But mounting U.S.-Japan hostility forced Nisei Week's leaders to retreat from the idea of biculturalism. The *Rafu Shimpo*'s English-language staff, for example, veered away from Japanese nationalism. Tanaka claimed that the decision was based on both the fallout from rescinding the trade agreement and the results of a survey that revealed the impressive Nisei commitment to the United States. The English section split from the paper's Japanese staff to launch an editorial policy encouraging the Nisei to drop biculturalism in favor of a "single American political loyalty." The Nisei were urged to support the JACL's Americanism, buy U.S. defense bonds, and forgo dual citizenship with Japan.[72]

The U.S.-Japan conflict even eventually spurred the Issei leadership to join the Americanization crusade. Tanaka observed the Issei's renewed push to acquire naturalization rights for Japanese immigrants and to assure their brethren that the American government would not consider them enemies in the event of a crisis with Japan. "It has always been my opinion," wrote Gongoro Nakamura, one of the most respected Issei in Little Tokyo, "that we Japanese residents in America, who were legally admitted into the United States as permanent residents, and who are fathers and mothers of American citizens of Japanese ancestry, and who admire and respect American institutions, ideals and traditions, and who have been endeavoring to promote the general welfare of the community in contributing to the American way of life through our respective occupations and professions, will be treated as residents and not as alien enemies."[73]

In these circumstances, Nisei Week became a way to ensure that Japanese Americans would not be confused with their relatives overseas. The *Kashu Mainichi* in 1940 situated the festival within the diplomatic crises of the day and portrayed it as a defining moment of Nisei Americanism:

> Nisei Week this year comes at a time when the world is troubled with a great turmoil. Where once was festivity in other lands, today their youths march in stiff uniforms, their minds and bodies weary with the burden of war. . . . [O]nly here [in the United States] can we celebrate the Nisei Week, free from the roar of invading bombers. . . . We welcome you all! Men and women of all races. Welcome to Little Tokio. And when you come, please notice that behind the glamour of the festivities there is seriousness and earnestness in the young people who have planned this celebration. They, like all other Americans, are eager to do their part in the building of this great country, to assume responsibility for its defense against all enemies and to safeguard its great institutions. For when the nation of birth is troubled, you will find these American citizens of Japanese extraction ready to do their part.[74]

In the early 1940s JACLers redoubled their efforts to fix the image of the ethnic community as unquestionably loyal to the United States. No longer was bridging the Pacific with Nisei biculturalism their highest priority. "In view of the present national emergency," JACL president Ken Matsumoto proclaimed in a 1941 radio address, "we feel that the important thing is not what our racial background may be but what we can do as Americans." The 1941 Nisei Week booklet captured this patriotic expression. Its centerpiece featured a Shirley Temple look-alike twirling a baton while leading a parade of Boy Scouts. The girl emphasized the Nisei's innocent embrace of their native land. Another photograph featured a gigantic American flag hoisted by hundreds of Japanese American youth, as if to symbolize their overwhelming loyalty to the United States. A third photograph showed Nisei Week beauty contestants seated around a replica of the Statue of Liberty with an accompanying text that read "America is our home."[75]

Patriotic intent also influenced the display of other national icons. Herbert Wada announced that Nisei Week's parade in 1941 would emphasize the "spirit of the American people" and that the "official attire" for the ondo dancers would be made from cotton in honor of the boycott of Japanese silk. The *Rafu Shimpo* went so far as to suggest that Japanese garments, regardless of their material composition, contradicted Americanism, and therefore recommended that kimonos not be worn in public. It also cautioned the ethnic community that there was "only one proper flag" to be displayed: "the stars and stripes."[76]

But beyond this consensus on loyalty to the United States, American-ism did not mean the same thing to different groups of Nisei. For the left-ist *Doho*, loyalty provided a means of unifying with capitalists to oppose the rise of fascism overseas. "The youth of today want peace and op-portunities. . . . They want democracy rather than concentration camps, they want work and play rather than drills and bullets." The newspaper claimed that the "real enemies" in Little Tokyo were the "apologists for Japanese militarism."[77] In an editorial entitled "Whose Talking for Whom?" Sam Hohri turned the spotlight on the JACL. He criticized them for pledging the Nisei's support for President Roosevelt's policies against Japan. "For the sake of democracy," he wrote, "we hope that the League realizes that it must recognize a minority or even a majority who are not wholly persuaded by the President's logic." Hohri insisted that the Nisei not support war in the Pacific, which did not make them "any less American than the fire-eating, snorting nabobs of the J.A.C.L."[78]

Such internal differences, however, were lost on key outside observers who before the Pearl Harbor attack tended to uphold Nisei loyalty. Ken-neth Ringle, the naval intelligence agent assigned in 1940 to assess the loyalty of Japanese Americans in Los Angeles, took the JACLers as rep-resentative of all Nisei. Ringle had studied Japanese language for three years when he was with the United States embassy in Tokyo and before coming to Los Angeles was familiar with the ethnic community in Hawaii. His ease among Japanese people was evident in the close contacts he forged with JACLers, who provided him with "valuable antisubversive information" on suspicious elements within Little Tokyo. Ringle's analy-sis concluded that "the entire 'Japanese Problem' has been magnified out of its true proportion, largely because of the physical characteristics of the people." The threat of espionage among Japanese Americans, he noted, "is no more serious than the problems of the German, Italian, and Com-munistic portions of the U.S. population" and therefore "should be handled on the basis of the *individual,* regardless of citizenship, and *not* on a racial basis."[79]

Public statements also underscored the loyalty of Japanese Americans. The *Los Angeles Times* encouraged its readers to attend Nisei Week be-cause Japanese Americans "had no part in and no responsibility for causing war clouds to gather in the Orient." Fletcher Bowron, the mayor of Los Angeles in 1941, echoed this sentiment. In the speech that opened what became the last Nisei Week before World War II, Bowron not only implored Japanese Americans to show their patriotism but also reas-sured them that "we know you are loyal."[80]

Almost everyone in the ethnic community wanted to believe him. But no amount of flag waving or volunteer intelligence work could convince Kane and other die-hard racists that the Nisei were trustworthy. Ringle viewed alarmists like Kane as "exceedingly dangerous" because their "half-truths" could arouse "violent anti-Japanese feeling among Caucasians of all classes" who do not distinguish between officers of the Japanese military and Japanese Americans.[81] The attack on Pearl Harbor proved him right. In the middle of January 1942, as the idea of internment was being considered, Kane predicted that "the Nisei who have been waving Old Glory around so long" would finally get what anti-Japanese foes long thought they had deserved.[82]

The American front that the Nisei Week festival of these years promoted received its greatest challenge after the Japanese attacked Pearl Harbor in early December 1941. Suddenly, the United States was at war with Japan; America's Pacific fleet lay in ruins, and the nation's people, stunned by the audacity of Japanese aggression, exploded with outrage—and fear. A mixture of racial chauvinism and national pride prevented most Americans from questioning the failures of their country's defenses or acknowledging the strength of the Japanese forces. Instead, the general public preferred to believe unfounded accusations blaming the losses at Pearl Harbor on the treachery of Japanese Americans. Bowron, who had praised the loyalty of the ethnic community at that year's Nisei Week, was one of many political leaders who succumbed to rampant anti-Japanese hysteria. "Right here in our own city," he warned his constituency, "are those who may spring into action at an appointed time in accordance with a prearranged plan wherein each of our little brown brothers will know his part in the event of [an] attempted invasion or air raid."[83] Growing fears about a racial conspiracy culminated in the decision to forcibly remove Japanese Americans from the West Coast, thus uprooting Little Tokyo and ending the early years of Nisei Week.

The relocation and internment of 110,000 Japanese Americans from the West Coast was considered a "military necessity." Stunned and embarrassed by the defeat at Pearl Harbor, Army leaders became overzealous in their attempts to prevent a potential Japanese invasion. General John L. DeWitt, commander of West Coast defenses, maintained that Japanese Americans were an "enemy race," who, partly because of their primordial ties to Japan and partly because of the ill-treatment they had long received at the hands of white Americans, could not be trusted to support the United States. Neither DeWitt nor any of those responsible for the internment were dissuaded by the lack of proof that Japanese Americans had been disloyal. It was as if the attack on Pearl Harbor had unleashed the ghosts of Nat Turner, Gabriel Prosser, and other leaders of slave rebellion. White Americans on the West Coast now feared—with paranoid proportions—the servile population they had once loathed, belittled, and exploited.

Although the ethnic community was scattered among the ten internment camps built to incarcerate the displaced population, many Japanese Americans from Los Angeles were sent to the Manzanar relocation center about two hundred miles north of Los Angeles. More than 80 percent of the internees at Manzanar were from southern California, including a sizable proportion of Little Tokyo merchants, employees, and Los Angeles JACL leaders.[84] The name *Manzanar* derived from a Native American term for the apple orchards that covered the lush Owens Valley before the city of Los Angeles deprived it of water in the 1920s and 1930s. A discarded paradise far away from the populations and military installations on the coast—save the Los Angeles aqueduct—it was an ideal place for a prison.[85]

PART 2

Camp

THREE

War and the American Front

Collaboration, Protest, and Class in the Internment Crisis

On December 6, 1942, more than two thousand Japanese Americans at the Manzanar internment camp renounced the Americanist campaign that had punctuated the last years of Nisei Week. At twilight, in the firebreak on the edge of camp, they gathered in protest, hailing the Japanese emperor and damning the "white man's democracy." The most vituperative contempt was reserved for those Nisei leaders believed to have betrayed their own race. Fred Tayama, Tokutaro Slocum, Togo Tanaka, and other Los Angeles JACLers were placed on a death list for actively collaborating with the Manzanar administration.[1]

At nightfall the protesters sought to murder Tayama, who was recovering in the camp hospital after being beaten the night before by six masked men.[2] But these efforts were stymied when a quick-thinking physician hid the JACLer from the angry mob. Meanwhile, another group of protesters laid siege to the Manzanar police station, demanding the release of Harry Ueno, the man accused of leading the attack against Tayama. Armed soldiers assembled in a line between the internees and the station. After hours of negotiation failed, the soldiers exploded tear gas into the increasingly hostile crowd. In the smoky confusion, shots were fired as the protesters scrambled in different directions. One was killed immediately. Another died a few days later. And eight were seriously wounded in what would later be known as the Manzanar riot.

Military police at Manzanar killed two internees during the conflict that
ensued on December 6, 1942. Such government force would obscure the class
relations among the internees that contributed to the crisis. *Courtesy National
Archives, photo by Clem Albers.*

The crisis at Manzanar revealed how much the ethnic community had
changed since the last celebration of Nisei Week. What festivities and
cultural performances there were at Manzanar took on decidedly different overtones. For example, the "community fair" celebrated in fall 1943
was in many respects a carbon copy of later Nisei Week observances,
complete with patriotic demonstrations, Japanese dances, arts and crafts
exhibits, a beauty pageant, and the everpresent welcoming of white
American guests. But the Manzanar fair was a faint imitation of the original, lacking the complex diversity of opinion that could be expressed
within the freedom of prewar Little Tokyo. Such an event was starkly
utilitarian, reiterating the chorus, "We *are* American. . . . We are *not* Japanese." This contrasted with the earlier hope, still alive in the hearts of
many Japanese Americans on the eve of Pearl Harbor, that the young
JACLers would become cultural bridges between Japan and the United
States. The fair's mono-Americanism, of course, also concealed a great
many internees whose faith in the second generation's rights as American citizens had been considerably shaken and in many cases shattered.
Consequently, neither it nor other festivities at Manzanar did justice to
Nisei Week's ability to embody the deep social conflicts within Japanese
American life.

Activists raise the American flag at Manzanar, May 1942. A large part of the ethnic community was detained at Manzanar, during the internment period; the identity politics that punctuated the prewar Nisei Week festival were challenged and radically transformed during World War II. *Courtesy National Archives, photo by Francis Stewart.*

In a more general sense, however, the practice of Japanese American identity during the internment was not a total departure from the story about Nisei Week. The festival's inversion of Little Tokyo authority— with children leading parents—proved a revealing rehearsal for the ethnic group's reaction to the war. As citizens of Japan, the Issei generation were in no position to soothe the public's wrath, let alone protect their rights as "enemy aliens." The JACLers—most of whom were not yet thirty years old— quickly assumed positions as the leaders of the ethnic community. The youngsters urged the community to complete the retreat from biculturalism that had begun in the late 1930s. In an attempt to prevent the internment, they cooperated freely with government and military officials. When these efforts failed, they became stalwart volunteers for the internment camp administration. As they had done during Nisei Week, the JACLers sought to counter outside hostility against Japanese Americans by demanding strict discipline and conformity of opinion within the ethnic group. But the heavy economic losses and emotional trauma caused by the sudden evacuation made it impossible for many Japanese Americans to rally behind the ideals of civic virtue, national

The evacuation forced Little Tokyo businesses to shut down and swiftly uprooted the ethnic community with devastating economic and emotional consequences. *Courtesy National Archives, photo by Clem Albers.*

sacrifice, and racial integration. To prove the group fully loyal to the United States, the JACLers fractured the solidarity that once was at the top of their agenda.

The conflicts that split the internees were predicated upon internal differences that were not new to the ethnic community. In the camps, support for the JACL remained strong among urbane, college-educated, and second-generation professionals and entrepreneurs. It was these people who were first to swear unconditional allegiance to the United States, volunteer for military service, and comply with the War Relocation Authority's attempt to resettle the internees outside the West Coast. The less cosmopolitan parts of the community were the least enthusiastic about both the JACL and their efforts to prove loyalty. The more culturally Japanese, the less educated, and those from rural or agricultural backgrounds were more likely to participate in the Manzanar riot and afterward to remain within the camps rather than to relocate (with government blessings) outside the West Coast. Upon being freed from the camps, they typically returned to their homes in southern California and participated in reestablishing Little Tokyo.

FRIEND OR FOE?

The Issei leaders never expected that the young people they put in charge of Nisei Week would some day turn against them. But beginning in early 1941, the JACL's "anti-Axis" committee provided "valuable antisubversive information" enabling American intelligence agents to pinpoint hundreds of Issei whom they believed might be dangerous in the event of a U.S.-Japan war.[3] In the wake of Pearl Harbor's destruction, the FBI used this information to incarcerate most of Little Tokyo's leadership, including officials of ethnic and business associations, journalists and newspaper publishers, Japanese-language teachers, and Buddhist priests. At the moment of these arrests, the JACL vowed to continue the search for subversives by investigating and turning over to authorities "all who by word or act consort with the enemies." The idea of the Nisei as a bicultural linkage across the Pacific had totally collapsed, as the war forced them to decide if they were a "friend or foe" of the United States.[4]

The JACLers suddenly supplanted the immigrant leadership. They urged the ethnic community to donate to the Red Cross, buy war bonds, and engage in public relations portraying the ethnic community as unquestionably American. Government officials supported the new leadership by recognizing the Nisei as the official spokespeople for Japanese

America. In Los Angeles, the U.S. Postmaster General appointed the JACL the official censor of the Japanese American press. Under its watchful eye, the *Rafu Shimpo* replaced the rising sun on its masthead with large block letters pledging, "WE ARE 100 PER CENT FOR THE UNITED STATES."[5]

With little hope of overturning the internment order and a desperate need to display its loyalty to the United States, the JACL proclaimed its absolute support of the evacuation of the ethnic community. According to Togo Tanaka, there was "no evidence of serious consideration to proposals that the organization resist mass evacuation once the President's Executive Order had been published." One JACLer urged his fellow members to cooperate fully with the internment. "No matter what kind of persecution we will have to go through," he proclaimed, "the American Flag will always be our symbol to carry on, and we know that when this thing is over, we will be mighty proud that we are American citizens of Japanese ancestry."[6]

There were different ways in which Nisei leaders sought to prove their loyalty. Fred Tayama distanced himself from the Issei generation and maintained what naval intelligence agent Kenneth Ringle regarded as an "intense desire to conform" to American culture. The JACLer had told Ringle that the Nisei "suffered" from their parents' inability to speak English and their unwillingness to get involved in their children's schooling or to attend the "normal community activities in which the Caucasian American participates." The Nisei, Tayama assured him, had done better by their children. He and his wife valued their daughter's "association with her [Caucasian American] teacher and playmates above everything else" and had "no intention of ever sending her to any [Japanese] language school."[7]

Tokutaro Slocum corroborated Tayama's insistence upon Issei-Nisei differences. Chairman of the JACL's "counter-espionage" activities, Slocum also prized relationships with white Americans and used the JACL as a means of Americanizing the ethnic group. But as an orphan from Japan raised by a white family in North Dakota, he had little experience or familiarity with Japanese Americans. He earned American citizenship by serving in World War I and apparently never wavered from the love of country that he displayed as a soldier. Although he left the JACL in the early 1930s, the news of Pearl Harbor ended his estrangement from the ethnic community, as the former sergeant boasted about going "over the top again" leading his FBI and naval intelligence "buddies" into the "ratholes" of Little Tokyo to arrest the Issei leaders

Tokutaro Slocum outside the Los Angeles JACL office in April 1942. As part of the organization's counterespionage activities, Slocum helped the FBI imprison Issei leaders after Pearl Harbor. *Courtesy National Archives, photo by Clem Albers.*

of a "nefarious, spying organization." For this, and especially for his purported friendship with Ringle and government officials, the war veteran was welcomed back to the JACL.[8]

But not every JACLer's allegiance to the nation put him at odds with the older generation. Togo Tanaka, newly installed as the *Rafu Shimpo's* editor in chief, dismissed the attack against the Issei as "witch hunting" and questioned the right of JACLers, "as private citizens without the facts, to set ourselves up as judges of our fellow men."[9] Although he acknowledged the problem of subversives within the ethnic community, he was convinced that the bulk of the immigrants were trustworthy. He knew this from his own father, who, despite his sympathy for Japan and animosity against white America, was in no way a threat to national security. Tanaka had said as much to Attorney General Francis Biddle and First Lady Eleanor Roosevelt a month before Pearl Harbor, when he lobbied in Washington, D.C., on behalf of the Issei leadership.[10] For his outspoken support, he was one of the few Nisei to be arrested in the FBI sweep after the Pearl Harbor attack. After a brief stint in jail, he resumed his campaign through his column in the *Rafu Shimpo*. Conversations with his Issei cellmates made him more certain that the "Issei fathers," if eligible for citizenship, would make "good Americans" and that the idea of them as enemy spies and saboteurs was nothing more than "hysterical baloney."[11]

The question of patriotism, however, was not the JACL's only concern within the ethnic community. Here the Nisei organization was also preoccupied with fending off challenges to its leadership, for despite the rapid increase in members after Pearl Harbor, the JACL represented no more than 20 percent of the ethnic community's adult males.[12] The most vocal critics were the leftists who had long condemned, and been condemned by, the probusiness JACLers. Ironically, World War II brought these antagonists together, as they shared an even greater antagonism to the fascist regimes in Germany, Italy, and Japan. But the leftists did not join a "united front" with the JACL only to be placed behind the lines of leadership.[13] Groups like the Nisei Writers' and Artists' Mobilization for Democracy criticized what it saw as the Los Angeles JACL's ineffective and unrepresentative leadership of the Nisei population. Led by Isamu Noguchi, who would gain international acclaim as a sculptor after World War II, the mobilization maintained that the JACL's "few old Nisei businessmen" had alienated the immigrant generation and made them apathetic toward the future. "Now instead of looking to the JACL as the only political organization for direction and guidance," Noguchi feared that the Issei "have been demonstrating a tendency to withdraw all support." [14] As was Togo Tanaka, the writers and artists were concerned about the widening schism between the Issei and Nisei, but, unlike Tanaka, they saw the JACL as an inappropriate vehicle for community leadership.

Another challenge to JACL leadership came from the center. The vast majority of Nisei organizations in southern California had been inclined to leave discussion of political issues to the leftists, the JACLers, and especially the Issei leadership. But the war and Los Angeles Mayor Fletcher Bowron, who reportedly ordered the JACLers to create a more representative group of Nisei, compelled their involvement in community governance. The result was the establishment of the United Citizens Federation, a coalition of twenty-one Nisei groups including the JACLers and leftists, but also Buddhist and Christian organizations, Boy Scouts, a labor union, a workers' club, a farmers' cooperative, a veteran's association, and an athletic league. On the day that Roosevelt signed Executive Order 9066 (the evacuation order), February 19, 1942, more than a thousand Nisei attended the federation's first meeting and heard the chairman, Togo Tanaka, wonder "if it is now possible, out of the numerous organizations which are represented here tonight[,] to coordinate into a body." Although still a JACLer, Tanaka made clear that this new organization would supersede the local JACL in both membership and political clout. But the attempt to forge a truly united front proved too little too late. The JACLers, excluding Tanaka, rejected the plan to share their authority with the bulk of the Nisei. Naval intelligence agent Kenneth Ringle observed the tension between the JACL and the federation and concluded that Nisei organizations lacked any basis for consensus. [15]

The harshest criticism of the JACL condemned its cooperation with the internment order. Perhaps the best example of this position was Joseph Kurihara. Born in 1895, he was at least twenty years older than the average Nisei and a veteran of World War I. Although he was a college graduate and a trained accountant, he became a fisherman by trade as a result of a business failure. In his new occupation he had worked with the JACL and written an occasional *Rafu Shimpo* column to combat measures that would ban the Issei from commercial fishing. After Pearl Harbor he offered his services to the organization to resist the internment, but to his surprise he found that "the goose was already cooked and there was no alternative." In his unpublished autobiography he recalled feeling "sick" about the JACLers' cooperation with the evacuation order. "They've accomplished not a thing," he wrote. "All they did was to meet General DeWitt and be told what to do. These boys claiming to be the leaders of the Nisei were a bunch of spineless Americans." To Kurihara, the only way to avenge the "weak-kneed" JACLers was "to fight them and crush them in whatever camp I happened to find them." [16]

Kurihara's was the bitterness of a patriot scorned. He had decided to renounce his American citizenship the day after he learned about the internment. The government's actions deeply hurt and offended him, and he was astounded that not even the "voices of the former World War [I] veterans" were good enough to prove the group's loyalty. "When the Western Defense Command assumed the responsibilities of the West Coast," he wrote, "I expected that at least the Niseis would be allowed to remain. But to General DeWitt, we were all alike. '[A] Jap is a Jap. Once a Jap always a Jap.'" Consequently, he "swore to become a Jap 100 percent, and never to do another day's work to help this country fight." [17]

There were other reasons, however, to oppose the JACL. Togo Tanaka reported that Little Tokyo denizens developed a firm mistrust of the organization due to its high profile as the government's loyalty police. The JACL's "counter-espionage" activities were seen as a patriotically veiled crusade against the Issei, and its members were referred to as the servants (dogs) of the white man. [18] Whether this view was accurate or not, the Nisei leaders were also implicated in schemes that took advantage of the most vulnerable within the ethnic community. Much of the outrage and accusations in Los Angeles centered on the ethics of Fred Tayama. His legal services office was rumored to have exploited the Issei, who were required to register as "enemy aliens" and often were desperate to get their estate in order before the evacuation. In addition, Tayama was accused of using his high position within the JACL to further his own business. But the most severe charge against him was that he could not account for hundreds of dollars raised to provide relief for the fishing community that was the first to be evacuated. [19] Like the JACL in general, Tayama's reputation for undermining the Isseis' authority made him an easy scapegoat for those Japanese Americans devastated by the sudden relocation.

Confronted with internal challenges to their leadership, the JACL sought to monopolize community ties with the U.S. government. At a meeting with military officials, one JACLer implied that his organization should be the only liaison with the government. There "is too much confusion," he complained, "because so many Japanese American organizations, regardless of their size and influence, insist upon going directly to certain governmental agencies and requesting advice and information."[20] When asked about the "jealousies" among the Nisei groups, Fred Tayama criticized those who "incite trouble" and "foment dissension" within the community. He portrayed the "dissenters" as they were portraying him: self-serving, greedy, and elitist. They "always considered themselves above working with groups for the common good, but because of the present difficulties, in order to protect their own best interests, they are attempting to usurp the leadership of those who have served their communities for a long time and use these organizations for their own selfish ends."[21]

Officials of the War Relocation Authority, the civilian agency that inherited the internment camps from the U.S. Army in May 1942, enabled the JACLers to continue their leadership of the ethnic community in the internment camps. WRA director Dillon S. Myer came to count on the JACLers as one of the agency's main allies in leading the ethnic group toward more "American" values, norms, and political orientations.[22] This outside support for the JACL belied the organization's deteriorating reputation within the ethnic community. The JACLers, Tanaka claimed, were in an "impossible situation" because they had not earned a constituency but had "inherited" one from the FBI and naval intelligence at a time of a "great deal of fear, uneasiness, mistrust, and suspicion." Although the military leaders behind the internment cast Japanese Americans as a monolithic race, the Japanese Americans entered the internment camps more divided than ever before.[23]

THE REVOLTING CONDITIONS AT MANZANAR

Nowhere did the ethnic community's internal conflicts appear more dramatically than at the internment camp in Manzanar, California. The increasing tension between the newly anointed Nisei leadership and the community they sought to Americanize culminated in the deadly protest that erupted in December 1942. Although newspaper headlines portrayed the crisis as a "Jap uprising" in honor of the first anniversary of the Pearl Harbor attack, WRA officials knew better. The principal finding and position of the researchers within the internment camp were that the protesters were motivated by legitimate concerns about the conditions at Manzanar. In studying the origins of the riot, Morton Grodzins found little support for the claim that it was a "Jap uprising," which he attributed to confused perception of the camp's new director. The riot, maintained Grodzins, stemmed predominantly from a broad-based outrage at the Manzanar administration. "The question could be put as . . .

involving administrative integrity and fairness to the evacuees. Loyalty had nothing to do with it." [24]

Togo Tanaka, in his report to the WRA's community analysis section, also blamed the riot on Manzanar's "ill-advised and ill-prepared administrators." Constant changes in personnel and outright anti-Japanese hostility on the part of key white officials, Tanaka claimed, made it hard for the internees to trust camp authorities. Fueling the mistrust was a degrading color line. Whites enjoyed better residences, food, and dining arrangements and higher pay for the same work performed by the internees. Under these circumstances, Tanaka could not "see how it is possible for any human being of normal impulses to . . . not be touched by the bitterness and disillusionment all around him." [25] Yet some internees were more bitter than others. The conditions at Manzanar, Tanaka argued, pushed a majority of the internees to support a small yet articulate group of pro-Japan ideologues. Championing the Japanese spirit served as a rallying cry for anyone who had a grievance against the internment, the administration, or the JACL. Perhaps the administration's greatest blunder, in Tanaka's eyes, was not to punish or remove this group from camp. Its lax enforcement of camp regulations encouraged open contempt for law and order and placed pro-American JACLers in constant jeopardy of being bullied and attacked.[26] The Nisei leaders were seen as apologists for a dishonest and ineffectual administration and, hence, were rejected as leaders of internee government and were the only ones placed on a death list during the Manzanar riot.

But no one who studied the riot maintained any illusions about the JACLers' ability to mold internee opinion. A white schoolteacher at Manzanar noted that the majority of the internees at that time were hostile to the Nisei organization. She reported that when the Nisei leaders "attempted to represent the people as a whole and acted as spokesmen for the entire Japanese community, it was only natural for resentment to follow." [27] The animosity against the JACL, Morton Grodzins noted, was so marked that "every discomfort at Manzanar could be traced back to the JACL's acceptance of evacuation." Fred Tayama was especially linked to the organization's negative image for having boasted about being an FBI informer and for allegedly using his leadership position, before the internment, for personal financial gain. All the analysts agreed that the Manzanar riot was ignited by the administration's appointment of Tayama to represent Manzanar at a meeting between WRA leaders and internees from each of the ten internment camps.

The researchers typically placed the internees' hostility toward the JACL in the larger context of generational competition. The Issei, explained Morris Opler, an anthropologist who headed the WRA's Manzanar research after the riot, had the upper hand before Manzanar because they controlled the enclave economy. But they "were wary of those [N]isei who were determined to become owners and competitors rather than work steadily and faithfully for the elders." These fears, Opler asserted, were realized when the Nisei took control of the ethnic community during World War II. Now the Issei were at the mercy of leaders who were younger, better educated, and more willing to conform to American culture. The elders did not handle this gracefully. They constantly insisted that the Nisei lacked the experience and fortitude for leadership. "In the eyes of many Issei," Opler maintained, "the Nisei were 'soft' and 'pleasure bound,' lacking in the 'pioneer spirit' and resiliency which characterized the older immigrant generation." [28]

At Manzanar, Issei and Nisei competed for internee leadership, with the younger generation gaining the upper hand only after the WRA restricted internee governance to American citizens. When the *Kibei,* those born in the United States but schooled and socialized largely in Japan, sought to serve as proxy for the elder generation, they were excluded from the political process by their inability to express themselves adequately in English, a WRA requirement adopted for the benefit of the Nisei. In the month preceding the Manzanar riot, the competition between the generations had turned decisively in favor of the Nisei. On the eve of the December 6 conflict, a prominent Issei leader asked the JACLer Togo Tanaka, "Why it is that the Nisei seem to want to control this camp? Why is it that they are out to persecute the Issei?" [29]

Yet the case of Nisei Joseph Kurihara, the man who vowed before the evacuation to fight the JACL in the camps, reveals a more complex picture of internal conflicts at Manzanar. Kurihara refused to support a government that mistrusted his loyalty. "I'm an American citizen," he pronounced at a meeting planned to protest the exclusion of Kibei from camp governance. "I've served under fire with the Army in the First World War. I haven't done anything wrong. Why should I be put in here?" [30] Kurihara tapped into wellsprings of frustration and bitterness among the Kibei. His vociferous criticism of JACLers, Manzanar administrators, and American racism also appealed to embittered Nisei, especially to those "rowdies" once condemned at Nisei Week and now easily swayed to rebellion. Kurihara told them that the internment resulted from pure racial hatred—"It is because we are what we are, Japs!" This older Nisei insisted that America was a "white man's land"; therefore attempts to prove loyalty by becoming American were in vain. The only viable option for internees was to prepare themselves for returning (or, for the Nisei, emigrating) to Japan by becoming "Japs . . . through and through to the very marrow of our bones!"[31]

Considering disillusioned Nisei like Kurihara, historians Arthur Hansen and David Hacker portrayed the Manzanar riot as a profound clash between cultures. In the most thorough analysis of the December 6 crisis, they argued that at its core the protest symbolized the primordial urge to reconstitute the ethnic community. This meant not just restoring the Issei to community leadership but also recentering Japanese traditions, folkways, and language forbidden in the camps. Hansen and Hacker maintain that the so-called pro-Japan element, which set off the riot, arose in response to repeated and concerted attempts by the Manzanar administration, working closely with the JACLers, to restrict the rights and cultural and linguistic expression of the Japanese-speaking internees. The riot, then, was not against the administration or the JACLers per se but against coerced assimilation. It was, in this sense, an attempt to re-create what Hansen and Hacker call a "Little Tokyo of the desert."[32]

As a whole, the above explanations of the Manzanar riot—excepting the idea that it was driven by the celebration of Pearl Harbor's anniversary, which can be dismissed out of hand—emphasize the importance of reactionary forces, compelling the protesters to seek to re-create the old social order of Little Tokyo. The goal, according to this perspective, was to place Issei leaders in command of a community distinguished by generational hierarchy, retention of Japanese traditions, and the primacy of the Japanese language. But the image of an autonomous, traditionally organized prewar ethnic community obscures the more complex picture of indigenous power relations discussed in chapters 1 and 2. While the Issei, in cooperation with the Japanese consulate, were the formal authorities in Little Tokyo, in the 1930s they had allied themselves with the Nisei, who promoted rather than contested the immigrant leadership's cosmopolitan notions of biculturalism and then Americanization. The first- and second-generation elite had come together as ethnic leaders to resist attacks from outside the ethnic community (through the assertion of placating ethnic identities of biculturalism and Americanism) and to purge, reform, or condemn indigenous enemies (rowdies, communists, supporters of organized labor, and overly "clannish" Nisei), regardless of generation or cultural orientation. As the next section argues, it was these dominated classes of internees, not the Issei, Kibei, or the culturally Japanese per se, who were most inclined to subvert the JACLers' American front (through beatings, gossip, disruption of internee programs, or, more commonly, utter disregard for them). In fomenting the Manzanar crisis, they then traded in these evasive "weapons of the weak" for the extremely risky strategy of direct assault.

LIKELY SUSPECTS

The class dynamics of the Manzanar riot were different from the ideology of working-class politics often associated with the organized labor and revolutionary parties. The riot, as Joseph Kurihara made clear, was to punish the alleged Nisei informers, free Harry Ueno, the man arrested for attacking Fred Tayama, and more generally to improve internee life. Indeed, many of the WRA collaborators had a greater commitment to working-class politics than did the protesters. The collaborators were leftists (communists, labor organizers, artists, writers, free thinkers) who, through a twist of fate and popular front dictates, found themselves at Manzanar allied with, rather than in their usual position of opposing, the JACLers. Looking for an overt antagonism between rich and poor, worker and owner, and high and low social status within the ethnic community leads to a dead end. As the above analysis of the crisis reveals, the explicit fault lines among the internees were nation, culture, and generation. If its significance is to be glimpsed at all, class must be recognized as the implicit, perhaps even unconscious, distinction from which more obvious conflicts were manifest. The focus here is not on the decision to rebel or cooperate, but on the class backgrounds and positions (and process of socialization inherent to these) that made it likely for internees to identify with one side or the other in the Manzanar protest.

The most visible WRA supporters embraced the cosmopolitan, educated, and cultured idealization of Western society that had defined prewar ethnic leadership. Enough has been said about the elite status of the JACLers, the young businessmen and professionals whose occupational status, college education, and Christianity made them more accepting of (and acceptable to) white America than most of the second generation. The leftists, targets as well of the Manzanar protesters, shared the JACLers' disdain for the "backwardness" of Japanese Americans and sought (for different reasons, of course) to bring them into the

light of the modern world. These were the antecedents of socialists like
Katayama Sen, who saw immigration as Japan's great chance to display
modernity. For example, John Sonoda, who was beaten up during the
Manzanar riot, was a Kibei insurance agent, whose liberal education in
Japan and bilingualism (speaking unaccented English) enabled him to
mix freely with white Americans. According to Togo Tanaka, Sonoda
was an effeminate "scholarly type opposed to doing any sort of manual
labor."[33] Sonoda and other leftists, Tanaka observed, coalesced around
the camp's newspaper, the *Manzanar Free Press*. This group included
Tomomasa Yamazaki (Issei), James Oda (Kibei, communist), Chiye Mori
(Issei, beautician, domestic worker, and communist), Satoru Kamikawa
(gardener and writer), and Choyei Kondo (a well-educated Issei).[34] Other
known leftists at Manzanar were Joe Blamey (postgraduate, Eurasian
immigrant from Japan), Koji Ariyoshi (college-educated, American-born),
Karl Yoneda (Kibei, communist, and labor organizer), and his wife Elaine
Yoneda (white, communist, labor organizer).[35] The picture that emerges
of the Manzanar left is of an international, bilingual community of intellectuals. If not for ideology, many leftists would have fit the mold for
ethnic leadership.

The Manzanar protesters also shared a similar social background
and status. The social profiles of twenty-one protesters arrested after
the Manzanar crisis reveal that they were much more likely than the
JACLers to come from the farming classes in Japan and to remain close
to the soil in their employment in the United States. Furthermore, they
were less likely than the pro-WRA faction to have gone to college, to be
Christian, and to live in cities. In short, they were like the majority of
Japanese Americans who remained apart from white Americans, relying upon the ethnic community for their economic, cultural, and social
livelihood.[36]

The social scientists working within the camps were not blind to
these sorts of class differences among the internees. Morris Opler noted
that the resentment against the collaborators was based in a prewar tension between Issei store owners and a rising group of Nisei competitors
who were better educated than the older generation business leaders and
practiced "superior business methods." While the Issei "were eager to
employ these bright youngsters as their clerks, . . . accountants, and as
mediators between themselves and the American business world . . . ,
they were wary of those Nisei who were determined to become owners
and competitors rather than work steadily and faithfully for the elders."
In a separate study of Manzanar protesters, Opler found that they came

disproportionately from rural communities and specific types of occupations such as gardening, farming, fishing, and small business.[37]

It is important to note that Opler did not recognize socioeconomic differences among the internees as evidence of a class conflict. Rather, he connected them to clashing cultural orientations—in short, the "troublemakers" remained more Japanese because their rural backgrounds and agricultural occupations isolated them from cosmopolitan forces in the cities that assimilated the pro-Americans. Hansen and Hacker, on the other hand, entirely ignored socioeconomic differences at Manzanar. The case of Togo Tanaka is instructive. His close ties to the WRA and his bold public statements encouraging internee collaboration resulted in his name being placed on the death list during the December crisis. This enmity toward Tanaka, Hacker and Hansen suggest, was an inevitable response to someone who deliberately chose to cooperate with his oppressors. From this perspective, Tanaka and the collaborators in general were overzealous American patriots who helped the FBI imprison innocent Issei leaders in the wake of Pearl Harbor. While Hansen and Hacker recognized the complexities of Tanaka's collaboration, they still give credence to the protesters' claim that his unshakable support for the American government revealed a "false consciousness" causing him to sell out *his people* in Japan and the United States and at Manzanar.[38]

Tanaka's collaboration with the WRA was motivated by hope rather than self-hatred. He was optimistic that America would win the war, and he therefore saw the internment as an opportunity to train a new generation of ethnic leaders to overcome anti-Japanese racism in postwar America. Resisting the internment, to him, would only alienate the silent majority of white Americans who were not antagonistic to Japanese Americans. Tanaka's cooperation with Manzanar authorities, then, was rooted in a remarkable faith in the goodness of white America, remarkable because many, perhaps most, internees—such as his father—had experienced enough racism at the hands of whites to be quite mistrustful of them. Tanaka, too, suffered his share of discrimination; indeed, after the war he vowed never to return to racist California again. But it was his class background and cosmopolitanism that predisposed him to distinguish good whites from bad.

Tanaka grew up in the middle-class white community of Hollywood, California, about five miles away from the center of the Japanese American community. His parents ran a retail fruit and vegetable market that catered primarily to white Americans. His father insisted that the family live outside the segregated ethnic enclave, and it was he who instilled in

Tanaka a sense of pride in the family's Samurai background and former wealth and property. Trained in the Chinese classics, the father also ingrained in his son a passion for ideas and education that led the young Tanaka to graduate Phi Beta Kappa from UCLA. But unlike his father, Tanaka did not become a "racial chauvinist"; his best friends were white, as were many of those on whom he relied for career and spiritual guidance. A convert to Christianity, he urged the ethnic community to turn the other cheek to its persecutors. He saw those internees who returned hate with hate as no better than the racists responsible for the internment. Both were victims of a narrow-minded, emotionally charged, belligerent clannishness that was at odds with the intelligent, rational, open-mindedness he believed was at the core of American society.

The uniqueness of Tanaka's social background becomes readily apparent when contrasted with that of another central player in Manzanar protest, Harry Ueno. Ueno, the protester whose arrest ignited the December unrest, openly challenged Tanaka's cooperation with Manzanar officials and his faith in white Americans. But, at the same time, he deferred to Tanaka's social prestige. In an interview published in 1986, Ueno recalled his respect for Tanaka's decision to fight for his country of birth, pointing out that Tanaka was from the Samurai class and therefore was held to a higher standard of loyalty to his birth country than Ueno was.[39]

Ueno's social background provides clues to his actions at Manzanar. He was born on a plantation in Hawaii and raised there until sent at the age of eight to live with his grandparents in Japan. Like most Japanese immigrants, his parents came from the farming classes and saw migration as a means to get rich quick, then return triumphantly to their homeland. When Ueno was fifteen years old, his parents did indeed return to Japan, but by that time the young man was estranged from them. Within a year he discontinued his schooling and returned by himself to the United States. His seven years in Japan estranged him from American society as well. He struggled with English and found it difficult to communicate with his brother who had grown up entirely in the United States. Eventually Ueno settled in Los Angeles and worked in the produce industry that employed the Tanaka family. Yet, unlike Tanaka, he did not establish intimate ties with white Americans and, surprisingly, was also not at home within the ethnic community. He excluded himself from Little Tokyo associations because of what he called his "limited educational background." It was only at Manzanar that Ueno began to embrace, and indeed feel embraced by, the ethnic community.[40]

The disparities between Tanaka's and Ueno's social backgrounds suggest two different ways that racial and class formations intersected among Japanese Americans. Despite their modest income at the fruit stand, Tanaka's parents enjoyed a high degree of cultural capital that they passed · on to him by refusing to live in a segregated community (which, in turn, allowed him to forge key contacts with middle-class whites) and by emphasizing education, discussion of ideas, and the written word. In this sense Tanaka's identification with nonracist, college-educated, Christian, white America was not a false consciousness. It revealed a porous notion of ethnic identity enabling the recognition and exchange of cultural capital between Japanese Americans and whites. What really upset Tanaka about the internment was that it denied him, even more than the racist society before the war, privileges and entitlements that should have been accorded to his class status. In 1999 he recalled a conversation that he had with a fresh Army recruit at Manzanar that made his frustration particularly clear. How is it, Tanaka asked the sentry, that "you haven't even graduated high school and I have a degree from the University of California, Los Angeles," and yet "I'm in prison and you're my guard?" After all, "under normal circumstances you might come to me for a job."[41]

Tanaka expressed a similar class distinction in regard to the Manzanar resisters. In his analysis of the December crisis, he described Harry Ueno as a typical "race conscious" Kibei who had worked as a clerk at no less than six fruit stands before becoming a cook at Manzanar. Ueno's defining trait was that he "is not the academic or educated type." Tanaka portrayed another protester as "the 'hard-working Japanese gardener type,' fairly solid, dark complexioned, with hands that were hard, apparently from gardening work." Finally, he described Joseph Kurihara, the head spokesman for Manzanar protesters, as an extremely bitter person who, despite his college degree, commanded a following of gangs of juvenile delinquents, truck drivers, food handlers, warehouse workers, rubbish haulers, and anyone who performed manual labor.[42]

Ueno's social background carried much less cultural and economic status in the United States than Tanaka's. This may explain why his parents returned to Japan and why they placed their own economic goals before their son's. This may also explain why Ueno, with his "limited background," excluded himself from involvement in the ethnic community before the war. At Manzanar, Ueno's campaign against Americanization revealed the hope of a transnational recognition and exchange of his more modest level of cultural capital. Like most resisters, he ex-

Togo Tanaka at Manzanar in July 1943. Tanaka's defense of
the Issei, support for the American government, and criticism
of both internment officials and Manzanar protesters reveal
the complexities of JACL collaboration. *Courtesy National
Archives, photo by Dorothea Lange.*

pected Japan to win the war and that he then would be recognized for his
loyalty by the Japanese emperor. Moreover, he believed that Japan's victory would validate and reward his particular linguistic and cultural competence to a degree that had heretofore been impossible in the United
States. When America was defeated, the protesters were fond of saying,
they would hang the collaborators, implying that they would assume
their socioeconomic status.

In this sense, the cases of Togo Tanaka and Harry Ueno reveal relationships between class sensibilities and ethnic, racial, cultural, and gen-

erational identities at Manzanar. Class conflict in and of itself did not produce internee protest, and it was not necessarily more fundamental to Japanese Americans than race, ethnicity, culture, or generation. But it did work in different ways than these other variables. The significance of class went unrecognized by both historical actors and their historians and thus illuminates an unconscious dimension to the December 6 unrest.

CRISIS OF MASCULINITY

If class background divided Manzanar internees into collaborators and protesters, so, too, did gender roles. Assignations of social responsibilities made on the basis of interpretations of biological differences between men and women influenced who would be on the front lines of the struggle. At Manzanar, internee governance and protest remained almost exclusively a male preserve. This is not to say that women played no role in camp politics; they rang bells to show their support for the rioters, wore black armbands to commemorate the slain protesters, and participated in the general strike that shut down the camp for a month. But all of the principal players in the crisis were men. So the riot reproduced the gendered division of labor that placed women as helpmates and men as their natural leaders. Such a division reflected a paternalistic ideology proscribing women to tasks inside the home and men to responsibilities outside it. The Manzanar protest, then, reproduced these traditional gender roles, but, more importantly, it did so at a time when such roles were undergoing a dramatic transformation.[43]

It has long been observed that the internment produced a crisis in Japanese American families. The camps' structured and controlled environment diminished the authority of the Issei patriarch, since the government assumed his role as provider of the family's food, shelter, and clothing. Many Issei fathers were separated from their families for as many as four years, forcing women to become de facto heads of households, responsible for weighty decisions such as whether the family should remain in the United States or repatriate to Japan. At the same time, the internment freed middle-aged and older women from cooking and other domestic responsibilities, enabling them to have a degree of leisure impossible outside the camps. Younger women, too, took advantage of wartime opportunities to establish a greater measure of self-reliance and independence. Nisei women, historian Valerie Matsumoto reveals, empowered by the wage parity of male and female workers in the camps, were encouraged to break away from parental authority by participating in WRA-sponsored programs that sent them to college, the military, or to jobs outside the camps. This new status within the family bolstered the growing refusal among Nisei women for arranged marriages and increased the expectation that their husbands be less chauvinistic than their fathers.[44]

But how did Japanese American men respond to the changing roles for women? What scholarship there is on gender in the camps views men as passive victims in the re-creation of Issei and Nisei womanhood. There is little literature on the relationship between war and male identities that has drawn much attention within fields of cultural and gender studies. Cultural critic Susan Jeffords, for example, reads texts and representations of the Vietnam War in American culture as mechanisms for asserting a particularly masculine sensibility that opposed and subverted the insurgence of feminism and women's rights. In so doing, narratives in films, literature, and journalism have portrayed the Vietnam War as a crucible through which racial, ethnic, and class differences among American men were supplanted by common bonds of masculinity—"brothers in arms." Jeffords's notion of war as a tool for "remasculinization" affords the opportunity to juxtapose the relative freedoms women achieved during the internment against the resurgence of masculine bonds within the Japanese American community. Yet for the internees, masculinity remained tied to racial formations in ways that Jeffords's analysis cannot explain. The symbolic castration of the Issei patriarch, brought by internment, set the stage for reassertions of manhood predicated on the return to a social order in which women were kept separate and subordinate to men.[45]

Consider the negative effect that the internment had on Ko Wakatsuki, as recounted by his daughter in the popular memoir *Farewell to Manzanar*. Wakatsuki was an ambitious Japanese immigrant who studied law in Idaho and dreamed of being elected to the U.S. Senate. Like many Issei, he was rounded up by the FBI in the wake of the Pearl Harbor attack and then interned in a separate camp from his family. Nine months later he rejoined them at Manzanar. "He had aged ten years. He looked over sixty, gaunt, wilted as his shirt, underweight, leaning on that cane and favoring his right leg." Wakatsuki was plagued by the shame of being considered untrustworthy by the American government (the one he dreamed of serving as a senator) and by those internees at Manzanar who saw him as an FBI informer. "This whispered charge, added to the shame of everything that happened to him [during his internment], was simply more than he could bear. . . . He exiled himself, like a leper, and he drank." Wakatsuki also took out his frustrations on his wife, Riku, blaming her for his self-imposed isolation inside the family barracks and accusing her of cavorting with other men solely because she had the liberty of interacting with the outside world. At times he threatened to kill her. "We watched many scenes like this since his return, with Papa acting so crazy sometimes you could almost laugh at the samurai in him, trying to cow her with sheer noise and fierce display. But these were still unfamiliar visits from a demon we had never seen when we lived in Ocean Park [in Santa Monica, California]." [46]

The pressures of the internment pushed another Issei to do more than threaten his wife. A Manzanar police report revealed that in September 1942, Ryosuke Onita, a forty-one-year-old Issei, retaliated against his wife for allegedly carrying on an adulterous affair by killing her and then taking his own life. In a suicide note addressed to Onita's coworkers at one of Manzanar's mess halls, he explained his actions as a "man's prerogative." His wife, he implied, had been unable to stop seeing her lover in spite of promises to do so. "In that respect I am doing only what a man should do. I was forced to commit this act." Onita's diary entries two weeks before he killed his wife provided insight as to what precisely motivated his action. He confessed that "as a man, I absolutely cannot bear the shame which results from my wife comparing me to my rival." But more than affronting his male ego, she violated gender norms for women and especially mothers. Women, he believed, were different from men because they were supposed to place their families and children before their own happiness. In a suicide note addressed to relatives, he explained that "I try to keep her by making her think about the children, but it is no use." [47]

Once his wife's indiscretions had become public, Onita felt himself to be the laughingstock of the internee community. "The whole society called me a fool. My wife and her lover called me a fool to my face." For two months Onita wrestled with the urge to strike back. "Should I restrain myself because of my wife and my children whom I love, or should I take resolute manly action?" he pondered at one point, but later on regretted that he didn't kill his wife's lover given an earlier opportunity, since "I would have been more manly to do so." While wavering between restraint and murder, Onita also came to see self-control as a manly characteristic. A diary entry dated a week before his ultimate act described a happy moment spent with his wife and children in which Onita was "filled with gladness." After a night's rest, he realized "there is no use in asking her to change her mind [about the affair]. But for the sake of preserving the welfare of the family, *and as a man,* I will take the humiliation" (emphasis added). Here it becomes clear that masculinity checked as well as fueled Onita's rage.[48]

What do we make of this extreme instance of domestic violence? Since it was the only case of its kind at Manzanar, it is fair to say that it reflected the singular personalities and individual experiences of those involved. Onita, after all, was in a highly agitated state of mind. The person who translated his writings from Japanese to English noted that one of the suicide notes was "written [while Onita was] in a very excited condition"; a social worker who counseled Onita and his wife remarked that he was "too nervous to talk connectedly," and even a friend testified that Onita was a "little extreme in his point of view." This instability, however, could not account for Onita's sense of gender roles, which were different only in degree from Ko Wakatsuki's response to the internment. Both Issei men felt an intense degree of community shame: Wakatsuki for being accused of being a traitor and Onita for being made a fool of by his wife and her lover. And both, albeit with very different consequences, took out their aggressions upon their wives, whom they blamed for their downfall. Finally, like Wakatsuki's, Onita's troubles were rooted in the tragedy of the internment. He claimed that the Manzanar environment, "where the Japanese are congregated and where immoral relationships exist all over because there is nothing else to do," easily corrupted his wife, since she already had a penchant for extramarital affairs. "This Manzanar," he concluded, "is wild for our family."[49]

Onita's justifications for his actions are also significant because they shed light on the rhetoric of Manzanar protest. For instance, Joseph Kurihara, the leading spokesman for the December 6 protesters, argued that the internment had forced the hand of the internees by breaking the covenant between the American government and its law-abiding Japanese American citizens. In a protest speech he declared that "after all these years of hard work in which Japanese Americans placed every confidence in the arms of the government of the United States, their hope, their trust, and their rights were pulverized. It is the most sacred bond of matrimony. We, the rightful offspring of American Democracy, have been orphaned by the government." This remarkable quotation articulated a gendered understanding of internee protest. Kurihara uses the peculiar phrase "arms of the government" to personify the state as the protector and caretaker of Japanese Americans, who appear as trusting, hard-working, and loyal subordinates, either as spouses (those in "matrimony" with the state) or as "orphaned" children. In this sense, two very different actions, Kurihara's protest of Manzanar conditions and Onita's murder of his wife, each sought to uphold the sanctity of marriage and family. The obligations that a state has to protect its law-abiding citizens and those that a wife has to honor a dutiful husband combined in a broad-ranging paternalism in which internee men appeared trapped in a double jeopardy: rejected by both the government (father) and Japanese American women (wife).[50]

A third dimension to the paternalist order was obligation to children, and in this respect internee resisters and collaborators found fault with each other. Harry Ueno explained that his opposition to the Manzanar administration sprang from his avuncular relations with the camp's children. As a mess-hall cook, he took special care to bake unauthorized treats that were a small but important joy for Manzanar youth. Through this endeavor, he discovered a shortage of sugar in the mess hall, which led him to accuse camp administrators of corruption. So it was that Ueno's resistance, through which he was transformed from outsider to protector-cum-father figure of the internee community, stemmed from concerns about the welfare of the children. The same concerns, of course, led Togo Tanaka in the different direction of supporting the WRA program, if not always the Manzanar administration. For him, the issue was not so much what happened to the children in the camps but what would happen to them after the war. Convinced that the United States would prevail over Japan, he thought it was wrong for the resisters, and internees in general, to cling to cultural traditions that would ill-prepare Japanese American youth for the possibility of postwar assimilation.[51]

If the return to a stable set of paternalistic relations was a goal for resisters and collaborators, then masculinity was a means to achieving it. Here, too, Onita's justifications for murdering his wife bear an instructive resemblance to the language of Manzanar protest, for both cases reveal a duality between manly resistance and manly restraint. Joseph Kurihara was the most outspoken in this regard, labeling the "baby-faced" Fred Tayama, whose beating instigated the unrest, a coward "to the very core of his bones" because he refused to "meet me like a man in public debate" and, instead, "sneaks around and spies on us." The soldiers who fired on the mob of internees were ones whom Kurihara would have shot, "if only I had [had] a gun." In the end, he questioned the masculinity of the Manzanar director, Ralph Merritt, since he failed to throw the JACL "stool-pigeons" out of the camp and was not a "man big enough" to admit that the protest was justified. Apparently, the protesters were the only ones brave enough to stand up against the "spineless Americans" who were taking unfair advantage of the Manzanar internees.[52]

This manliness was also expressed after the protest had been squelched and Kurihara and tens of others were in the county jail in nearby Bishop, California. According to Kurihara, some prison guards "admired our guts, and others feared [them]." Another way in which the prisoners apparently showed their mettle, Kurihara boasted, was by not succumbing to the bleakness of their confinement. "Whatever methods the officials may employ in trying to break our morale have failed. The inmates have readily adjusted to the situation and spent the days leisurely and rather happily. None of us weakened. Instead we all took it like a man, and amused ourselves by entertaining each other with stories and songs." Kurihara's "grandest" Christmas and New Year's Eve were reportedly spent in prison. The idea that the resisters could take their oppression mirrored an earlier criticism of the collaborators made before the Manzanar protest by the camp's underground resistance (it is unclear whether Kurihara and Ueno were members). The criticism maintained that the collaborators were too cowardly to endure the oppressing conditions of the internment and instead flapped around "like a fish on a board" trying to escape the inevitable torture.[53]

The resisters even shared masculine bonds with white Americans and the dreaded internee collaborators. Kurihara respected collaborator Tokutaro Slocum's "guts" for having served in World War I, and he esteemed both Slocum and Togo Tanaka for their ability to speak their minds in public. Furthermore, he lavished praise upon the director of one of the special prison camps (Leupp) where he and his fellow protesters had been sent, calling him a "real American" whose "true sportsmanship" fostered a "genuine friendship which prevented the hatred naturally existing between individuals of belligerent countries."[54] Harry Ueno, too, had the capacity to recognize manliness across battle lines and, like Kurihara, singled out Togo Tanaka from other pro-WRA factions accused of being FBI spies and collaborators. Recalling a face-to-face encounter with Tanaka, Ueno said that he did not think Tanaka was a spy. "Not considering the way he talked openly. Whatever he believes in, he tells you openly. He's not ashamed, or scared, or anything. . . . I believe in him. I don't think he would do anything behind our [protesters'] backs." Yet Ueno did not trust Tanaka's friend because he remained silent throughout their encounter. He did not trust some of his own comrades in protest for the very same reason. Because of their silence, he wasn't sure whether they supported the United States or Japan. Siding with America was bad enough, but being secretive about one's loyalty violated a deeper sense of manly honor.[55]

Collaborators also acted for purportedly masculine reasons. Tokutaro Slocum was fond of army metaphors, seeing support for the camp administration as his way of serving his country and commander-in-chief. He went to Manzanar, he boasted, because "my President told me to," accusing anyone who criticized the internment or the administration, even a fellow war veteran such as Kurihara, as a coward afraid to die in battle.[56] Tanaka further underscored the manliness of the collaborators by contrasting them to Manzanar leftists, who, it should be remembered, had vied with the JACLers for internee leadership. To be a "red," Togo Tanaka reported, was associated among the internees with having "loose morals" and partaking in "unconventional behavior," especially with respect to sexual and masculine transgressions. For example, he highlighted disparaging rumors about the editor of the *Manzanar Free Press* not only because she was a known communist but also because she was twice divorced, which was certainly uncommon for Japanese Americans at that time, and currently living with a third man. In another case Tanaka described a staff member of the *Free Press* as a well-educated supporter of the WRA program but who, unlike the collaborators, had an aversion to manual labor. Finally, Tanaka noted that Karl Yoneda, an outspoken collaborator at Manzanar, was a communist, and he was married to a white woman, who, according to many internees, did not follow Japanese customs. Yoneda himself noted that one of the criticisms against him at Manzanar was that he performed domestic duties (e.g., washing clothes) while his wife worked and attended political meetings outside the home.[57]

In the final analysis both protesters and collaborators at Manzanar struggled over the meaning of masculinity and in these efforts reinforced the exclusion of women from community decision making. In protesting against, or in collaborating with, the WRA, Japanese American women, like the earlier Nisei Week queens, were merely supposed to follow and submit to male authority. Although strained by the imperatives of internment, the boundary separating men's and women's roles at Manzanar was strengthened by the internee's political conflicts.

THREE ROADS TO FREEDOM

The conflicts forged at Manzanar would continue to split the ethnic community into distinct, oppositional factions. In the wake of the Manzanar protest and an earlier clash at the internment camp in Poston, Arizona, the WRA was forced to abandon its strategy of "barbed-wire democracy." The agency's officials were now convinced that the only way to rid the internees of the group solidarity and values that made them such an easy racial scapegoat was to free them from the camps. Predictably, the Manzanar internees responded to the prospect of freedom in different ways that underscored their internal diversity.

In December 1942, WRA director Dillon Myer knew that the idea of freeing the internees while Allied victory in the Pacific remained uncertain would be hotly contested. The general public was in no mood for clemency, especially after newspapers heralded the Manzanar unrest as a "Jap uprising" in celebration of the anniversary of the Pearl Harbor attack. The Army, as it had done to justify the internment in the first place, confirmed such misinformation by insisting that the ring leaders of the Manzanar protest, along with those who stirred up trouble in the rest of the camps, were inherently disloyal to the United States. The most suspected internees were the Kibei, Issei bachelors, Issei couples without children, and those who petitioned for repatriation to Japan.[58] The WRA, however, resisted pressures to distinguish between internees based on these social categories. If it was so easy to distinguish the loyal from disloyal, Dillon Myer asked, then why did the Army not do so when it evacuated Japanese Americans from the West Coast? The director maintained that the "artificial environment" of the camps threatened to sour, rather than nurture, the democratic spirit.[59] The crisis at Manzanar lent urgency to Myer's decision to break down the internees' ethnic solidarity by integrating them into white communities far from the West Coast. To facilitate this dispersal, he established guidelines that allowed the internees to leave the camps "indefinitely" as long as they secured a job, informed the WRA as to their whereabouts, proved they would be accepted in their new community, and were cleared of any disloyalty by the FBI.[60]

To speed up the release of the internees, the WRA implemented its own loyalty test in January 1943. In cooperation with the Army, which sought volunteers for an all-Nisei combat team, the agency devised a "leave clearance" application required for all internees over age seventeen to complete. Buried in this form were two questions used to determine the internee's loyalty and, for American citizens, their willingness to register for the draft. Question 27 queried draft-age Nisei men whether they would "serve in the armed forces of the United States on combat duty, wherever ordered"; and Question 28 asked each internee to "swear un-

TABLE 3.1   LEAVE STATUS OF INTERNEES FROM INCEPTION
TO CLOSING OF MANZANAR INTERNMENT CAMP

Leave Status	Number	Percent of Total
Indefinite leave (Resettlement)	2,380	21.5
Transfer to Tule Lake (Segregation)	2,216	20
Terminal departure (Remaining)	5,706	51.5
Transfer to another camp	760	7
Total	11,062	100

SOURCE: War Relocation Authority, *The Evacuated People: A Quantitative Description*, Table 4.13 (Washington, D.C.: United States Department of the Interior, 1946).

qualified allegiance to the United States of America and faithfully defend the United States from any or all attack by foreign or domestic forces, and forswear any form of allegiance or obedience to the Japanese emperor, or any other foreign government, power, or organization."[61]

The response to these questions determined the fate of the internees. The overwhelming majority at Manzanar affirmed their loyalty to the United States and were then given a choice to remain in the camp or be released on "indefinite leave." A significant fraction of the internees, however, refused to forswear allegiance to Japan, swear allegiance to the United States, or agree to serve in the nation's armed forces. These people were whisked away, along with their family members and those seeking repatriation or expatriation to Japan, to Tule Lake, the camp in northern California that was now set aside for "troublemakers."[62] Table 3.1 reveals that most internees at Manzanar decided to remain in the camp (or join family members at another camp) until they were forced to leave Manzanar after the war. Twenty-two percent of the internees chose to resettle in cities in the Midwest and along the East Coast, while a slightly smaller proportion of them were segregated from the rest of the internees in the maximum-security camp at Tule Lake. None of the three choices promised to lead the internees back to their homes in southern California. How did they decide which road to take?

At this point, the internees' primary objective was survival. Whether they elected to resettle outside the camp, segregate to Tule Lake, or remain at Manzanar, they expressed their desires in the language of the American front. All but a handful of the most ardent internees sent to the Tule Lake segregation center repeated their support for the United States like an incantation to ward off the constant charge of disloyalty. They chose their road to freedom not on the strength of their patriotic conviction but from the different options available to them as a result of their various social positions, including age, sex, generation, economic standing, and family circumstances.

ROAD ONE: RESETTLEMENT

The most likely by far to leave Manzanar on indefinite leave were young men and women in their late teens and early twenties. Forty percent of the American-born generation, compared to only 8 percent of the Issei, left the camp under the indefinite leave program until it ended in December 1944 with the rescinding of Japanese American exclusion from the West Coast.[63] A few of the men joined the Army's famous 442d combat team, which fought and earned highest honors in the European theater. Most of the resettlers left the camps not merely to prove their loyalty but to take advantage of economic, social, and educational opportunities that had escaped them before the war. A good number of them enrolled in colleges and universities throughout the East and Midwest. Those who had completed their education, like Roy Takeno, a graduate of the University of Southern California who found a job at a Denver newspaper, used the relocation as a means to finally begin their careers.[64] Carl Kondo, the prize-winning Nisei Week essayist in 1935, represented others who sought places like New York City, which were relatively free of the hostility that had plagued Japanese Americans in Los Angeles. "Race prejudice," he reported, "is not too welcome here in New York. It isn't safe with some ninety nationalities scattered about. All kinds of languages are spoken, and on the radio you get Italian and German language broadcasts. No one thinks anything of it. No one asks you your nationality. . . . So you can easily lose your identity."[65]

Sociologist Dorothy Thomas observed that most resettlers tended be college-educated, Christian or secular in their religious convictions, and from urban, nonagricultural backgrounds. What distinguished them was that they were the "most highly assimilated segments of the Japanese American minority," who embraced the "wider opportunities" that awaited them beyond their "segregated ethnocentered communities."[66] The same thing could have been said about the JACLers from Los Angeles, who, not surprisingly, played a prominent role in the indefinite leave program.

Tanaka encouraged the internees to leave the camps and assimilate with their fellow Americans after he fled Manzanar with his wife and child as a result of the December 6 unrest. He then worked with the Society of American Friends to resettle Japanese Americans and Jewish refugees from Europe in Chicago, where he was living.[67] For all his attempts to restore the internees' faith in democracy, Tanaka was deeply embittered about the racial prejudice he had experienced in California. He vowed never to return there. Living in Chicago convinced him that the environment there "was much more conducive to a stress-free life for our children and our grandchildren."[68] To the young Tanaka, Chicago posed an exciting opportunity to get away from the segregated communities that he was convinced exacerbated the racial misunderstanding that had led to the internment. His vision was to disperse Japanese Americans throughout the city so that "we don't put all on one block here on the South Shore or Hyde Park or on the Westside."[69] This, of course, was also the WRA strategy and, for that matter, the growing orthodoxy of the nascent Civil Rights Movement, which would soon make the idea—and practice—of racial integration a central tenet of American liberalism.

Tanaka was one of many JACLers who refused to return to Los Angeles with the ending of the exclusion order. Kiyoshi Okura, the leader of Nisei Week's flora-dora sextet, found a use for his master's degree in psychology as a social worker at Boys Town in Nebraska. His UCLA classmate, Kay Sugahara, the first president of the Los Angeles JACL, moved to New York City after he was discharged from military service. Ever the entrepreneur, Sugahara established a shipping business that would earn him the moniker "Nisei Onasis."[70] In her analysis of the 1950 census, Thomas found that Japanese Americans who remained in New York City and Chicago had an extremely high level of education compared to those returning to Los Angeles. In these two cities the ethnic population was twice as likely to be college educated as their white neighbors, whereas in Los Angeles, they pursued higher degrees at the same rate as whites. Thomas also noted that many more of those remaining east of the Rocky Mountains moved on to professional jobs than those returning to the West Coast, who continued "piling-up on the lowest rungs of the occupational ladder."[71]

The exigencies of World War II encouraged the Nisei elite of Los Angeles to break away from the ethnic solidarity that had been the foundation of their social, economic, and political objectives. For them, the ethnic enclave with its racial vulnerability, rigid internal hierarchy, and possessive investment in group conformity was a thing of the past. In Chicago, New York City, and other places where anti-Japanese politics had never taken root, highly educated people like the former Nisei Week leaders entered the mainstream economy. Fleeing the racial strictures they had experienced in southern California, they reaped the benefits of their knowledge, training, and abilities.

ROAD TWO: SEGREGATION

The internees at Manzanar who were segregated at Tule Lake shared a social profile that was the opposite of the resettlers; the segregants were more likely to be Issei or Kibei Buddhists from agricultural backgrounds.[72] Both Issei and Nisei men at Tule Lake also were significantly less educated than those choosing to stay at Manzanar or those venturing on to freedom.[73] Joseph Kurihara, who eventually ended up at Tule Lake after being accused of chasing Tanaka and the other JACLers away from Manzanar, was the exception to the rule; he was college-educated, came from an urban and professional background, and had few ties to Japan before the war. Kurihara, like many of the segregants, viewed the decision to go to Tule Lake as an extension of the December 6 protest. The question of loyalty to the United States was far less important than the issue of justice for the Manzanar internees.

Anthropologist Morris Opler documented the segregants' fervent criticism of the Niseis' lack of civil rights. He recorded their views at the loyalty hearings that the WRA held to coax potential segregants into changing their minds. "I'm supposed to be a citizen of the United States," said John Suzuki, a thirty-six-year-old Nisei who was married, had three children, and was the manager at a large produce firm in Los Angeles before the war. Suzuki refused to answer the loyalty questions because the internment had convinced him that his American citizenship was worthless, and thus it was fruitless for Japanese Americans to remain in the United States. "What security have we?" he asked the review board. "If this can happen now, why can't the same thing happen in five years?"[74] Opler made clear in his notes that Suzuki was fully American, speaking "perfect English," and exhibiting a "perfect American attitude" in protesting for his rights as an American citizen. One of the board members, who was assessing his loyalty, noticed that Suzuki showed "no interest in Japan" and thus queried him about his refusal to affirm loyalty to the United States.

BOARD MEMBER: What has happened [to Japanese Americans] is unfortunate. But other minorities have had to face discrimination too. In my part of the country the Germans are probably treated worse than the Japanese.

SUZUKI: It's all right to be of a minority as long as you're of the same race.

BOARD MEMBER: I can't see that. If you're discriminated against because you belong to a minority group, it's as bad whatever race you happen to belong to.

SUZUKI: This is the reason you look at it differently; you are a white man. At the end of the war, animosities will be high. There will be high feelings against us. There will be a boycott of us if we start in business. At the end of the last war, the bad feeling didn't continue against the Germans. But you can't tell a German from an Englishman when he walks down the street. But when I go down the street they say, "There goes a Jap." Perhaps it will be fifteen years before this feeling will die down. I disagree with you when you say that 100,000 Japanese can be assimilated now. I know the WRA personnel are doing what they can. But the one hundred thirty millions in this country are hostile.[75]

In addition to Suzuki's observations about American race relations, there was a more pragmatic reason why he and most of his fellow segregants transferred to Tule Lake. After the December 6 crisis, it was widely believed that Manzanar would be closed as a result of the turmoil. The idea of being "forced out" of camp and dispersed within white America was too much for Suzuki, who feared for the health of his sick mother and aged father. Opler noticed that the majority of Nisei segregants tried to safeguard themselves from the racists on the outside, even if it meant blemishing their records as loyal Americans, sacrificing American citizenship, and living in the foreign world of Japan. He maintained that the internees most likely to stay on were "those who have lost particularly heavily in the evacuation, those who have large families, those who are in poor health, those who would find difficulty in making an occupational adjustment outside and those who have misgivings about public opinion in localities where they might settle." The segregants from Manzanar, according to Opler, "represented the individuals weakest in health, wealth and future prospects, rather than those weakest in essential loyalty."[76]

Such pragmatic concerns were hardly unique to the segregants. Roy Takeno, Manzanar's documentary historian after Tanaka and Joe Grant

Masaoka left the camp, illuminated the small things that influenced the response to the WRA's loyalty questions. The reasons for "remaining loyal" included having Caucasian friends, loving American sports, maintaining an "unquenchable thirst for chocolate malts and ice cream sodas." Takeno noted that "it may be disappointing to American publicists and some of the best friends of the Japanese if it were known that most of those who are deciding to remain American aren't doing so primarily because of their loyalty, as such, to the nation's flag, to the Four Freedoms, or even to the principles of democracy."[77] Takeno addressed this point further in a discussion of segregants from Manzanar. He pointed out that white Americans have difficulty grasping that these people are merely "trying to be practical. . . . They feel that issues of loyalty or obedience bear little or no relevance to the matter of deciding their own future."[78]

ROAD THREE: REMAINING

The majority of internees who answered "yes" to the WRA's two loyalty questions and remained at Manzanar were also being practical. Thomas claimed that the remaining internees made up the core of the ethnic group that was "physically, emotionally, economically, and demographically incapable of finding jobs and homes in other areas."[79] The bulk of this population consisted of children younger than fourteen and adults older than fifty. Because resettlement to the East and Midwest had attracted so many internees in their twenties, the proportion of Manzanar residents older than sixty-five had increased more than two and half times.[80] Their unwillingness to leave the camp in 1943 and 1944 continued into 1945, even after Japanese Americans were allowed to return to the West Coast. An Issei internee expressed the concerns that perhaps most Manzanar residents had about the WRA's plans to finally close the camp. In a letter to Dillon Myer, he worried about his family's financial stability but also underscored his reluctance to remain on government assistance. At the same time he complained that the twenty-five-dollar travel stipend the WRA paid to each internee was not enough to begin their new life in Los Angeles.

> Mr. Myer, my family and I have gone through many difficulties and hardships, without any fault on my part or anyone in my family, since the war broke out. And our hardships and obstacles, especially financil [sic], will be confronting us for the days and years to come. . . . I am sincerely and re-

spectfully appealing to you that some adjustment be worked out so that the evacuees and war casualties will be treated not by the present impractical and inadequate assistance or forced [to relocate], but by the policy of cooperation, goodwill, kindness and friendship which are born [of] humanity and justice for which this great country of democracy stands.[81]

Fears of returning to southern California were well founded. During and just after the war, anti-Japanese groups and individuals initiated a campaign of terror to intimidate Japanese Americans from returning to the West Coast. The Native Sons of the Golden West, American Legion posts, labor unions, Hearst-owned newspapers, and other veterans of anti-Japanese movements once again unfurled their banner of hate. As in the past, California proved the state most unabashedly anti-Japanese. During World War II, an overwhelming majority of Californians wanted to amend the U.S. Constitution to permit large-scale Japanese American deportation. WRA agent Allan Markley sent a confidential report to Dillon Myer that identified two movements under way in southern California to oppose the return of Japanese Americans. The first consisted of "land owners pledging themselves not to sell or lease land to people of Japanese origin," and the second were "housewives in certain areas pledging not to do business with merchants or others of Japanese ancestry." Markley concluded, "Hundreds of community leaders and many civic organizations and trade bodies in the southern California area are still violently opposed to the return of any of the Japanese people until the end of the hostilities with Japan."[82] Indeed, after the internees were allowed to return to southern California, WRA officials recorded fifty incidents of anti-Japanese violence—which typically involved gunshots—and hundreds of less serious cases of assault and intimidation.[83] The *Rafu Shimpo,* which was reestablished in 1945, repeatedly advised its readers how to cope with such hostility. Columnist Henry Mori reassured Japanese Americans that they were innocent victims of senseless persecution. "Some West Coast people," he cautioned, "still hold tenaciously to the idea that returnees must at all times be the target of discrimination. War hysteria has niched [*sic*] their narrow minds so much their focus has become cross-eyed with contempt."[84]

Not even the Nisei who had served in the American military could avoid anti-Japanese antipathy. In Hood River, Oregon, an American Legion post removed the names of sixteen Nisei veterans from its honor roll commemorating the dead who had served in World War II. It took a national controversy, in which the legionnaires' actions were roundly condemned, before the post reacknowledged the contributions of Nisei veterans.[85] In California, state legislators demonstrated their continuing anti-Japanese sentiment by seeking to take away agricultural land from those Japanese Americans who were able to keep it throughout the war. As the internees began returning to their homes, Sacramento tightened enforcement of the Alien Land Act, the 1913 measure designed to thwart Japanese American settlement and economic advancement. California's attorney general received additional funds to prosecute violators, and, consequently, by late 1946 more Japanese Americans than ever were in jeopardy of losing their land.[86] Nisei columnist Larry Tajiri referred to the California situation as a great land grabbing of Japanese American farms.[87]

With bad news from the outside, many of the internees decided to stay in the camps even after Japan's August 1945 surrender. In fact, some internee leaders fought the WRA's plans to close all the camps six to twelve months after the war's end because they feared that many inmates had become dependent on camp life and could not readjust to the real world.[88] An opinion poll taken at one relocation center confirmed these fears. When asked why they wanted to remain incarcerated, respondents replied that they were worried that resettlement would bring financial and employment difficulties, discrimination, and family separation.[89] But once again government officials forcibly uprooted the internees—this time from the camps. Manzanar closed in November 1945, and Tule Lake, the last of camps to shut down, freed and exonerated most of its inhabitants of their wartime "disloyalty" in January 1946. As thousands of newly released internees made their way back to southern California, they faced different fears from those they had when they left the region three or four long years before: Would they still have a home? Could they reestablish a business or find a job? Would they be welcomed by former neighbors and business associates?

THE INS AND OUTS OF RESETTLEMENT

The answers to these questions were often, surprisingly, "yes." Within five years after they were released from their internment, the Japanese American population in Los Angeles reached its prewar level of thirty-seven thousand. Despite the WRA's attempts to disperse the ex-internees across the United States, the vast majority of them returned to the West Coast. Dorothy Thomas found that by 1950 fewer than one out of six of those resettling from the camps during the war remained east of the Rocky Mountains. Those who remained were the JACLers and other

Nisei elite who best exploited the economic opportunities available to Japanese Americans in places like Chicago and New York City. Eighty percent of the entire ethnic population in 1950 had resumed their concentrations in Washington, Oregon, and especially California. Bill Hosokawa, columnist for the JACL's news organ, the *Pacific Citizen*, observed a growing split between those who had and those who had not returned to the West Coast. He referred to these groups as the "ins" and the "outs" within Japanese American communities. The "ins," he asserted, remained among their own kind, while the "outs" braved to live and interact with white Americans.[90]

The Japanese Americans who pushed the goal of integration were more in step with the powerful currents of racial reform sweeping across American society. While the Nisei Week festival had underscored the Americanism of the ethnic community and had often reached out directly to establish good relations between Japanese and white Americans, it had stopped short of encouraging the diminishment of ethnic ties and obligations. In postwar America, however, this was de rigueur for many Americans who sought to overlook racial differences in an attempt to discredit the beliefs in white supremacy that fueled Nazi atrocities.

Outraged at the sins of segregation, Togo Tanaka opposed those, like Los Angeles journalist Harry Honda, who accepted ethnic and racial communities as a fact of human nature. "The minority-minded and race-conscious part of us that insists on doing everything among and with 'our own people,'" Tanaka wrote in 1947, "will welcome Harry Honda's declaration of war on those fuzzy idealists with starry eyes, long hairs, and dirty fingernails who want us to work at inter-group rather than in-group solidarity."[91] Los Angeles Nisei Sue Takimoto also derided those in her community who "remain aloof and separate, permitting as few contacts as possible with those of other groups," while other champions of integration complained of similar tendencies among Japanese Americans in Berkeley, Denver, and New York City.[92] Columnist Molly Oyama repeatedly chastised Los Angeles Nisei for being "clannish" and for hiding behind a self-imposed "silken curtain" separating them unnecessarily from other peoples. According to Oyama, self-segregation resulted in part from Nisei prejudices against Jews, Filipinos, Mexicans, and blacks, for "[w]e are often just as guilty as the white Caucasians in this respect, with [fewer] 'excuses' for our prejudices. Having been victims of race prejudice ourselves, there is less justification for the 'beam in our eye.'"[93] Oyama also instructed the Nisei that "you will have to take most of the initiative" in making friends with whites and recommended taking them out to eat. "Usually, the non-Nisei likes something exotic or unusual like a Chinese or even a Japanese dinner."[94]

The memories of the near and distant past, however, prevented most of the Japanese Americans in Los Angeles from trusting people beyond the ethnic community. Tomosa Sasaki documented this distrust in a series of reports he filed as part of the WRA's attempt to monitor the reintegration of former internees to Los Angeles. One Issei accountant told Sasaki about his difficulty in socializing with whites. "I don't have confidence in my English," he said, "and so although there are many things I would like to say, I don't." While this Issei was hopeful that Japanese Americans outside the West Coast were mixing more with whites, he was doubtful that those in Los Angeles would achieve full integration.[95] A Christian minister offered a similar assessment. Reverend Kowta believed that the "Japanese are not ready for [integration]" because "the people who have returned to the West Coast are the most conservative" who have only lived in Japanese communities.[96] A government study conducted by John Kitasako found that even the Japanese Americans who initially reached out to whites began to "shy away from integration." Kitasako reported that the time came "when the Nisei started becoming a bit weary of being headline attractions at functions arranged by well-meanings individuals, and there grew in them a desire for the quieter enjoyment and privacy of all-Nisei companionship. In this society of his own kind, he can relax, and he can conduct himself without feeling self-conscious, and without having someone say, 'Oh, I think you're all so American.'" Kitasako further revealed that some Nisei viewed integration as "almost a fighting word" because it evoked memories of wartime persecution and discrimination.[97] The *Pacific Citizen* summed up Kitasako's point when it concluded that the pendulum had swung back to "self-segregation after a period of artificial integration."[98]

The reestablishment of Little Tokyo was the ultimate expression of this dynamic. While Japanese Americans were interned, the former Japanese quarter had become a community for newly migrated African Americans known as "Bronzeville." The resurgence of the Japanese quarter proceeded rather quickly. Landlords in the area, often Anglo or Jewish, urged Japanese Americans to resettle there because, as one Nisei recalled in 1973, they "had this prejudicial point of view that the Japanese tenants always paid on time."[99] Yet the ex-internees harbored their own prejudices as well. In her study of the resettlement in California, anthropologist Katherine Luomala reported that the Nisei returnees had singled out blacks among those they called the "bogeyman." She maintained that the early resettlers to Los Angeles feared and avoided them, with some of these "scouts" predicting that blacks would riot and "forcibly resist" attempts by Japanese Americans to reclaim Little Tokyo.[100] Although no riot erupted, conflicts over crime and cleanliness pestered black-Japanese relations.[101] "The only places that look kept up are those owned by the Japanese," said one Nisei merchant upon reopening his store in Little Tokyo.[102] Another returning merchant noted that violent crime was rampant in the streets where children once played.[103]

Liberal integrationists, like Togo Tanaka, criticized those who stirred up "the emotions of Issei, Nisei and Kibei in Los Angeles by insistent references to criminals as 'Negro' or colored persons without recognition of the truth that color is only incidental to the fact that crime is always high in run-down, overcrowded, near-slum areas of segregation such as Little Tokyo–Bronzeville." Tanaka noted that Little Tokyo businessmen's "racially exclusive organizations and activities" threatened interracial harmony. But he did not blame Little Tokyo leaders entirely for their antiblack feelings. These Japanese Americans, Tanaka concluded, had been "maneuvered by members of the majority group to take issue with members of a minority group with which they have much more in common and with whose welfare their own is more immediately linked."[104] And although Tanaka would have decried it, the return of Little Tokyo (and the demise of Bronzeville) also reflected prejudices against white Americans. One Issei revealed a sense of racial superiority in explaining how Japanese Americans rebuilt their community:

> [I]t is because we are Japanese that within a years time we have been able to get back as much as we have. . . . No other race could have done that. You take the hakujin [white people]. . . . I'll bet they would still be in the relocation camps demanding compensation from the government. But the Japanese lost millions, and I'll bet within the six months that have just past, the Japanese have spent millions of dollars already to get back some of the things that they lost.[105]

This is a remarkable statement in light of the 1980s movement for Japanese American Redress, which culminated in monetary compensation for all living survivors of the internment. Asking the government for economic compensation in this redress movement was seen as a crucial development in the political mobilization of Japanese Americans—a "breaking the silence" about the painful memories of World War II.[106] But it is well to remember that 1946 was a world apart from the later period of identity politics (discussed in chapters 5 and 6). Certainly not everyone agreed with the view implicit in the above quotation: that the ability of Japanese Americans to bounce back from hardship without complaining or demanding compensation symbolized their superiority to whites. Yet the idea of resiliency as the basis of group pride was everywhere apparent during and after the internment crisis: It was apparent in both the JACLers' turn-the-other-cheek position and the Manzanar protesters' stance as manly, or model, prisoners; in both the resettlers' charge to integrate in Midwestern and East Coast cities and the returnees' attempt to reestablish their homes and businesses in southern California. Some might argue that resiliency operated as a code of honor rooted in the primordial mists of Japanese culture, but to do so is to neglect the precedent of Japanese American history, for this group always had been more concerned about getting their own house in order than in making demands upon the state.

The postwar proved no exception to this rule as the returnees to Los Angeles soon battled to reestablish community leadership. In July 1946, one Nisei noted that he was glad these groups had yet to return and that all the "big shots who lived here before . . . are pretty quiet." On the other hand, the Issei leaders, according to another informant, "are itching again for leadership, but they are debating whether they should come out or not because most of them were in internment and are afraid that if they do anything in terms of organization and leadership they may again be placed under suspicion."[107] Indeed, when the immigrant associations did return in August 1946, they took on an Americanized identity to distance themselves from the specter of anti-Americanism that surrounded them. The *Rafu Nihonjinkai* and *Nanka Shoko Kaigisho,* the two leading Issei groups that also had initiated the Nisei Week festival, become known as respectively, the Japanese Chamber of Commerce and the Japanese Businessmen's Association (later changed to the Little Tokyo Businessman's Association).

Following closely behind the Issei organizations came the "reactivation" of the Los Angeles JACL. In collecting data for the WRA, Tom Sasaki revealed that the accusations against the JACL had not ended with the internment. One informant noted that the Issei would not support the organization because its leaders had exploited so many of the older generation. "It's no wonder," he said, "that Fred Tayama got beaten up in camp. He should have been killed."[108] Tayama was the focus of community scorn, as he had been at Manzanar. Another informant told Sasaki, "The JACL before the war made a poor showing because many of the leaders were out for themselves. These various service organizations charged quite a bit for information and services that should have been given free. You take Fred Tayama. He could never make money. Just before evacuation he saw a chance to make the money, and he needed it because he liked to show off and pretend that he was worth quite a bit. Those people like him, thought that leadership meant having money and showing off." [109]

Nobody was more aware of the anti-JACL sentiment than the individuals who reestablished the Los Angeles chapter. Many of them had not been active in the organization before the war and did not want to live in the shadow of its past deeds. "Rather than saying that we are reactivating the JACL," John Saito suggested, "we ought to say that we are organizing a new chapter . . . to keep the stigma of the pre-war JACL from marring the reputation of the new JACL." [110] The membership agreed with Saito and decided not to invite Mike Masaoka, the JACL's national director, to speak in Los Angeles because of his reputation as a WRA collaborator. [111] But the new JACL still failed to drum up financial support from the Japanese American community. In late 1947 Frank Chuman, the chapter's recently elected president, concluded that the JACL continued to suffer from the "pre-war and evacuation misunderstandings in regard to the JACL's intentions." Chuman's response was to propose a "public relations program to 'resell' the JACL."

The attempt to revamp the image of the organization was more than cosmetic. The Los Angeles JACL transformed itself from the organization that had once sought to save Little Tokyo by promoting its Americanism. Gone were many of its most prominent and forceful leaders, and in their places emerged a younger cohort of Nisei who had come of age during World War II. Following the lead of the national organization, the local chapter removed ethnic qualifications to membership, welcoming white Americans into the group. [112] The Issei, however, remained excluded until they were allowed to naturalize as American citizens in 1952. Also in step with the national leadership, the Los Angeles JACLers embarked on a full-fledged commitment to racial integration. To reach this end, the local organization published a short-lived newsletter called the *Los Angeles Vanguard*. In its second issue, Fred Fertig, head of JACL's southern California regional office, maintained that the chapter's "policy makers are striving to have local persons of Japanese ancestry abandon their pre-war isolationists' ways." [113] In that same issue, Frank Chuman warned that for Japanese Americans to reject integration "is to condemn ourselves to the lives which we lived before the war—that of living on small individual islands within ourselves with no outlet to the mainland." [114]

There was no turning back for the Japanese Americans of Los Angeles. That life in which they had been bound to the ethnic enclave by the pressures of racial discrimination and the internal demands of group solidarity was gone forever. A new age had dawned in which the language of racial integration informed the competition to define Japanese American identity. After the war, the question was no longer whether the ethnic community should assimilate into mainstream society; it was how to break down its walls of exclusivity while still retaining ties of ethnic solidarity that for so long had defined it.

PART 3

Communities

FOUR

Defining Integration

The Return of Nisei Week and
Remaking of Japanese American Identity

Taro Kawa was one of the first Japanese Americans to return to Los Angeles after the exclusion order was rescinded in December 1944. His top priority was to reclaim the family's home, which had been leased while family members were interned and, subsequently, living in Chicago. He was so determined to do this that he loaned money to his tenants toward the purchase of their own homes. Later, Kawa was equally committed to reestablishing the family grocery store. To this end, he found one of the family's former employees in the WRA camp in Poston, Arizona, and, in his own truck, took the worker and his entire family back to Los Angeles. By October 1945, the grocer had regained the remainder of his prewar crew and, to his delight, would soon begin to welcome back the store's old Japanese American clientele.

A few years later, Kawa sought to restore yet another piece of his lost world. In August 1949, he formed a triumvirate of Little Tokyo businessmen with insurance broker Kiyo Yamato and travel agent Eiji Tanabe and under the auspices of the local JACL chapter revived the Nisei Week festival. The celebration was heralded as the capstone of Little Tokyo's reemergence, marking the end, as the festival souvenir booklet put it, to the "hectic evacuation years" and "the return again to familiar faces and old haunts." [1] The *Pacific Citizen* proclaimed that "the big story of Nisei Week is its reflection of the economic and social health of the displaced Americans who have returned home. The race-baiters have been routed and the songs and dances of Nisei Week serve to wipe out the memory of bitterness and frustration of the mass evacuation experience."[2]

In truth, the economic and emotional legacy of the internment experience, as the movement to redress this injustice would reveal in the 1980s, could not be so easily ameliorated. But the implication that the newly restored Nisei Week had witnessed a profound shift in racial sensibilities was accurate. World War II, as historian Ronald Takaki argues, was a watershed in the long struggle for Japanese American civil rights. Indeed, it took less than a decade after the end of the war for all major anti-Japanese laws and court decisions to be rescinded. No one in American society had expected such a dramatic reversal of political winds. Then, again, no one had imagined the suddenness in which the nation would be hurled into an intense, protracted, and massive military buildup with its former allies in the Soviet Union. One of the first American acts of the Cold War was the reconstruction of Japan. Here, the Americans kept the Soviets at bay and single-handedly occupied and rebuilt the nation of its former enemy. This relationship between victor and vanquished produced a mutual admiration and familiarity, a goodwill that would radically revise American attitudes toward Japan and, by extension, Japanese in the United States.

The 1950s and 1960s was an "era of good feelings" for Japanese Americans that transformed Nisei Week's "buy in Lil' Tokio" campaign into a quaint and distant memory. As a result, Nisei biculturalism, the orthodoxy insisting that Japanese Americans promote and protect the ethnic community's economic position in southern California, failed to return. As racial restrictions became legally barred from private- and public-sector jobs, most Japanese Americans no longer relied upon the ethnic enclave for their livelihood. And so while Nisei like Taro Kawa rebuilt Little Tokyo shops, there was no need to re-create the broader, horizontally and vertically integrated network of coethnic businesses. The postwar collapse of anti-Japanese restrictions also softened the need for the repressive strictures of the American front. No longer would the struggle be to gain *access* to mainstream institutions and due process of the law. Japanese Americans, instead, sought to gain *success* within social, economic, and political spheres that had previously been closed to them.

The new orthodoxy at Nisei Week was integration, which, like biculturalism and the American front, embodied conflicted and changing inflections. Such ethnic negotiations were evident in the regeneration of Nisei Week leadership, as well as within internal debates about keeping the festival in step with the social mobility and rising class status of Japanese Americans. Yet despite Nisei Week's lavish spectacles and expanding budget, there was a heightening ambivalence among Japanese Americans about their much touted "success" in advancing up the rungs of America's social hierarchy. Although no Japanese American wanted to return to Little Tokyo's prewar segregation, most of them stopped short of dismissing ethnic identity and community as merely symbolic gestures to an antiquated past. Integration at Nisei Week would mean *inclusion* into society's main institutions but not total *immersion* in white America, the severing of ties to Japan and Japanese culture, or, even worse, interracial marriage with whites. The policing of group identity fell upon the shoulders of those community leaders who would discipline *Sansei* (the third generation), women, youth delinquents, and others within the group for violating the fine line between the ideal of the melting pot and the practice of ethnic pluralism.

RACE FOR DIPLOMACY

The revival of Nisei Week in 1949 in many ways was a sequel to the last celebration that took place in 1941. Once again ondo dancers paraded down the streets of the Japanese quarter; young women vied to become "Queen of the Nisei"; street toughs were warned to be on their best behavior; and overall the festival looked and functioned very much as it always had.[3] Yet small changes in Nisei Week protocol said a great deal about what had occurred during the festival's absence. For example, a color guard of Nisei veterans replaced the Boy Scout troop that had traditionally led the festival parade. And in addition to visiting with Little Tokyo merchants, the festival's beauty contestants paid a call on Nisei GIs recovering at the local Veteran's Administration hospital. This veneration of Nisei servicemen was most evident in the festival's souvenir booklet. A full page of the booklet commemorated the Nisei war dead with a photograph of the memorial dedicated to them in a local cemetery. The accompanying text read: "The mixed transition years since the last Nisei festival in 1941 are most dramatically brought home by the silent sacrifices of the Nisei GI whose valor in World War II underwrote the eventual reintegration of Japanese Americans into the greater American community."[4]

The impressive record of Nisei soldiers gave Japanese Americans the proof of patriotism that had escaped them before the war. When the returning internees confronted racial antagonism in 1945, the War

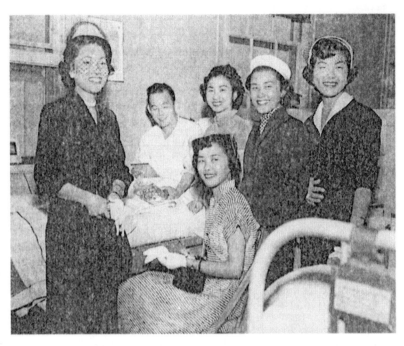

Visiting Japanese American veterans in hospitals was on the list of responsibilities of Nisei Week beauty contestants. *Courtesy Toyo Miyatake Studios.*

Relocation Authority solicited white military leaders for its campaign to fight anti-Japanese discrimination. Roger W. Smith, commander of the famed all-Nisei combat team, chastised the "West Coast acts of terrorism against the families of the men in our outfit" and remarked that he was especially "burned up" about Nisei soldiers being refused entrance into veterans organizations. "We thought we closed a deal when we finished the war on both fronts," he told an audience in nearby Orange County, California, "but this is rather debatable when some of the things for which we fought are being attacked here at home."[5] On this same issue, General Joseph Stillwell, the Allied leader in Europe, assured the people of Orange County that the Nisei soldiers "bought an awful big hunk of America with their blood."[6]

It was not surprising that the WRA, the agency seeking to resettle the internees in white communities, launched a vigorous postwar drive to remove the stigma of Japanese American disloyalty. Immediately after the victory over Japan, its southern California office applauded the people of the region for allowing the "vast majority" of the resettlers to easily "make themselves part of the American community." "Now that its over 'over there,'" the office maintained, "the public is aware . . . that the evacuees did everything in their power to cooperate with the U.S. Government" and "that they have proved loyal wherever trust has been invoked."[7] In 1951, Hollywood joined the bandwagon with the premiere of MGM's *Go for Broke,* a feature-length film starring Van Johnson as the commander of the famed all-Nisei combat team.

The popular embrace of Japanese Americans even included some of their worst political enemies. For example, Earl Warren, the governor of California, who in his previous position as the state's attorney general championed the wartime internment, welcomed back the former internees and promised—this time—to uphold their civil rights. Fletcher Bowron, still the mayor of Los Angeles, went even further than Warren by admitting that the internment was wrong and by apologizing to his returning constituents for having once questioned their patriotism. A few years later, he testified on their behalf at a congressional hearing looking into the need to compensate internees for economic losses. "I have been impressed with the fortitude of the Japanese people," he told the congressmen, "the way they took it, and then how they came back and reestablished themselves in this community."[8]

This positive view of Japanese Americans signaled a dramatic retreat from the internment experience. By 1946, American citizenship had been restored to the overwhelming majority of Nisei who had renounced it during the internment. A year later internee draft resisters, imprisoned for their protests, would receive a pardon from President Truman, and soon after, Congress would all but admit the injustice of the internment by approving a well-intentioned, but inherently flawed, attempt to compensate the internees for their economic losses. While these actions sought to make up for the internment, another set of public policies confronted the racism behind it. For example, in 1946, California voters rejected an initiative designed to make the Alien Land Law a permanent part of the state's constitution.[9] According to *Pacific Citizen* editor Larry Tajiri, this defeat represented the "final repudiation for the native fascists on the 'Japanese Issue.'"[10] His claim received even stronger backing in 1948 when the U.S. Supreme Court all but ruled California's Alien Land Law unconstitutional.[11] Most importantly, in 1952 Congress removed the cornerstones of anti-Japanese discrimination in the United States: the exclusion of Japanese immigration and the legal barrier preventing the Issei from becoming naturalized citizens. After that, the legal basis of anti-Japanese discrimination came crashing down.

It would be heartening to think that the nation came to its senses about Japanese Americans when confronted with overwhelming evidence of their loyalty, but the legacy of racial minority involvement in American warfare suggests otherwise. The heroism of black troops since the Civil War had never produced the sudden social acceptance that Japanese Americans received in the late 1940s and 1950s. Furthermore, the internment proved that Japanese American veterans of World War I also had made no lasting effect on racial discrimination. Why, then, did the Nisei's battlefield heroics spark a social revolution at home? The answer has less to do with their incredible deeds than with the government's ideological need to channel the nation's animosity against the Soviet Union during the Cold War. The "war hates and race hates [against the Japanese] did not go away," historian John W. Dower observes; "they went elsewhere." [12]

The surrender of Japan in August 1945, Dower observes, segued immediately into the start of the Cold War, as America counted on Japan as a key anticommunist ally. To cement this alliance, American policy makers had to contend with their own wartime propaganda, which had drummed into the American public the notion that the Japanese were bestial and subhuman. The perfect example of this, Dower reveals, is the postsurrender cartooned image of Japan as a little monkey sitting on the shoulders of a smiling American GI. During World War II, the simian metaphor portrayed the Japanese as powerful beasts or as intelligent yet duplicitous monkeymen; but afterward, as the above image conveyed, it cast the losers as a childlike race in need of American guidance, patience, and education. So it was that the overriding goal of the occupation forces, which remained in Japan for nearly six years after the war, was to train the Japanese to embrace the democratic institutions that the Americans had made for them.

In theory, the occupation's forced democratization was not much different from the WRA's "barbed-wire liberalism," yet the two campaigns took on antithetical meanings in Cold War America. The colonial-style rule of American forces in Japan was cheered as a monument to peace and security (and anticommunism). The racism of the internment, however, was castigated as a national disgrace. That Japanese Americans, as soldiers and internees, had established their loyalty to the United States certainly had something to do with this image. But in the larger picture, America's change of heart about the internment was rooted in foreign affairs. As Cold War tensions increased in the late 1940s, the state department feared that the discrimination of racial minorities in the United

States would damage the nation's reputation as the leader of the "free world." This fear prodded President Harry Truman to desegregate the armed forces and to use executive powers to outlaw racial inequities in federal employment. Moreover, as Brenda Gayle Plummer, Gerald Horne, and Mary Dudziak have shown, Cold War politics played a vital role in historic civil rights decisions, such as *Brown v. Board of Education of Topeka Kansas.*[13] Within this context, the internment became tied up with the segregationist world that was anathema to Cold War liberalism.

A 1955 feature in the *Saturday Evening Post* captured the contrast between the internment and the occupation. "California's Amazing Japanese" was a sympathetic essay focusing on the career achievements of a handful of Los Angeles Nisei. The article's author minced no words about the internment, calling the camps "rude" and repeating Mayor Bowron's apology that the executive order was a "great error and injustice."[14] As such, the internment stood as the baseline from which Nisei began to climb the ladder to "amazing" success. The occupation, on the other hand, was seen as an unquestionably positive step for Japanese Americans. According to one Nisei, being stationed in Japan had allowed white American GIs to understand and appreciate Japanese people and thus to get over their racism against Japanese Americans. The editor of *Scene,* a glossy Japanese American magazine, whose subscribers included former servicemen and families of American-Japanese mixed marriages, also championed the occupation's unexpected benefits. According to Masamori Kojima, the cultural immersion of thousands of whites who had been sent to Japan "has aroused American interest in things Japanese perhaps as much as it aroused Japanese interest in things American."[15]

A new genre of films highlighted the intimate relationships forged between Americans and Japanese during the occupation. Such productions included *Sayonara,* the 1957 adaptation of James A. Michener's best-selling novel about interracial romance in occupied Japan. The plot revolved around the racial education of Major Lloyd Gruver (Marlon Brando), a white American pilot who comes to prefer the quiet charms of Japanese women to the more aggressive demands of his white fiancée. This was Hollywood experimenting with sexy issues of race relations at a time when it struggled to maintain box-office sales in the face of competition from television. But in many ways, *Sayonara* (both the book and film) challenged racial hostility with racial stereotypes. Although he gets beyond his racist upbringing, Major Gruver falls in love with (and marries) a Japanese woman only given her ultimate submissiveness to his paternalistic benevolence.[16] In many respects, the occupation forces expected no less in their relationship with the Japanese people as a whole.

The Crimson Kimono, director Samuel Fuller's B-grade movie set in Los Angeles's Little Tokyo and climaxing against the backdrop of the Nisei Week festival, went further than Sayonara in imagining the post-war intimacy between Americans and Japanese. This 1959 film centered on the relationships between Nisei Joe Kojaku (James Shigeta) and two white Americans. The first relationship was with his fellow police detective and partner (Glenn Corbett), who served with him in World War II. The second one, which ultimately severs the first interracial bond, was with an attractive white co-ed (Victoria Shaw), who falls in love with Kojaku to the chagrin of his white partner. While films such as Sayonara had featured interracial romance between white men and Japanese women, not since the silent films of Sessue Hayakawa had a Japanese (or any Asian, for that matter) man and a white woman fallen in love on screen. The Crimson Kimono's interracial romance was undoubtedly shocking for many and revolutionary for others, but for B-movie masters like Fuller, who relied on shock value to compete against the major studios, pushing the envelope of racial and sexual standards was all in a day's work. Yet, in other ways, Fuller's film proved as conservative as any mainstream production. According to film critic Gina Marchetti, the Crimson Kimono's interracial romance advanced Fuller's "virulently anti-communist" agenda by portraying "America as a society striving for equality within its own ranks as it also waged a cold war against the Eastern Bloc and its allies."[17]

In linking Nisei race relations and Nisei Week to international diplomacy, Fuller unwittingly continued a well-heeled Japanese American strategy. After all, had not the inaugural Nisei Week in 1934 sought to fight local anti-Japanese discrimination by drawing attention to its negative repercussions for U.S.-Japan relations? But during the Cold War, the international significance of domestic racism seemed to have carried much heavier consequences than in the 1930s. The threat of a world overrun by communism, or (at its starkest) destroyed by nuclear weapons, pushed American policy makers and cultural producers to beat a speedy retreat from overtly anti-Japanese sentiments.

BEYOND LITTLE TOKYO

As whites came to embrace Japanese Americans as partners in the nation's anticommunist crusade, Japanese Americans, in turn, started to integrate

into white America, moving beyond the economically and socially insular world of the ethnic community. This, too, was evident in the revival of
Nisei Week. Obscured by the festival's hoopla about the return of Little
Tokyo was a controversy about the use of its profits. Previously such
monies went straight into JACL coffers. The trio of businessmen who
rejuvenated the festival, however, decided to use them to build a "community center" that would accommodate the Nisei's everpresent passion
for athletic competition. "The idea," wrote Harry Honda, "caught like
rapid fire" among the local JACLers, officials of community sports
leagues, and the increasingly influential veterans, who saw the center as
"something the boys wanted for their youngsters."[18] But where the center was to be built proved an unexpected bone of contention. When the
dream of such a facility began in the 1930s, the assumption was that it
would be located in Little Tokyo. By 1949, though, this no longer was a
foregone conclusion. In response to the city of Los Angeles's plans to replace part of Little Tokyo with a new civic plaza, some of those involved
dared to recommend that the project be moved outside the historic core
of the ethnic community.[19] Even after the city razed an entire Little
Tokyo block in 1950, debate continued until the issue became moot in
the mid-1950s when Nisei Week stopped turning a profit.[20]

The fate of the proposed community center revealed the inescapable
fact that Little Tokyo was no longer the hub of an expansive agricultural
economy. Sociologists Leonard Broom and Ruth Riemer observed that
postwar Japanese Americans in Los Angeles did not regain the "neatly
articulated system of production and distribution" that had defined the
prewar community. They found that "Japanese American farmers had
been able to establish claims on a relatively small proportion of prewar
holdings; wholesale produce dealers, with a small source of supply and
fewer outlets, were less numerous; and retail produce dealers had not
been able to assert themselves in successful competition with chain
stores."[21] The loss of the agricultural enclave forced most of the resettlers into the mainstream labor market. Although more than half of the
workers in the ethnic community were employed by Japanese Americans
in 1940, this figure declined to less than 30 percent by 1948.[22] Those
most likely to reestablish small businesses were Nisei between the ages
of twenty-five and forty-four, like Taro Kawa. But unlike Kawa, most of
them were independent contractors (especially landscape gardeners and
domestic workers) who did not re-create the nexus of business alliances
that was prewar Little Tokyo.[23] Table 4.1 indicates that the proportion
of those working in agriculture, nearly a third of all employed males in

TABLE 4.1   OCCUPATIONAL DISTRIBUTION
OF EMPLOYED JAPANESE AMERICAN MALES
IN THE LOS ANGELES METROPOLITAN AREA
(1942, 1950)

Occupation	1942	1950
Professional	7	5
Managerial	20	14
Clerical (sales)	15	8
Service	10	6
Farmer (farm labor)	27	15
Operative	—	11
Craftsman	—	11
Gardener	10	23
Other	11	7
Total	100	100

SOURCES: Percentages compiled by Lon Kurashige from statistical data in "WRA Form 26: Evacuee Summary Data ('Locator Index')," electronic data set, 1942, U.S. Department of the Interior, War Relocation Authority, RG 210 (Washington, D.C.: National Archives) and Steven Ruggles et al., Integrated Public Use Microdata Sample, 1950 (Minneapolis: Historical Census Projects, University of Minnesota, 1997).

the ethnic community before the evacuation, was cut nearly in half after the war. Equally remarkable was the rising significance of landscape gardening, which replaced farming and farm labor as the leading occupation for Japanese American men.

Notwithstanding the overwhelming economic losses, the destruction of the agricultural enclave could not have come at a better time. The American drive to win the Cold War ushered in unparalleled economic opportunities. The war economy that had pulled the United States out of the Great Depression continued after World War II, despite woeful predictions by the nation's leading economists. Instead, the massive government spending to contain communism around the world generated the longest sustained growth of the American economy. The rising affluence of the United States lifted even the most downtrodden of minority groups. But in the atomic age, economic opportunities were particularly prevalent for those, like the Nisei, who achieved advanced education. Sociologist Midori Nishi claimed that as early as 1949 most college-educated Japanese Americans "had no great difficulty in finding work along the lines of their training."[24] Nishi observed that the number of Nisei in professional and technical positions had doubled within four years of V-J day; many even found jobs in large corporations, public schools, and other sectors of the economy that had been previously closed to them.[25]

As a result of this expansion, the bulk of employment opportunities in the ethnic community no longer centered in the wholesale markets and immigrant firms in the downtown area. In 1950 Harry Honda bemoaned the fact that the food and prizes at the festival's carnival drew the crowds away from Little Tokyo restaurants and stores. To him, this indicated that Nisei Week had turned into a device to raise funds for community organizations, which sponsored the carnival booths, rather than to bolster the downtown businesses.[26] The next year Honda criticized the Little Tokyo merchants for failing to support the festival and suggested that it may have outlived its economic and civic purposes.[27] A year later, fellow journalist Carl Kondo also bemoaned the transformation of Nisei Week. He observed that in holding most of the events in the evening, the festival cut into the benefits for Little Tokyo stores. Even more disturbing to him was its lack of political consciousness and engagement. "Yesterday, the emphasis was closing the gap between the Hakujin community by contributing something colorful to the greater Los Angeles metropolis," Kondo asserted. "Today it seems the emphasis is upon the Nisei talent show."[28]

Nowhere was the end of the "buy in Lil' Tokio" campaign better revealed than in the Nisei Week beauty pageant. As early as 1949, Harry Honda warned that merchants from the outlying districts sought to abandon the "fundamental reason for Nisei Week" (which was to benefit the downtown stores) by asking that *their* customers be able to vote for the festival beauty candidates.[29] Despite Honda's distress, the following year's festival leaders expanded the boundaries of the merchandise voting beyond Little Tokyo. The issue did not go away, as the boundaries changed again in 1951, this time to the benefit of downtown merchants. But by 1953 the question was not who could supply votes but whether to do so at all. That year the *Rafu Shimpo* reported that merchandise voting did not seem profitable for Little Tokyo merchants.[30] A few years later this form of voting for the beauty contestants, which had always been marred by charges of bias and chicanery, was abandoned altogether. In its place came a system whereby contestants were nominated by Japanese American organizations from across southern California and the winner decided by an independent panel of judges.[31]

The fanning out of the ethnic population made it increasingly likely that the Nisei Week queen would represent communities well outside Little Tokyo. Once the former internees regained a footing in southern California, they left the old downtown neighborhoods, joining the postwar flight to the suburbs. Between 1949 and 1959, although the group's

Nisei Week queen Terrie Hokoda in 1949 sits in a pool of "ballots" that were cast through consumer purchases in Little Tokyo. *Courtesy Toyo Miyatake Studios.*

overall population in Los Angeles more than doubled, the number of Japanese Americans living in or adjacent to Little Tokyo declined more than 10 percent. By the latter date, the immigrant clusters of the past were less evident as the ethnic community now spread out over 90 percent of the census tracts in the city of Los Angeles.[32] "The Japanese population," explained one Nisei in 1970, "is scattered throughout southern California and to a large degree . . . their everyday needs are met in the same manner as those of other suburbanites. Their lives no longer revolve around Little Tokyo."[33]

The dispersal of the ethnic population was seen by many as one of the unexpected benefits of the internment. Joe Ishikawa spoke for many Nisei in addressing the "salutary effects" of World War II. "Not only have Japanese Americans been awakened to the possibilities of a future in other sections of the country," he wrote in 1957, "but those who have chosen to return to the West Coast have also developed an awareness that the old insularity was a stultifying thing."[34] The Nisei Week booklet in 1958 celebrated those "emerging from [a] 'ghetto' outlook toward a wider civic responsibility." In highlighting those contributing to the broader society (such as local PTA president Betty Kosawa and the city of Gardena's "Citizen of the Year" Sam Minami), the booklet concluded that the ethnic community was no longer an island unto itself: "That many more Nisei are giving freely of their time and talents for worthy community-wide causes seems to indicate that they are becoming increasingly aware of the world outside their prewar Li'l [sic] Tokio and are coming to realize that the welfare of any ethnic group is dependent on the general welfare of the city as a whole."[35]

Moving beyond the old insularity, however, did not preclude the establishment of new concentrations of Japanese Americans. The ethnic community in Gardena, the southwest part of Los Angeles, increased more than tenfold from 1940 to 1960, becoming the fastest growing concentration of Japanese Americans in southern California. On the city's far west side, near posh Beverly Hills estates, the ethnic population in 1960 more than doubled from what it had been before the war, primarily as a result of the increased opportunities for gardeners. A few miles east of downtown, entirely new suburbs developed in the San Gabriel Valley, which was an especially convenient place to live for Little Tokyo merchants and workers. Finally, on the near west side, the Crenshaw area grew to become the largest concentration of Japanese Americans in metropolitan Los Angeles.[36] The size of the community enabled the development of a thriving center for Nisei small businesses, known after 1960 for its annual "Oriental Festival of Culture," which was heralded as the second Nisei Week.[37] Although independent of Little Tokyo, save for affectionate ties maintained for the old enclave, the newer Japanese American communities reproduced its leadership, business district, and annual festival.

After half a century of being quarantined from America's social institutions and after the internment during World War II, that the integration of Japanese Americans proceeded unevenly is not surprising; both sides of the color line displayed reluctance and fear. Entering the middle-class, white-collar professions and suburban neighborhoods could not erase the legacy of ethnic solidarity.

REGENERATION OF THE SECOND GENERATION

The challenge of balancing integration and ethnic solidarity would fall mostly on the shoulders of a younger cohort of Nisei, who were born during the Issei baby boom of the 1920s. This was the large majority of the

TABLE 4.2   OCCUPATIONAL DISTRIBUTION
OF NISEI AND SANSEI MALES IN THE LOS ANGELES
METROPOLITAN AREA BY AGE COHORT
(1970)

Occupation	Older Nisei (Pre-1920) N = 40	Nisei "Boomers" (1920–29) N = 75	Younger Nisei/ Older Sansei (1930–39) N = 56
Professional	8	29	38
Gardener	20	19	5
Managerial	18	13	11
Craftsman	8	13	20
Clerical (sales)	18	12	12
Other	28	14	14
Total	100	100	100

SOURCE: Percentages compiled by Lon Kurashige from data in Steven Ruggles et al., Integrated Public Use Microdata Series, 1970 (Minneapolis: Historical Census Projects, University of Minnesota, 1997).

second generation whom the founders of Nisei Week heralded as the future of the ethnic community. Yet the future did not arrive in Little Tokyo until the revival of the festival after World War II. The return of Nisei Week was dedicated to this "newer generation of Nisei youth . . . who grew up in wartime America . . . [and] whose early formative lessons in democracy were learned in the confines of relocation camps."[38] Their leadership at Nisei Week marked the regeneration of the second generation.

More than their older siblings, Nisei "boomers" took advantage of the new career opportunities opened up to Japanese Americans. Table 4.2 indicates that age was inversely correlated with occupational status. In 1970, the census revealed that the strong movement of Japanese Americans into professional occupations typically did not include the older Nisei born before the baby boom of the 1920s. At that time, 8 percent of older Nisei worked in the white-collar professions compared to 29 percent of Nisei boomers and 38 percent of the younger Nisei and older Sansei who were born in the 1930s. The ethnic community's increasing interest in the crafts revealed a less dramatic, but still clear, age inversion, with the younger Nisei and older Sansei more than twice as likely to be counted as craftsmen than the older Nisei. The younger cohorts also tended to move away from jobs associated with small business, such as managers, proprietors, and clerical and sales positions. This phenom-

TABLE 4.3   INCOME DISTRIBUTION OF NISEI
AND SANSEI MALES IN THE LOS ANGELES
METROPOLITAN AREA BY AGE COHORT
(1970)

Income Level	Age Cohort by Birth Year		
	Older Nisei	*Nisei "Boomers"*	*Younger Nisei / Older Sansei*
	N = 43	N = 76	N = 56
Lowest	67	42	38
Middle	28	50	57
Highest	5	8	6
Total	100	100	100

SOURCE: Percentages compiled by Lon Kurashige from data in Steven Ruggles et al., Integrated Public Use Microdata Series, 1970 (Minneapolis: Historical Census Projects, University of Minnesota, 1997).
NOTE: Income level based on all males with income in the Los Angeles metropolitan area.

enon was most noticeable with the younger Nisei and older Sansei who almost totally eschewed landscape gardening, a career that employed 20 percent of older Nisei and 19 percent of the boomers. Hence, the older a Japanese American man was in 1970, the more likely he was to continue the ethnic community's traditional forms of employment.

The younger Japanese Americans also typically made more money than their elders. Table 4.3 reveals the income distribution of the aforementioned American-born age cohorts. The incomes of older Nisei were most likely to be within the lowest third of the ethnic community. Almost 70 percent of older Nisei earned the lowest amount of money compared to 42 percent of Nisei boomers and 38 percent of younger Nisei and older Sansei. While only a small fraction of each cohort earned the highest level of income, they were well represented in the middle ranks. This level contained 28 percent of older Nisei, 50 percent of the boomers, and 57 percent of the younger Nisei and older Sansei. So the majority of the youngest cohorts had entered the middle class, while the incomes of the oldest Nisei were overwhelmingly within the lowest bracket of the Los Angeles community.

The above findings corroborate researchers John Modell's and Edna Bonacich's conclusions about the professionalization of the ethnic community. On the basis of survey data from three generations of Japanese Americans taken in the mid-1960s, they argued that successive cohorts of the ethnic group were leaving the pattern of immigrant entrepreneurship and entering the mainstream "corporate" economy. They found that less than a third of those born after 1934 were inclined toward small business, while almost 70 percent of the older Japanese Americans in Los Angeles continued this economic form.[39] Modell and Bonacich maintained that "the Nisei who had, as adults, experienced the Issei ethnic economy (and indeed has often participated in it) are appreciably the most likely to have worked to reestablish it, in modified form, after the war."[40] But the impressive professionalization of the younger cohorts, they contended, meant that the efforts to rebuild the ethnic economy would seemingly die out with the older generations. They concluded that the enclave's inability to perpetuate itself spelled its inevitable doom— as well as that of the economic basis of Japanese American solidarity. Moreover, they believed that the decline in small businesses would reduce anti-Japanese antagonism, as white and other ethnic entrepreneurs would no longer be in competition with a Japanese American bloc. Taken together, these conclusions led Modell and Bonacich to predict that the ethnic community would soon be totally immersed in white America.[41]

Such a prediction, while identifying the altered structural basis of Japanese American identity, ignored the creative ways in which Nisei Week's new leaders would define integration. After its revival, the festival soon fell out of the hands of the Los Angeles chapter of the JACL. By the mid-1950s, a number of Nisei organizations shared the responsibility for putting on Nisei Week. Two of the most active newcomers to festival leadership were recently established veterans' associations. As the reputation of the World War II Nisei combat team spread, the leading organizations for American veterans not only discouraged the anti-Japanese antics of their chapters but also actively recruited Japanese American members. By late 1949, the first all-Nisei chapter to appear in southern California was the American Legion's "Commodore Perry" post, which had actually been established in 1935 by Issei and Nisei veterans of World War I but had its charter revoked after Pearl Harbor. A few months after the Perry post reemerged, the Veterans of Foreign War (VFW) sponsored the entirely new Los Angeles Nisei Memorial Post 9938. Both of these groups were centered in Little Tokyo and concentrated their efforts on defeating anti-Japanese legislation. With firm backing from their national headquarters, the former soldiers fought against racially restrictive housing covenants. By lobbying the California legislature, they helped eliminate anti-Japanese licensing practices and overturn the Alien Land Act. Their status as war heroes was also used to break down the immigration and naturalization exclusion for

Japanese immigrants, which Congress finally abandoned in 1952. Within the ethnic community, the veterans sponsored youth programs, kept an active social calendar, and, of course, became central to the planning of the Nisei Week festival.[42]

But the veterans alone did not replace the loss of the immigrant mutual-benefit associations. In the early 1950s, many Nisei wondered who would resume the Issei's concern for Japanese American welfare. "There was really a 'pent up' need," recalled Little Tokyo businessman Edwin Hiroto, "to have some central thing that would draw [the Nisei] into providing services and feeling they were doing something worthwhile for the community."[43] The Japanese American Optimist Club was established in 1954 to fill this need on the part of the Nisei generation and, following the veterans' associations, entered into Nisei Week leadership. Like the veterans, the Optimists belonged to a primarily white organization (the International Optimist Club) that connected them to a vast network outside of the ethnic community. Following the international organization's motto "Friend of the Boy," the Optimists sought to resolve and prevent issues of juvenile delinquency among Japanese Americans. "Their belief," said the Nisei Week booklet in 1955, was "that active participation in programs of sports and scholarship will keep youngsters from becoming wards of the public in future years."[44]

The postwar expansion of Nisei Week leadership also enabled women's organizations to participate in festival planning. One of the most significant of these in the 1950s and 1960s was the Montebello Women's Club, which grew out of the yearning for social outlets by Nisei housewives in suburban San Gabriel Valley. In 1953 these women founded the first all-Nisei body of the Greater Federation of Women's Clubs, thus continuing the community's attachment to venerable mainstream organizations. The federation, as it had done since its creation in 1925, allowed its members to escape the isolation of the domestic sphere. Together the Nisei clubwomen engaged in communal projects (such as sewing bees), celebrated and commiserated about the experiences of motherhood, and expanded their knowledge of cooking and beauty techniques. The federation also exposed its Japanese American members to a world beyond the ethnic community. Although Yae Aihara was familiar with women's auxiliaries within the ethnic community, becoming a clubwoman in 1955 was her first brush with the customs and protocols of civic life. What "impressed" her immediately was that Nisei women could conduct a formal meeting, complete with bylaws, Robert's Rules of Order, and designated roles for club officers. As club president in the early 1960s, Aihara attended federation conferences and continued its mission to donate money for local charities. Indeed, it was the need to raise funds that spurred the club's involvement in Nisei Week.[45]

Thus the festival's new leadership rested upon important pillars of integration; never before had so many community organizations been firmly ensconced in white America. Yet these ties to mainstream organizations in no way diminished the leadership's support for the ethnic community. The new organizations involved in Nisei Week insisted on retaining a Japanese American identity. The Optimists especially resisted requests to have their group take on a geographic identity (e.g., Downtown Optimists) that would require them to accept members from outside the ethnic group. According to charter member Edwin Hiroto, his group believed that, ideally, Japanese Americans should give up their ethnicity and blend into the melting pot, but in reality they had been mistreated too many times by white Americans to feel fully at ease in their company.[46] Hiroto himself exemplified their preference to remain within Japanese American circles. After graduating from the University of Southern California in 1951, he became an independent insurance salesman because no mainstream company would hire him. He established an office in Little Tokyo because, as he put it, "I never thought I could be successful selling to other than Buddhaheads." Hiroto continued his commitment to the ethnic community in 1958 when he became the top administrator of City View hospital, which was run by and for Japanese Americans.

After he returned from the Army, VFW member Robert Hayamizu also graduated from the University of Southern California only to have his career ambitions thwarted by racial restrictions. He was pained to discover that not even a master's degree in public administration and top placement scores would land him a job in the federal civil service. He then decided, like so many of his friends, to go into business for himself as a gardener. The decision was not hard to make since, at that time, he knew gardening to be one of the best-paying jobs for Japanese Americans. This was confirmed in 1961 when health considerations forced him to accept a position with the Los Angeles County, at half his former income. Throughout his career pursuits, Hayamizu remained committed to the ethnic community, which he served through his leadership of the VFW. Since there were other posts in southern California that served their own region, Hayamizu believed, it was "up to us to support the Japanese community primarily." In running Nisei Week, he continued the VFW's campaign against anti-Japanese sentiment by making it clear that "we weren't all slant eyes . . . we were just the normal Americans."[47]

Though not as political as the veterans, the Montebello clubwomen were no less supportive of Japanese American concerns. The club's first charity project was aimed to improve the lives of war widows in Japan. This they saw as not just a humanitarian gesture but a responsibility of their ethnic heritage. By the late 1950s, the clubwomen had ceased donating to mainstream American charities, concentrating instead on an orphanage that housed Eurasian children from occupied Japan, a convalescent home for aged Issei, and the newly established City View hospital.[48] Yae Aihara noted that she and the rest of the members did not feel compatible with white Americans and so eventually engaged in fundraising projects only within the ethnic community. Despite the rhetoric of integration, most of the clubwomen had few chances to interact with whites throughout their schooling, inside the internment camps, or within the secluded world of postwar suburban domesticity. Ironically, the Greater Federation of Women's Clubs, like the other mainstream organizations that had recruited Nisei members, became a means to continue a voluntary form of ethnic segregation. So it was that Nisei Week's new leadership maintained solidarity within the Japanese American community, while, at the same time, anchoring it in mainstream society.

SECOND WIND

The opportunity for Japanese Americans to function outside the ethnic community, however, still had costs for Nisei Week. After all, not everyone was as committed to its continuation as were the ethnic organizations composing the festival leadership. Sociologists Gene Levine and Colbert Rhodes found that in the mid-1960s more than a third of Japanese Americans nationwide were highly assimilated or "monocultural." This "American type," according to their survey analysis, tended to avoid events, such as Nisei Week, that revolved around ethnicity or cultural heritage. Signs of this monoculturalism were clearly apparent at Nisei Week. For example, in 1964, a *Kashu Mainichi* columnist warned that the festival had become an empty gesture lacking any "community spirit behind the project. . . . It seems that the Festival," he observed sarcastically, "is just put on because it needs to keep up the tradition." At the same time, another columnist saw a new hope spring from the community's declining interest in Nisei Week. Although agreeing that interest in the festival was dying among Japanese Americans, George Yoshinaga argued that it was receiving a "second wind" from the rising influence of Japan and Japanese culture and consumer goods in the United States.[49]

The rebuilding of war-torn Japan spurred the revival of Nisei Week. Although the festival's success relied on strong support from outside Little Tokyo—namely from the Los Angeles mayor's office and city agencies, the mainstream media, and many of "our Caucasian friends"—just as important, noted the festival's chairman in 1958, was America's "good international relationship with Japan." Japanese commercial products, he noted, "are welcomed in average American homes, whether it be artwares, pictures, furniture, food, music, architectural designs, or gardens. Thousands of ex-GIs and tourists remember what they saw in Japan," and there "is a tremendous surge of good motion pictures, television shows introducing things Japanese very favorably."[50] The chairman advised that Nisei Week capitalize on this "Japan boom"; "all the events should be restudied in order to produce . . . a more refined show" emphasizing the cultural arts of Japan. He called this a major "turning point" in Nisei Week history.[51]

The 1960s promised to revive and extend the Pacific Era in American international trade damaged by World War II. As in the 1930s, Japanese Americans recognized their strategic position between America and Japan and sought to benefit as liaison promoting business and cultural exchange. Southern California Nisei leaders began to reidentify with Japan, to reclaim their Japanese heritage, and to reconstruct themselves as a "bridge of understanding" between the trading partners. Warming U.S.-Japan relations reintroduced a wealth of Japanese merchandise, culture, and influence. Nowhere was this more evident than in southern California. The expanding metropolis of Los Angeles—with its economic opportunities, proximity to Japan, and large Japanese American population—became the Pacific Rim's American capital. Thus, although postwar immigration from Japan retained minimal Nisei connections to Japan and although Sansei often grew up with little Japanese influence, U.S.-Japan business relations proved the main Japanizing agent in southern California. The beginning of the Pacific Rim era reopened prospects for Japanese American biculturalism and reduced the need for hyperpatriotic expression.

By the late 1950s, cracks had begun to appear in the hard shell of Nisei Americanism. Since the late 1930s, most Nisei leaders had turned away from Japan, hoping to find sanctuary from anti-Japanese discrimination in super-American patriotism. More than a decade after World War II, some Nisei apparently still harbored deep resentment toward Japan. A famous Japanese author commented on the chasm between his compatriots and Japanese Americans. "Since Japan was defeated in the war," Shohei Ooka remarked, "the immigrant's way of thinking has changed so much that there is not a way of bridging the gap between theirs and ours. Nisei fought us and are now preoccupied with how to adapt themselves to American life." Ooka implied that Nisei were closed minded to Japanese culture and history.[52]

Nevertheless, there were many signs that Nisei Americanism had begun to relax and that identification with Japan was no longer taboo. A strong supporter of Nisei veterans, George Yoshinaga called for the once universally despised Tomoya Kawakita's release from Alcatraz, where he was sentenced as an American traitor of war. Yoshinaga sympathized with Kawakita, the Nisei–turned–prison-camp–keeper, and other Japanese Americans stranded in wartime Japan. He regarded strandees as victims of extraordinary circumstances. Kawakita should be set free, argued Yoshinaga, because by 1961 war hates had healed and should be played down in the current "era of good feelings" between Japan and the United States.[53] It was also Yoshinaga who stirred up Nisei enthusiasm for Japan's beauty contestants. He sided with Japanese candidates over all others (including Americans) in international beauty competitions. His and the community's response to Japanese bathing beauties approached the prewar Nisei passion for Japanese athletic accomplishments. In either case, the Nisei celebrated Japanese victories over Western nations.

The Nisei Week festival exhibited Japan's refurbished image in Japanese America. Soon signs of Japanese economic and cultural merchandise punctuated the celebration. In 1959 the festival parade's main attraction showcased Toyopet cars from the budding Japanese automobile manufacturer Toyota. Six years later, parade officials used tiny Datsun convertibles instead of large American-made cars to carry Nisei Week dignitaries. Beginning in the 1960s, Japanese corporations supplied parade floats advertising, among other businesses, the Bank of Tokyo, Japan Airlines, and Yamasa soy sauce and fish cakes. Nisei Week leaders also added to the parade venerable Japanese traditions, such as the ritual of the *mikoshi*. The mikoshi is an ornate, golden Japanese shrine invested with Shinto religious significance. The Nisei Week ritual began with a Shinto ceremony in which a priest anointed the shrine; then a group Japanese-clothed young men hoisted the mikoshi on their shoul-

A Nisei Week parade float in 1960 represents the growing influence of
Japanese multinational corporations in southern California made possible
by American efforts to rebuild the Japanese economy and restore formal
U.S.-Japan relations. *Courtesy Toyo Miyatake Studios.*

ders and ran with it through Little Tokyo streets screaming good cheers.
The success of the mikoshi ritual sparked the creation of a youth version, complete with a scaled-down shrine. Divested of much religious significance, the mikoshi tradition contributed a unique and exotic element
to a festival otherwise laden with predictability. Even so, it proved Nisei
Week's most notable inclusion of Shintoism, known to Americans as the
emperor-worshipping religion that fueled Japan's war effort. During the
postwar occupation of Japan, Shintoism had changed in the American
imagination from anti-American fanaticism to playful exoticism.[54]

Nisei Week also proved an opportune time to celebrate U.S.-Japan
friendship. The year 1960 marked the centennial of diplomatic relations
between the two nations. Japanese American leaders held a special event
during Nisei Week to honor the occasion. The Japanese Chamber of
Commerce, Japanese American Optimists, Nisei Veterans Coordinating
Council, JACL, and other leading community organizations sponsored a
U.S.-Japan centennial celebration and invited the mayor of Los Angeles
and other prominent politicians and businessmen. The event proved a

grand opportunity for Japanese Americans to resituate themselves as liaison between Japan and the United States—to profit literally and figuratively from their connection to both nations. The main performance dramatized the role of Japanese Americans in the history of U.S.-Japan relations. The piece presented this history in four parts: It began with the first Japanese delegation to meet a U.S. president in 1860, skipped to the arrival of Japanese immigrant women in 1908, acknowledged the contributions of an Issei doctor and other scholars to Western science, and concluded with a victory march of the famed 442d all-Nisei battalion. The event's program proclaimed, "The epic of the 442nd, the most decorated unit in U.S. military history, breathed new life into the friendly relations between the United States and Japan."[55] The production thus placed Japanese Americans at the center of U.S.-Japan relations. United States and Japanese officials, on the other hand, would not have recognized—let alone emphasized—the role of Japanese American immigrants and their offspring in promoting good relations between the two nations. As before the war, Japanese Americans sought to benefit from biculturalism. The Nisei Week booklet claimed that Japanese Americans "deserve credit for their part in the spread of Japanese influence. Living in the void between East and West, they serve as bridges between the two in whatever their occupations may be."[56]

Evidence of U.S.-Japan trade relations in Nisei Week increased significantly throughout the 1960s. In 1963, the mayor of Nagoya served as grand marshal to the festival parade. Around that time Los Angeles officials had negotiated a "sister city" agreement with their Nagoya counterparts, bringing closer cultural and economic ties with Japan and including many Japanese Americans in the city's Los Angeles–Nagoya Sister City Association. In 1965, Nisei Week leaders named a leading Japanese industrialist as festival grand marshal. Head of a corporation including the electronics giant Panasonic, Konosuke Matsushita was the first Japanese businessman to receive this honor previously awarded to Hollywood celebrities and regional politicians. That same year, Japanese movie star Miiko Taka was Nisei Week parade marshal, which marked the first time Nisei Week honored Japanese nationals as both festival and parade marshals. The following year the president of the Japan-America Society of Southern California also earned an honorary title in Nisei Week. Yet the largest Japanese corporate influence was largely invisible to the festival guests. Before 1964, the festival received most of its financial backing from Little Tokyo merchants and community donations, but in that year Nisei Week leaders solicited contributions from Japanese corporations for the first time. The support of the Japan Traders Club of Los Angeles (later to become the Japan Business Association) grew substantially over the next three decades. In 1968, Japanese businesses, including Toyota, Honda, Nissan, Mitsubishi Bank, Japan Airlines, and Sumitomo Bank, became the festival's largest contributors. Seven years later the Traders Club would contribute a third of the entire Nisei Week budget.[57]

With Japanese corporate backing, Nisei Week became a showcase for Japanese culture and businesses. Kiyomi Takata, a queen's contest leader, reportedly explained that beauty contest entrants had received extra coaching in Japanese manners because Nisei Week "has become an introductory show on the customs and mores of Japan to increasingly large numbers of Western[er]s."[58] In 1960, columnist George Yoshinaga complained that festival press releases were increasingly written in Japanese and not English. He exclaimed: "Nisei Week is for the Nisei. . . . Just how many Nisei can read Japanese?"[59] Two years later, fellow columnist Henry Mori observed the growing trend of Japanese corporate and other "outside" interests taking over Nisei Week. "The future Festivals," he noted, "will be more international in scope[,] and if the present trend keeps up they may continue to be centered in Little Tokyo[,] but there will be more outside interests having their say in the promotion. The fact that more cultural events are being held successfully points also toward that direction."[60] Fred Taomae, writing in that year's Nisei Week booklet corroborated Mori's findings. "The biggest and most spectacular event in the spreading of Japanese influence is Nisei Week, without a doubt, and Lil' Tokio in Los Angeles is the biggest center of Japanese activity in the Southland and the continental United States." Taomae went on to describe a bright future for Japanese Americans. "Coupled with the charm of Japanese culture, the quality of Japanese products, and the exceedingly good relations between Japan and the United States at present, its seems that Japanese influence in southern California is destined for greater heights."[61]

Thus starting in the 1960s, Nisei Week produced and was produced by increasing U.S.-Japan trade relations. Community leader Saburo Kido acknowledged that festival leaders had taken advantage of the "Japan Boom" in the United States and geared Nisei Week toward cultural as well as commercial promotion. "No longer is the art and culture of Japan something to be considered merely 'quaint' or 'strange,'" wrote Kido. "When the American public is in a receptive mood to learn and understand, every effort must be made to accommodate them." The Nisei Week booklet characterized the festival as a "cultural medium" for inter-racial and international peace—an act of "cultural diplomacy." [62] But not everyone appreciated the direction of Nisei Week's and Little Tokyo's Japanese revival. Henry Mori cautioned Japanese Americans about in-creasing Japanese investment. "There is . . . a growing number of invest-ors from Japan," wrote Mori, "whose unlimited source of revenue—much greater than those holdings of the local property owners—can revamp the physical appearance of Lil' Tokio." Mori continued that "[g]iven five more years in Little Tokyo, we would not doubt that there would be only a handful of Japanese American workers holding jobs on First and San Pedro Sts. . . . Eventually Lil' Tokio may not be as 'little' as it implies today." [63]

"BATHING SUITS SHOULD BE A MUST"

Another way to ensure the longevity of Nisei Week, without relying solely upon an integrating Japanese American community, was to capture the interest of the general public. This, of course, harkened back to the pre-war attempt to heighten Little Tokyo's tourist appeal. It was not sur-prising then that one of the proponents of "orientalizing" the enclave in the 1930s voiced a similar concern in discussing the future of Nisei Week in the 1950s. Columnist Carl Kondo maintained that "our section isn't any too different from the many other neighborhood sections within the city, for we have businesses carrying American-made and advertised brands, and very little of the exotic." [64] Within the affluence of postwar society, the exoticization of Nisei Week meant increasing its produc-tions, visibility, and glamour. Its leaders sought to transform the com-munity celebration into a class of professionalized entertainment that would mark Japanese Americans on the cultural calendar of southern California, alongside the Rose Bowl Parade and Cinco de Mayo. Even as the festival was revived in 1949, columnist Harry Honda declared that it already "has become too big for its infant shoes." [65]

The professionalization of Nisei Week occurred gradually and often without comment. Very few seemed to notice, or care, that in 1954 the celebration of Issei pioneers no longer honored all of the most elderly immigrants. Instead, Pioneer Night singled out only those deemed wor-thy of community appreciation. [66] Gongoro Nakamura, honored by the festival in 1956, was a typical example. Nakamura was the most recog-nized Issei leader in southern California before the war, serving as president of the community's most powerful political associations. He received a law degree in the United States, and using his English language skills, he had served as a liaison between the Issei and Nisei and between Japanese Americans and white America. It was in this spirit that in the fall of 1941, he traveled to Washington, D.C., with Togo Tanaka to assure government leaders that Japanese Americans were loyal to the United States. In addition to his status within the community, Nakamura was also recognized by the festival for being among the first Issei to become a naturalized American citizen.[67]

In this way, the pioneer honor reflected a new construction of the Issei. When the nation was in the midst of the depression, it was fitting that Nisei Week idealized Japanese immigrants as survivors of economic and social hardship—and thus the oldest Issei, who had presumably survived the longest, received the most applause for their struggles. But in the postwar, as Japanese Americans (and the nation) were freed from the economic desperation of the past, Issei came to symbolize the desire for social status and respectability. So it was that Pioneer Night became an exclusive engagement for ethnic leaders to fete, and be feted by, their own kind.

The ethos of community participation that had characterized the earlier Pioneer Night was also compromised in the festival ondo. In 1954, the *Rafu Shimpo* observed that the ondo had become a performance by students of Japanese dance and no longer symbolized Issei and Nisei cooperation by welcoming broad community participation. A letter to the *Kashu Mainichi* editor in 1959 complained that the "private" dance schools held a privileged position in the ondo, while the "non-private" participants were "shoved to the rear and crowded together so badly that they looked awful by comparison."[68] Even Japanese dance teachers regretted the festival's professionalization. The choreographers who had led the Nisei Week ondo before the war both admitted their distaste for the competition between dance schools that occurred at the festival. Each year they were loathe to buy more expensive costumes so their students would outshine their opponents. But few of those watching the ondo performance complained about the lavish kimonos worn by the ondo dancers. Nor were they disappointed in the growing number and size of parade floats winding their way through Little Tokyo or the increasing number of Hollywood celebrities and political figures waving to them.

Nisei Week's promotion of Japanese American respectability was most clearly apparent in the festival beauty pageant. In addition to ending merchandise voting and having ethnic organizations nominate candidates, the queen's contest, to a degree never before attempted, was self-consciously modeled upon professionalized beauty pageants like the Miss America contest. The coronation ball, where the Nisei Week queen was crowned, was moved out of the downtown area and held at some of southern California's most prestigious hotels and landmarks (including the Beverly Hilton and the Hollywood Palladium). Well-known actors, such as Chuck Connors and John Forsythe, were hired to host a dinner program modeled after Las Vegas stage shows. And to remove the taint of nepotism that marred earlier contests, the judges were typically selected from outside the ethnic community. The apparent objectivity of the new judging protocol set up a revealing contrast with the much-maligned system of merchandise voting. In retrospect, the notion of selecting the festival queen via Little Tokyo receipts seemed to characterize the "backwardness" of the ethnic community's petty commercialism. The expert judges, on the other hand, reflected its movement into the professionalism of white-collar society.

Another addition to the beauty pageant was the swimsuit competition. After appearing in traditional Japanese garments, contestants paraded on stage wearing swimsuits that revealed their figures for the judges. This competition was also modeled after the Miss America contest, which had had its contestants appear in swimsuits since its inception in 1921. Columnist Harry Honda's response to swimsuits in the Nisei Week contest suggests why there was no such competition before World War II. When the idea was tried out in 1950, Honda maintained that Nisei Week should continue to showcase the kimono and the demure qualities of Nisei women that set them at odds with "bathing beauties." To fellow columnist George Yoshinaga, however, the swimsuit competition had more to do with Americanism than it did with womanhood. The issue was simple: the Nisei were American, therefore their beauty pageants should be no different from those in mainstream society—Japanese traditions, and inhibitions, be damned! For a new generation of women, Yoshinaga asserted that the "modern day Sansei lass looks more at home in a swimsuit than a kimono. . . . With some of these girls, the first time they wear a kimono is in Nisei Week and they look pretty awkward."[69]

Yoshinaga embodied an apparent contradiction within the integration orthodoxy. Like the monocultural JACL Nisei, his wartime internment and subsequent service in the U.S. Army had cemented his feet in the American front and pushed him to assert his Americanism at all times. But like so many other Nisei in southern California, Yoshinaga kept close ties to the ethnic community. He worked as a journalist for various Japanese American newspapers and maintained the prewar ideal of Nisei biculturalism by using his bilingual skills to broker business deals between Japan and the United States. But after the American occupation of Japan, "Japan-boom" in American society, and the "Americanization" of Japan, he admitted that sort of biculturalism was becoming increasingly routine and unremarkable. Indeed, at this time it was possible for Yoshinaga, and Japanese Americans in general, to look to Japan as a role model for the Nisei Week beauty pageant.

The inspiration came in 1959 when a Japanese woman became the first representative of an Asian nation to become Miss Universe. Sponsored by an American swimsuit manufacturer, this international competition, unlike its rival, the Miss America pageant, made no pretensions to being more than an occasion to judge and appreciate women's bodies.[70] But standards of beauty, with their implicit assumptions about sexuality, were more than aesthetic concerns. For a Japanese woman to be recognized as more beautiful than whites was tantamount to saying that the Japanese, as a race, were just as sophisticated and cultured as anyone in the Western world. This is why the local Japanese American press, which had pulled for Japan's entry since the Miss Universe contest began in the early 1950s, cheered the victory as if it marked the end of an era of anti-Japanese discrimination. Reportedly, many Japanese Americans wept with joy upon hearing the news. Consequently, the jubilation proved a golden opportunity to promote swimsuit judging in the Nisei Week beauty contest. Based on the victory of Miss Japan, Yoshinaga asserted that the "Nisei has reached the station where judging in bathing suits should be a must."[71] To his delight, a few years later the beauty pageant contestants in 1962 elected to make swimsuits a permanent part of the competition.

The swimsuit issue exemplified Nisei Week's movement away from an ethnic standard of beauty. No longer did the queen symbolize the blending of East and West, and although she was still required to wear a kimono, the garment served more as an emblem of heritage than a mark of cultural competence. At the baby contest, the standard of beauty was even more clear-cut, as the contestants were formally judged for Western features such big eyes and curly hair. This appreciation (indeed, emulation) of mainstream ideals was not without precedent. From its inception, Nisei Week had promoted the middle-class propriety and civic virtues of Japanese Americans; that it now celebrated their physical and cultural similarities with the majority of Americans was an extension of this drive for social acceptance. The sudden collapse of anti-Japanese restrictions after World War II and the group's unexpected social success emboldened Japanese Americans to portray themselves as more than simply loyal subjects. Rather, they asserted that the ethnic group was the epitome of the "American dream." Their Americanism had switched from a defensive prewar posture designed to retain the ethnic enclave to an aggressive postwar drive to claim as much of white America as they desired and now felt they deserved.

But, as in all Japanese American expressions of integration, there was ambivalence about how Japanese American women should look. Columnist Henry Mori noted that white beauty standards disadvantaged even "assimilated" third-generation women. "Unfortunately, the Sansei still lacks in height . . . as far as beauty contests go," Mori quipped. "Standing next to a non-Nisei beauty who stands 5′7″ with a 36−24−36 tape, the race could be a stopper for the Japanese American entrant. Not to mention her gams at a distance."[72] There was also the question of how far Japanese Americans should go in competing with whites. As early as 1947, columnist Bill Hosokawa frowned upon the idea of Nisei with bleached hair and surgically enlarged eyes. Later on, Yoshinaga would agree. Although pushing the queen's contest to be as American as possible, he still believed that "aping" Western ideals by trying to appear more white violated the "natural beauty of Japanese women."[73] The ultimate warning about Anglo conformity came with the seemingly true report that the Japanese winner of the Miss Universe contest had received breast implants. Some Japanese Americans, the *Kashu Mainichi* noted, pitied the woman and implicitly the many other Japanese who received cosmetic surgery to look more Western. But other Japanese Americans thought that the "bust-job" marked her as a "money-hungry, do-anything" opportunist.[74]

The image of Japanese women prostituting themselves to the West was reminiscent of the controversial relations between Japanese women and American GIs during the occupation. Although some Japanese women, in honored service to the defeated nation, volunteered to meet the sexual needs of the conquering forces, most of those who cavorted with the enemy did so in exchange for desperately needed money, food, and consumer items. As a result, these latter women were looked upon with envy and contempt by many Japanese who saw such interracial relations as a sign of their country's powerlessness. Those who went so far as to marry an American were often shunned by their relatives and society in general. After these war brides immigrated to the United States, Japanese Americans reacted to them in a similar manner. Historian Paul Spickard maintains that Japanese women married to white and black men "were stigmatized as immoral women." They were rarely encouraged to join community organizations and even avoided the fellowship of Japanese American churches.[75] Nisei Week provided a case in point regarding the ostracization of war brides. Its festivities, while celebrating Japanese immigration in general, never welcomed the newest migrants into the ethnic community. The festival booklet would applaud the influx of Japanese from Hawaii to southern California but remained conspicuously silent about the women who would prove to be the largest postwar migration of Japanese to the United States.[76]

In this way, the ultimate symbol of Japanese American integration—the mixed marriages between war brides and former servicemen—was forsaken. As the Nisei Week booklet observed in 1953, interracial marriage, while practiced by the more integrated Japanese Americans back East, "is not yet sanctioned" on the West Coast. Here most Nisei "approve theoretically of intermarriage because it signifies equality, but the approval is usually for the other fellow, not for himself."[77]

SPOILS OF SUCCESS

The limits of integration were also revealed by delinquent youths. In the late 1950s, the vernacular newspapers alarmed the community with reports of teenage gangsters wielding mysterious-sounding weapons such as "zip guns" and "bottle bombs," injuring people with shotgun blasts, getting high on "red devil" amphetamines, and of course stirring up commotion at Nisei Week.[78] The murder of a Sansei in 1958 initiated a community response to juvenile delinquency. JACL and Japanese Chamber of Commerce leaders helped start an organization to examine youth problems. Known as Japanese American Youth, Inc. (JAY), this group sought to prevent gang activity by promoting and coordinating youth activities.[79] But concerned Japanese Americans formed their own opinions about the roots of Sansei delinquency. The *Kashu Mainichi* argued that residential dispersion was responsible for youth problems. While faulting the segregated prewar enclave for being "unsophisticated," the paper praised it as a "safe" and "happy" community with well-adjusted youth. The end of segregation in the postwar era, on the other hand, had enabled Sansei to socialize with "lower classes" (especially working-class blacks, Chicanos, Anglos). "Sansei kids got into trouble when they integrated too well into the community around them and mingled with youth of other races and nationalities and who were below them socially, economically, and educationally."

Thus while the *Kashu Mainichi* encouraged "integration" with upper or similar classes, it strongly discouraged "downward integration" by warning of its negative effects on Japanese American youth: "Their English and speech suffered[;] their social life veered toward gangs and similar 'exciting' activities. They accepted the standards of the more delinquent 'beatniks' of the new generation. They [ended] up with pushers who haunt junior and senior highs, playgrounds, theaters, and even have the temerity to hang around legi[ti]mate youth organizations in attempts to 'push' or peddle marijuana and other narcotics. Nisei and Sansei girls got into trouble, involved in sexual delinquency and so forth."[80]

Others in the community blamed the Nisei for their children's deviance. Community youth organizations like JAY criticized parents for being too busy to involve themselves in delinquency prevention programs.[81] One of the most ardent and controversial articulators of this position was Ellen Endo, a Sansei columnist. Over a period of several years beginning in the mid-1960s, Endo wrote at length about Sansei deficiencies and Nisei culpability for them. An older Sansei, Endo alerted the community that its youth were becoming a lost generation susceptible to criminal activity, drugs, and antisocial behavior. Disturbances at Nisei Week often generated her concern. Endo predicted that Japanese Americans eventually would become afflicted with the same social problems affecting black Americans.[82] While recognizing her community's achievements, she cautioned that with success came problems—that despite its positive features, assimilation was the harbinger of crime, deviance, disorder. The columnist often accused Nisei parents of spoiling their children, of practicing a "give-them-anything attitude" that made Sansei prime targets for drug pushers. "Children too frequently see their parents strive not only to keep up with the Joneses," observed Endo, "but trying to keep one step ahead. It is natural for young people, in view of this fact, to question their parents' motives when status symbols, such as a fancy college or car, are involved." According to her, the postwar Nisei quest for status drove them to both pamper and pressure their children. Spoiled Sansei were victims of overly high parental expectations. "A possible cause of the problem of juvenile delinquency among Sansei may be the fact that JA parents ask a great deal of their children in the way of school work and behavior. Those who can, do, and those who can't rebel." In short, Endo wrote, "Mom and Dad's insistence that their offspring be the best in all endeavors appears to have the opposite effect these days."[83]

According to Endo, the spoils of success had ironically unveiled a lack of integration. She maintained that Nisei social mobility masked their psychological stagnation and that the second generation inherited from their immigrant parents an inability to express feelings and show affection. This "Oriental make-up," Endo contended, limited Sansei assimilation; while third-generation youth possessed ample material goods, they envied their white classmates' demonstrative parents. One of Endo's fans chastised Japanese Americans for repressing emotion, a problem she claimed led to juvenile delinquency, antiblack hostility, and domestic unrest.[84] Furthermore, Endo wrote that "thoroughly Americanized" youth feel "self conscious" around hakujins because "[i]n many Sansei minds, the Caucasians are viewed as better conversationalists, possessing more dynamic personalities and having some sort of built-in guarantee to success in life because of their white skin." The columnist faulted Nisei parents and implicitly Nisei society's exclusivity for Sansei feelings of inferiority. She said that Southland youth "feel complacent and comfortable in their exclusively Sansei crowd and would rather sit back and criticize the Caucasian community . . . for sentencing them to this second-class existence than to compete [with them]." Ultimately, Endo warned Japanese American youth to "stop feeling sorry for themselves and quit insisting they are 'second-class'" so that "they won't condemn the next generation to the same hang-ups."[85]

Although not necessarily shared by most southern California Japanese Americans, Endo's criticisms were revealing. An older Sansei, she identified neither with the second nor third generation. Clearly, she was an "integrationist"; her scolding of Japanese Americans harkened back to the late 1940s' and early 1950s' condemnation of enclave culture "clannishness."[86] Yet Endo wrote after Nisei had made great strides toward integrationist social and economic goals. Nisei success in many ways compromised her faith in integration. Like those who warned of "downward integration," Endo saw social mobility as having mixed effects on Japanese Americans. But unlike her integrationist predecessors, she lacked the sanguine faith in the effects of assimilation. A strong sense of irony drove her narrative of Sansei degeneracy—second-generation success contributed to third-generation deviance. The most shocking evidence of this declension argument came from the rise of radicalism among Japanese American youth.

FIVE

The New Cosmopolitanism

From Heterodoxy to Orthodoxy

At the beginning of August 1965, Nisei Week leaders were gearing up to celebrate the festival's twenty-fifth anniversary. It would be an auspicious moment, Nisei Week's chairman proclaimed, to herald the festival's "maturation" and its achievement in reaching "a high level of sophistication where we can be proud to share this week with the entire American community."[1] As it turned out, however, the celebration was marked by tragedy rather than triumph. On August 11, four days before the festival was to begin, the nearby ghetto of Watts, California, erupted in a storm of destruction and racial warfare. This crisis, the nation's worst urban unrest since World War II, prompted ethnic leaders to postpone the festivities, fearing that the events, like the Nisei-owned stores that were vandalized and looted during the conflict, would invite trouble from "angry blacks." In this way, the occasion planned to commemorate the hard-won achievements of one racialized minority was disrupted by the explosive frustrations of another.

In the aftermath of the Watts riots, the apparent contrast between "successful" Japanese Americans and "angry" African Americans would become fixed in America's racial consciousness. In 1966 the *New York Times* was the first of many mainstream publications to hold up Japanese American integration as a lesson for black America. The feature essay in the *Times Sunday Magazine,* written by sociologist William Petersen, contended that the history of Japanese Americans proved that even the most persecuted of racial groups could attain social mobility through

Nisei Week beauty contestants in 1965 read about the Watts riots, which caused the festival's postponement and began the era of the "model minority." *Courtesy Toyo Miyatake Studios.*

hard work and quiet determination. In some respects, this image of Japanese Americans as the "model minority" echoed the postwar portrayal of heroic Nisei soldiers, which vindicated those in the ethnic community who had refused to protest the internment and, instead, stood behind the American front. Indeed, during the contentious era of civil rights and new left politics, Japanese Americans themselves embraced the notion of the model minority. Consequently, the *Pacific Citizen* reported that Nisei and Sansei who supported struggles for African American civil rights had not "won popularity contests in the community." [2]

And yet it was those few Japanese Americans inspired by black struggles who sparked an ethnic revival that would once again transform the meanings and contours of the group's identity. Beginning in the early 1960s, young, highly educated Nisei and Sansei worked within the ethnic leadership, especially through the national JACL organization, to push Japanese Americans to support the Civil Rights Movement and other political issues beyond their own ethnic interest. At the end of the decade, these "JACL liberals" found common cause with student radicals who generated a social movement among Asian Americans emanating from college and university campuses. The leaders of this Asian American movement, like the Issei leaders who exalted the cosmopolitan West and the JACLers who began Nisei Week, represented a new generation of intellectuals calling for a drastic revision of group orthodoxy, leadership, and relations to white America. Although earlier Issei and Nisei revisionisms sought to escape the "backwardness" of Japanese traditions by embracing white America, the "young turks" from college and university campuses rearticulated ideals of integration and Americanism as debilitating, narrow-minded, and parochial. Theirs was a new and radical cosmopolitanism that championed the progressive spirit of the group's indigenous heritage and culture and historical connections to other racialized minorities and Third World peoples. At the same time, this new identity rejected the subordination of women within the ethnic community as well as signs of the group's slavish accommodation to white America.

Testifying to the power of the Asian American movement, Nisei Week in the 1970s and 1980s attracted political debate more than any other period in its history. But the festival would not embrace the movement's new cosmopolitanism until this identity itself was rearticulated. Although the line between the integrationist orthodoxy and the option of student radicalism was clear at the outset of the Asian American movement, this distinction became blurred and permeable as Nisei Week leaders, and Japanese Americans as a whole, joined the ethnic revival, echoing the activists' call for ethnic pride and cultural retention. In so doing, Nisei Week transformed radical cosmopolitanism into the fuzzy, reformist, and even patriotic orthodoxy of cultural pluralism.

REVIVAL OF THE FITTEST

In August 1972, an intrepid group of high school students brought the Vietnam War home to Japanese America. As the final entry in that year's Nisei Week parade, the students marched in honor of a North Vietnamese patriot, calling themselves the Van Troi Anti-imperialist Youth Brigade. As they reached the center of Little Tokyo, a team of Chinese lion dancers joined them, thrashing a caricatured head of President Nixon and undulating a long body tattooed with antiwar slogans. Mean-

Asian American youth disrupt the Nisei Week parade in 1972. As the Van Troi Anti-imperialist Youth Brigade, they encouraged Japanese Americans to oppose the Vietnam War and both American and Japanese forms of imperialism around the world. *Courtesy Japanese American National Museum, gift of Nobuko Miyamoto-Betserai (98.211.3).*

while, a cadre of supporters unfurled a banner from a nearby balcony, which urged the ethnic community to "Support the Victorious Struggle of the Vietnamese People." Before a grandstand of dignitaries and special guests, the youth brigaders set fire to a Japanese war flag, while their supporters on the balcony rained down leaflets declaring death to the "rising sun" of Japanese and American imperialism. The sudden explosion of firecrackers panicked the nervous crowd, prompting the immediate expulsion of the students from the festivities.[3]

Nisei Week supporters criticized the youth for having betrayed their promise to keep politics out of their performance. "While we agree with the brigade's fervent desire to end the conflict in Vietnam," one festival official wrote, "we can't agree with their methods which smack of fanatical end-justifies-means thinking."[4] For columnist Ellen Endo, the problem was not how the students protested but where their efforts were focused. She dismissed the attempt to bring Nisei Week in step with the political consciousness of American youth, counseling that those seeking to politicize a commercial-cultural event like Nisei Week are "wasting their time."[5]

The rebuke to the Van Troi group exemplified the reaction against the Asian American movement in Little Tokyo. "There is little doubt," Nisei leader Mike Masaoka noted, "that many JACL leaders and members are uncomfortable with the militants, the activists, and the protesters among the young Japanese Americans today." Most of the organization's predominantly Nisei members, Masaoka added, are "conservatively oriented in their activities and in their outlooks," preferring to maintain the "established order."[6] The Nisei's vociferous response to the radicalization of Japanese American youth obscured the younger generation's own opposition to social protest. Although sympathizing with the goal of ethnic retention, one Sansei respondent to the *Pacific Citizen* opposed the protests and rioting that erupted in the name of black autonomy. "I think the Japanese American should continue to obey the law while withholding sympathy and support from those who don't," he wrote. "It is because our parents and grandparents were busy doing quiet, important, worthwhile things instead of screaming and burning and demonstrating that we are today accepted by American society, yet able to maintain our Japanese identity."[7] The image of the Nisei as model citizens was also used by another Sansei to dismiss the "younger members of my generation [who] think they have a valid excuse to raise a little bit of hell." In a letter to the *Rafu Shimpo,* she noted that the Nisei had every right to be bitter about American society, but instead they worked "their tails off to give us what we have today!"[8]

A national survey conducted in 1967 found Nisei and Sansei equally opposed to social protest. Funded by the JACL and designed by sociologists at the University of California, Los Angeles, the Japanese American Research Project (JARP) asked more than two thousand Nisei what advice they would give to African Americans struggling to overcome racism. The findings revealed that the vast majority of Nisei recommended a quiet, nonthreatening route to social mobility. Nearly 40 percent of them advised African Americans to improve their situation by obtaining more formal education; 26 percent thought they needed to improve their attitude and conduct toward others; and almost 20 percent said that to gain social mobility they either needed to work harder or stop "unruly" civil rights struggles. The survey of more than eight hundred Sansei posed a more direct question about their response to black protest by asking the degree to which the respondent favored "black power." Mirroring the conservatism of their parent's generation, more than 84 percent of the Sansei were against "black power," with the vast majority of those finding the idea "very unfavorable."[9]

TABLE 5.1   RELATIONSHIP BETWEEN SANSEI
INTEGRATION AND APPROVAL OF SOCIAL PROTEST

	Integration	Approval of "Black Power"	
	Race of Two Best Friends (%)	Favorable (N = 65)	Unfavorable (N = 357)
Japanese American	39	19	43
Non-Japanese American	61	81	57
Total	100	100	100

SOURCES: Compiled by Lon Kurashige from Gene N. Levine, "Japanese-American Research Project (JARP): A Three-Generation Study, 1890–1966" (computer file), 2d ed. (Los Angeles: UCLA, Institute for Social Science Research, and Chicago: National Opinion Research Center [producers], 1985; Ann Arbor, Mich.: Interuniversity Consortium for Political and Social Research [distributor], 1992).

Clearly, the Asian American movement and its Nisei supporters made up a small, yet critical, mass of the ethnic community. In the only systematic study of the Sansei activism, Minako Maykovich revealed that about 20 percent of third-generation college and university students in California were involved in social protest to some degree.[10] These students, Maykovich suggested, tended to be more Americanized than most of their generation. Sample data from the JARP offer some evidence to support this claim. The index of integration in Table 5.1 is the race of the subject's two closest friends. Those whose friends were not Japanese American (typically white) were assumed to be more integrated, while those with Japanese American friends were considered more ethnic. That the majority of the Sansei sample (61 percent) counted whites as their two best friends confirmed that Japanese Americans in the 1960s were developing closer ties with white Americans. But, as the figures show, this integration seemed to be indicative of more liberal views about social protest. Eighty-one percent of those who were favorable to "black power" counted whites as their two best friends, as opposed to only 57 percent of those who were unfavorable to "black power." In other words, support for radical politics tended to draw a larger percentage of highly integrated Sansei than the opposition to radical politics.

Table 5.2 reveals a similar relationship between integration and social protest among the Nisei. The best index of integration here was level of education and occupational status. Since the JARP did not ask the Nisei about "black power," I have used a question about protest during the internment as a measure of the Nisei's support for radical politics. The

TABLE 5.2 RELATIONSHIP OF NISEI EDUCATION,
OCCUPATION, AND APPROVAL OF SOCIAL PROTEST

Education	Protest (N = 350)	Order (N = 1808)
High school graduate	25	40
College graduate	19	12
Postgraduate	27	10
Other	29	38
Total	100	100
Occupation	(N = 339)	(N = 1757)
Professional/technical	51	30
Ownership/managerial	15	17
Clerical	6	7
Sales	4	6
Crafts	9	11
Operative	3	5
Domestic service	13	25
Total	100	100

SOURCES: Compiled by Lon Kurashige from Gene N. Levine, "Japanese-American Research Project (JARP): A Three-Generation Study, 1890–1966" (computer file), 2d ed. (Los Angeles: UCLA, Institute for Social Science Research, and Chicago: National Opinion Research Center [producers], 1985; Ann Arbor, Mich.: Interuniversity Consortium for Political and Social Research [distributor], 1991).

findings reveal that those in support of protest during the internment tended to be better educated and employed in higher-status occupations. They were nearly three times more likely to have received a postgraduate degree (27 percent protest, 10 percent order) and almost twice as likely to work as white-collar professionals (51 percent protest, 30 percent order). In contrast, those advocating order and cooperation during the internment were much more likely to have stopped their schooling after high school (40 percent order, 25 percent protest), and they were about twice as likely to work in domestic service (25 percent order, 13 percent protest). What the JARP suggested for both Nisei and Sansei in the 1960s was that the more integrated they were, the more likely they were to be sympathetic to social protest. Put another way, the socially concerned Nisei and Sansei shared social backgrounds as well as political convictions.

The attempt to radicalize the JACL also illuminated the link between the two generations in favor of social protests. Almost a decade before the emergence of student radicals in the late 1960s, a new cohort of JACL leaders had been pushing the ethnic community to support black civil rights struggles. In 1963, a JACL contingent marched on Washington, D.C., with Dr. Martin Luther King Jr. in support of his famous dream

JACLers join the "March on Washington" in 1963, reflecting the political liberalism of a handful of the national organization's leaders. *Courtesy Japanese American National Museum, gift of K. Patrick and Lily A. Okura (98.158.1).*

of an integrated America. As president of the national organization, Frank Chuman proposed to raise two million dollars to fight the nation's poverty, discrimination, poor education, and lack of jobs. By 1966 the *Pacific Citizen* reported that the majority of the organization's leadership embraced black struggles but were hamstrung by the conservatism of the larger membership.[11]

Nevertheless, the leadership kept nudging the JACL to the left. As the incoming national president in 1966, Jerry Enomoto proposed to "expand its horizons and get in step with the times." Enomoto was younger and much more liberal than past JACL leaders. After completing bachelor's and master's degrees in social welfare from the University of California, Berkeley, he joined the administration of the California prison system and by 1971 was the first Asian American to head one of the state's correctional centers. Relations with prisoners taught Enomoto that social problems could not be overcome simply by urging disadvantaged groups to imitate the quiet mobility of Japanese Americans. "No Nisei," he proclaimed, "can deny the values and hard won fruits of our parents' struggle," but "these values aren't going to mean a thing to many of our less fortunate Americans, unless we can come out of our glass houses, and demonstrate their actual meanings." [12]

Such pleadings carried a sense of urgency in the aftermath of the Watts riots. The Los Angeles unrest convinced others like *Pacific Citizen* editor Harry Honda that Japanese Americans had to "start changing our attitude, or at least improve our understanding of what the issues are with respect to blacks." Like most JACLers, Honda was no radical, nor had he been especially concerned with the problems outside the ethnic community. He had stood behind the American front during World War II and after returning to southern California was accused by the integrationist Togo Tanaka of refusing to share Little Tokyo with the black residents and businesses that had moved in during the war. The Watts riots, however, had come close enough to his Culver City home to draw his attention to the world outside Japanese America. Considering the notion that "JACL's role is to provide a steadying influence for its members," Honda replied that the organization has been "so 'steady' during the past decade that many believe we've actually fallen asleep." He insisted that the leadership's role in a "troubled America" was "not 'forcing involvement' in a 'controversial issue' but trying to lead and motivate chapters and individual members to recognize the principle that minorities (the Negro especially) are entitled to work out their own destinies as freely as the majority in America." [13]

Urging Japanese Americans to stand up for the cause of civil rights was more than a matter of principle. JACL liberals hoped that sharpening the organization's political teeth would attract new members from the younger generations. A survey of the organization's southern California membership in 1969 revealed an acute absence of Japanese American youth, with more than 80 percent of its members married and more than 90 percent above age thirty. The JACL's attempt to recruit Sansei through its youth arm, "Jr. JACL," was seen by the organization's leadership as a complete failure. The main problem, one youth leader complained, was that the "field of civil rights and human relations has been sorely neglected in most junior chapter programs." Those who did join the JACL often reproduced the conservatism of their parents' generation by discouraging Japanese Americans from embracing movements for political and cultural liberation. "Clean cut and well groomed," one Jr. JACLer boasted. "That's JACL." [14]

The student radicals offered a compelling alternative. Sensing that it might boost youth membership, Enomoto invited them into the JACL, insisting they be given free rein to change the organization as they saw fit.

"Instead of asking for us to make JACL fit youth," he argued, "it may be useful to ask youth to mold JACL in the patterns it feels are relevant." [15] Former JACL president Roy Nishikawa also welcomed the youth movement, seeing it as a means to revive JACLers from a troubling complacency. "Is it any wonder," he asked rhetorically, "that the more aware and involved Sansei are saying that the great bulk of JACLers remain uninformed, unaware, unconcerned, uncommitted and uninvolved? That JACL is insensitive to the truly relevant needs of the community? Is it any wonder that JACL is considered dead and dying?" [16]

Jeffrey Matsui, second in command of JACL's administration, also saw the youth movement as a means to revive the aging Nisei organization. Like other liberals, Matsui was not afraid of jeopardizing the model image of Japanese Americans. His editorials in the *Pacific Citizen* consistently berated his generation for being "one of the last minorities to know our place" and prodded them to "open their minds" to social issues outside Little Tokyo. Having grown up in Hawaii, where Japanese Americans were politically powerful, Matsui did not understand why the "mainland Japanese were always there to show the white Americans that we are as American as apple pie." To him, the protests by Sansei students opened an important channel of communication with "young people, not just Jr. JACL members." As a social worker, he hoped the youth movement would provide a "mechanism . . . so that young people frustrated in society can come in [to JACL] and straighten things out." [17] But Matsui did more than identify with the student radicals; he hired them on to the staff of the JACL's southern California office, persuading them that it was more practical to change the Nisei organization from within rather than to attack it from outside.

The student radicals were pragmatic as well. Victor Shibata, founder of a grassroots drug abuse–recovery program for Asian American youth, joined the JACL staff because he was seduced by the organization's ability to mount large-scale political campaigns. He thought that with nearly twenty-five thousand members, a paid staff, and a full-time lobbyist, the organization might provide the best means to awareness about drug problems within the ethnic community. Warren Furutani too sought to direct the JACL to his own ends. The reason for joining the JACL, he wrote, was not to take it over, but to use it as a "legitimate front . . . where we could air the views of the [community's] more progressive elements." For Furutani the JACL provided a "vehicle" for the youth movement, while liberals like Jeffrey Matsui and Jerry Enomoto "greased the wheels." [18]

With critical support from JACL liberals, the young staff pushed the organization to address social problems within the ethnic group. We "looked everywhere [in the community] that we weren't supposed to," Furutani recalled, "and kept finding problems."[19] With Shibata's experience with drug-abuse issues in mind, the staff launched a "drug offensive" in which they criticized the ethnic leadership for covering up drug-related problems among Japanese Americans. "Our community was trying to hide the problem," Furutani maintained, "but the problem kept opening up because kids were dying." *Gidra,* the leading Asian American movement periodical in southern California, reported that official statistics for Gardena, a middle-class Japanese American suburb, confirmed the problem of drug abuse among Japanese American youths. In 1970, the Gardena police reported eight suicides by Japanese Americans, seven of them brought about by drug overdose. Two years later, the Gardena Memorial Hospital reported at one point handling five drug overdoses a week by Asian Americans.[20] While Japanese Americans most likely were not more susceptible to drug abuse than the average American youth, the JACL staff often exaggerated the extent of the problem to combat the community's entrenched model minority image.

The liberal-radical alliance also exposed the powerful legacy of the wartime internment. In late 1969, the staff organized a pilgrimage to Manzanar to put the ethnic community in step with blacks and other racial minorities who had marched in the name of civil rights. The staff was almost entirely ignorant about the history of internment and did not know better than to stay overnight at Manzanar in the dead of winter. The youth relied on Nisei like Edison Uno for insight about the wartime hardships that Japanese Americans endured. In 1970, Uno urged the JACL to petition the American government to admit the mistake of incarcerating Japanese Americans during World War II. With critical support from Sansei radicals, Uno and other Nisei liberals planted seeds within the JACL from which a movement to redress the injustice of the internment would grow.[21]

But the young staff would not harvest the fruits of their labor within the JACL. In July 1972, the radicals, including their mentor Jeffrey Matsui, lost hope of reforming the organization and therefore resigned their positions. What prompted their leaving was the national JACL's refusal to hire a fellow radical for its top administrative post. The organization, Furutani concluded, had reached a "fork in the road" with the old guard focusing on services for JACL members, while the radicals emphasized the social welfare needs of the broader ethnic community.[22] Matsui was

Asian American activists organized the pilgrimage in 1969 to the site of the former Manzanar internment camp in order to "break the silence" about the wrongful incarceration of Japanese Americans during World War II. *Courtesy Visual Communications Archives.*

particularly shaken by the JACL's inability to "become a vehicle responsive to the needs of all segments of the Japanese community in the United States." This revelation, he confessed, "sucked all of my trust for the leadership of the JACL."[23]

In truth, neither the radicals nor liberals were convinced that the so-called civil rights organization was a viable tool for reform, let alone radical change. The staff's resignation, one Nisei liberal explained, only confirmed that the JACL was a "middle-class, establishment organization" and was not concerned with "lower class, 'problem people.'"[24] The radicals themselves had reached this conclusion before they resigned. By 1972, Furutani had become frustrated with community reforms, seeing programs like the drug offensive as merely "Band-Aids" unable to resolve the larger issues in society. For the broader picture, he turned to Marxism and Leninism, which encouraged him to leave the "reform stuff behind and just be [a] revolution[ary]." Fellow staffer Ron Wakabayashi confirmed that the staff felt comfortable with leaving JACL; it made it seem as if the old guard was "the bad guy rather than putting light on some of the ideological conflicts starting to arise."[25]

The staff's resignation revealed the limits of radical-liberal cooperation. Although JACLers and student activists found common cause
within the ethnic community, they were motivated by different conceptions of social responsibility. The liberals saw Nisei parochialism as a
disturbing sign of complacency; in the words of one editorialist, the
ethnic community had become "fat and satisfied." Their goal was for
Japanese Americans to give back to society by aiding the less privileged
within and beyond Little Tokyo. The radicals, on the other hand, maintained that the "success" of Japanese Americans was an illusion concealing their continued domination as racial outcasts. Their challenge
was to encourage the ethnic community not to give back to American
society but to remake it by tearing down its core values and institutions.

THE NEW HETERODOXY

The case against the community's integrationist orthodoxy was made
at the outset of the Asian American movement. In one of the earliest
expressions of student radicalism, Yuji Ichioka, a graduate student in
Berkeley, California, declared that the "crucial question facing us today
is not that of integration." Rather than focusing on the problems preventing Japanese Americans from blending into white America, Ichioka
directed the spotlight upon the "society which we have sought, too often, with ludicrous fervor, to become integrated into." [26] What resulted
from becoming American, Warren Furutani explained, was that "we
have acquired all the worst characteristics of America's majority: the
racism, prejudice, selfishness and arrogance which is a reflection of a
people that has made it at the expense of others." [27]

The relationship between the assimilation of Japanese Americans and
the "others" to whom Furutani referred was spelled out clearly in Amy
Uyematsu's manifesto for student radicalism, "The Emergence of Yellow
Power in America." Using writings by Stokely Carmichael and other
black nationalists, Uyematsu addressed the antiblack prejudice within
her own ethnic group. She argued that in seeking to become truly accepted in American society, the ethnic community had remained silent
about the discrimination against African Americans. This silence, she
wrote, perpetuated "white racism" by allowing "white America to hold
up the 'successful' Oriental image before other minority groups as a
model to emulate. . . . By being as inconspicuous as possible they keep
pressure off of themselves at the expense of blacks." [28]

Wearing the mask of white America, however, carried a high price for

Japanese Americans, according to Uyematsu. In gaining economic security and mainstream acceptance, they had been forced to "deny their yellowness" by denigrating "their own languages, customs, histories, and cultural values." "They have become white," she suggested, "in every respect but color." Yet no matter how hard they tried to become like the majority—even by altering their appearance—Japanese Americans continued to be put at risk because of their racial markings. Assuming "white identities," she insists, perpetuated racism by causing Japanese Americans to develop an "extreme self-hatred" about being nonwhite. The only way out of this trap was to come to terms with one's "mistaken identity" by recognizing the futility of assimilation in a racist society.

Thus were the identity challenges propelling the Asian American movement. After conducting hundreds of interviews and an extensive study of movement publications, historian William Wei notes that student radicalism stemmed from the deep disillusionment of being socialized in American culture and values and yet denied the fruits of assimilation by continuing to face discrimination in mainstream society.[29] Even a glance at the writings of student radicals confirms this point. An entire section of the anthology in which Uyematsu's essay appeared was devoted to identity concerns. The thrust of the submissions details the problem of being American and yet looking Japanese. One author admitted to never considering "myself 100-percent American because of obvious physical differences," while another acknowledged that realizing "you are not quite as White as the White society you wish to identify with . . . can be painful experience."[30] The poem "I hate my wife for her flat yellow face" addressed the perils of assimilation most powerfully.

> I hate my wife for her flat yellow face
> and her fat cucumber legs, but mostly
> for her lack of elegance and lack of
> intelligence compared to judith gluck.[31]

Problematizing the Anglo ideal was not an end in itself. The student radicals exposed the shame of having a "flat yellow face" to highlight the importance of creating an indigenous identity valuing Japanese Americans on their own terms. "Yellow power," Uyematsu explained, "advocates self-acceptance as the first step toward strengthening personalities."[32] The vision also promoted a broad notion of nonwhite value by embracing the political struggles of blacks, Native Americans, Chicanos, and other racial minorities wrestling with the limits of assimilation. The bounds of race extended as well to peoples in Asia and the Third World.

The youth movement idolized Mao Zedong and Ho Chi Minh as race rebels who resisted the colonial aggressions of white powers. The radical conceptions of racial minorities in the United States and colonial subjects abroad were rooted in the principle of self-determination. "We see the Vietnamese people's struggle as a just struggle," proclaimed the Van Troi youth who disrupted the Nisei Week parade in 1972, "for they are only fighting for their basic fundamental rights as humans rights . . . to live in peace without foreign intervention and to be able to determine their own lives." [33] While the larger antiwar movement emphasized the importance of bringing American troops home, the student radicals sympathized with the plight of their Vietnamese "brothers and sisters."

Self-determination also meant the creation of an indigenous set of aesthetic criteria. "Yellow people," Uyematsu confessed, "share with . . . blacks the desire to look white. Just as blacks wish to be light-complected [sic] with thin lips and unkinky hair, 'yellows' want to be tall with long legs and large eyes." She claimed that women in particular "ape white standards of beauty" by lightening black hair, padding bras to appear to have larger breasts, and taping eyelids to make eyes seem bigger. [34] The call to appreciate the physical attributes of Japanese Americans on their own terms encouraged the Van Troi protesters to condemn Nisei Week's beauty pageant as well. Addressing the white men who often judged the contestants, they asked if it was "human and dignified to have those of the opposite sex and different race to judge our sisters according to standards and values that are not our own?" [35] The answer went beyond creating a new ethnic aesthetic to asserting a racial separatism demanding that only Japanese Americans could judge other Japanese Americans fairly.

Radicals who advocated these fictive bonds of identity could not ignore divisions within the ethnic group, for a main part of the new cosmopolitanism involved tearing down the existing one. Here the Van Troi protest was also illuminating. The youth raged against the honored position in the Nisei Week parade given to the veterans of the famed 442d battalion who fought in World War II. That the ex-soldiers led the parade through Little Tokyo was seen as a statement in favor of the JACL's American front. "The 442d," the student radicals asserted, "reflects only one side of the response to the crisis that our people faced . . . during the concentration camp experience. They represent that segment . . . Japanese Americans who, in order to survive, joined the U.S. military to prove their patriotism to America." Yet in focusing attention upon the veterans, there was no "mention made of others who refused to serve in the

U.S. military . . . who were torn between loyalty to the people of Japan and their shaky status in America" (Thai Binh Brigade leaflet).

The Asian American movement stood up for the economically as well as politically silenced within Japanese America. They treated two of the festival's honorees in 1972 with the same scrutiny as the war veterans. The Japanese consul general in Los Angeles and JACL leader Mike Masaoka were said to "represent very clear political lines of Japanese corporate interests both in the community and abroad" and yet "they ride in big cars and fancy floats in a supposedly non-political parade," while "the police were called on to disperse us" (ibid.). The attack was grounded in the threat to independent businesses and low-income residents in Little Tokyo posed by foreign investment (the subject of the next chapter). Beyond their opposition to Japan's support for the Vietnam War, the Van Troi brigade burned the "rising sun" flag to condemn the corporate takeover of the immigrant community. It was no coincidence that the youth hung their antiwar banners and tossed firecrackers from the Kajima building, Little Tokyo's newest and most celebrated symbol of overseas investment. Burning the war flag also was intended to send a message to Japanese American youth who had come to adopt it as a moniker of ethnicity. "This is NOT our symbol," the protesters urged. It is a sign of militarism and "false identity" that misserves the ethnic community's working-class legacy (ibid.).

The new cosmopolitanism was committed to resisting the domination of women as well as racial minorities, colonial subjects, and Little Tokyo's stores and denizens. But on this issue, the level of commitment varied within the movement. Like civil rights and black power organizations, the Asian American movement restricted women from leadership positions and reproduced traditional gender roles. One female activist in Los Angeles recalled that in the early stages "it became clear that even within the movement, where we were talking about creating a different kind of society . . . there were problems with women not being taken seriously, or their work not being looked at in the same light, or women being accepted as leaders by men." [36] Another activist noted the "inherent chauvinism" that had women "doing the typing while the brothers are out doing the organizing in the communities." [37]

It was often left to women to raise the youth movement's gender consciousness. Borrowing insights from white feminists, Georgia Lee, for example, went beyond criticizing the Nisei Week beauty pageant as enacting a white standard of beauty or being a "sexist tool of capitalism" because it served corporate interests. To her, the issue was the beauty pageant itself. Such contests, she argued, contributed to the conception of women as commodities to be consumed by men. The queen contestants were presented as a "line of impaled sweet young things . . . so alike with apricot cheeks and cotton candy hair, gowns aglitter with sequins, and smiles frozen in place from hours of practice." These "packaged girls," Lee continued, "all walk with identically perfect posture; with uniform grace they lower their uniform perfections into their chairs and assume identical attitudes, knees together, ankles close, one foot slightly in front of the other, hands in lap, back straight, chin up, and smile." This conformist ritual, she concluded, was "dull, overly-serious, pretentious, hypocritical, and silly"—something avoided altogether by the "real girl." [38]

It was also left primarily to women to theorize the intersections of racial and gender inequality. One activist identified two sources of sexism within the movement. One was that "male chauvinists . . . feel that women should be subordinate in the political movement because they are mentally and physically weaker than men"; the other was that men "so 'emasculated' by white racism cannot stand to see women in roles of equality or leadership." [39] As Susie Ling's study of women activists in Los Angeles reveals, this sympathy for the emasculation of "their" men kept them from identifying with white feminists. Indeed, their interest in the women's liberation movement was mostly to use its insights to strengthen their racial struggles. Although one woman acknowledged the sexism within the youth movement, she reminded "yellow females" that "no matter how much we allow [our men] to degrade, discriminate, and mold our social expectations," they needed to become feminists because being "sweet or shy will not help you or your people find freedom from economic and psychological oppression in white society." [40]

To prescribe the new cosmopolitanism, then, was to urge Japanese Americans to abandon the orthodoxy of integration that shied away from addressing national and global currents of anticolonialism, panethnicity, racial politics, and feminism. This was no small task, as the Van Troi protesters discovered much to their dismay. The failure of student radicalism to reach a broad base within the ethnic community, however, would not be permanent. By Nisei Week's fiftieth anniversary in 1990, the beauty-pageant judges were no longer exclusively, or even a majority of, white men, while the festival honorees as well were predominantly Japanese American. Organizers of the Nisei Week parade deliberately sought to foster good relations with neighboring racial minorities by inviting participation from groups of blacks, Latinos, Chinese,

and other Asian Americans. Most surprisingly, the festival embraced political protest by becoming a vehicle for the movement to redress the
government for the wartime internment of Japanese Americans. Clearly,
the language and sentiments of the Asian American movement had eventually caught on within the ethnic community and by the 1980s were
competing with the orthodoxy of integration. The success of the new
cosmopolitanism, however, came at the expense of the student radicalism that had founded it. The festivities and spectacles at Nisei Week
would embrace the ideals of ethnic pride and self-determination in a
very different way than had the Asian American movement.

IDENTITY IN THE STREETS

In the 1980s a later generation of Japanese American youth disrupted
the Nisei Week carnival rather than the parade. While the older generation managed the activities inside the carnival, their teenage and college-
age children packed the sidewalks outside the festivities to watch a
spontaneous procession of stylized cars. Festival authorities complained
about the traffic jams caused by so many vehicles driving past the carnival and about the loud noises produced by gunning engines and screech-
ing tires. The most urgent concern, recalled one official, was the fear of
cars spinning out of control while "racing down the street eighty miles
an hour." In 1980 the chairman of Nisei Week's carnival called upon the
Los Angeles police to shut down the unofficial spectacle of car cruising.[41]
Seven years later the LAPD warned that they had established a "Cruiser
Task Force" to patrol the festivities.[42] In 1984, however, festival leaders
themselves sought to regulate car cruisers by making their vehicles an
official part of the festival. In the 1990s, the Nisei Week car show cor-
ralled the cruisers into a space where they could be displayed, admired,
and discussed—but not driven.

As a form of youth resistance, car cruising seemingly had nothing in
common with student radicalism. Parading cars or watching them be
paraded were not overtly political acts. They were not orchestrated, nor
did they invoke or even criticize an explicit ideology or ethnic orthodoxy.
Tim Mochizuki remembers that the two-hundred and fifty members of
his club of car cruisers had little or no awareness of political issues for
Japanese Americans. Indeed, Mochizuki himself exhibited none of the
identity dilemmas preoccupying Uyematsu and other student activists.
For him, growing up in Gardena, California, a large suburban community of middle-class Japanese Americans, was a multicultural experience

in which he made friends with Japanese Americans, whites, blacks, Hispanics, and members of other Asian groups. He never encountered racial prejudice, nor did he suffer from the "self-hatred" of wanting to be white. On the contrary, his bilingualism in Japanese and English, which developed from speaking Japanese with his immigrant mother, and biculturalism from annual visits to Japan was something that he and his friends esteemed.

But if the car cruisers had no political consciousness, they shared with student radicals a resistance to Anglo conformity. In regions like southern California, with its expansive nexus of freeways and decentralized urban landscape, cars became vehicles of ethnic identification. Perhaps the most renowned blending of car and ethnic cultures was the low-rider, the stylized vehicle associated with Chicano communities. The low-rider, observes anthropologist James Diego Vigil, although appreciated and imitated throughout Mexican America, continues to be principally an expression of gang members and culture. He describes this distinctive car style as having "lowered rear ends (or all around), either permanent or temporary (with hydraulic lifts of the type that raise and lower truck tailgates). This lowered vehicle can be an older 1940s or more recent 1970s model (usually a General Motors vehicle, especially Chevrolets); it may be regular in appearance or highly decorated (multicolored paint jobs, sparkly wheels, rich leather or velvet upholstery, and so on). The image of the driver is slumped-back[,] low silhouetted[,] and the drive is smooth and slow."[43]

Just as Chicano gangsters fashioned a car culture unto themselves, so too did Japanese American youth modify vehicles in ways that expressed their subculture. While young men long had engaged in street racing, the car cruising in the late 1970s and early 1980s introduced a new Japanese American style: what I call the "Buddhahead car." Unlike low-riders, which were typically American-made cars, Buddhahead cars were primarily Japanese imports. One "road racer" explained that these cars were lowered to the ground, without hydraulic lifts, and usually were painted without much flash or sparkle. They had wide tires neatly tucked under the car body's flared wheel wells and an extended rearview mirror across the top of the front windshield. This style derived from professional road racing cars especially produced by Datsun and Toyota. The goal, recalled one former car cruiser, was to have a "clean car without unnecessary frills, body adornments, or trinkets making it appear unsuitable for racing." But these cars, he affirmed, were also designed to be distinctively ethnic: "It might be a Chinese-character good luck charm dangling [from the rearview mirror] or a Japanese war-flag displayed on a window, but somehow they said 'I am not the average white American. I am a Japanese American.'"[44]

Buddhahead cars were known for being maneuverable rather than fast. Sansei took pride in a vehicle's ability to round tight corners and curves rather than show a burst of speed in a straight line. The latter goal was identified with white youth who were said to be more interested in building powerful "muscle cars" modeled after dragsters with the back hiked up and the front sloping down. Tim Mochizuki, on the other hand, took pride in having his Toyota Corolla outperform American-made cars with much larger engines. He recalls with particular delight the times when the "Jap beer cans" and "rice burners" of his car club beat white competitors in a standing quarter-mile race.[45]

But car cruising was more than a means of overcoming whites and whiteness. It was part of a subculture of Japanese American youth centered around community events such as basketball games, Asian fraternity and sorority activities, Buddhist community, or obon, festivals, and of course Nisei Week. The car cruisers would follow a social circuit from one Japanese American festival to another, culminating in the cruise at Nisei Week. To Dan Kuramoto, leader of a popular jazz-fusion group, this spectacle symbolized the identity and culture of the new generation. His song "Cruisin' J-Town," performed by his professional band "Hiroshima," characterized car cruising as a struggle to create a Japanese American identity embracing their ethnic heritage and ties to other racial minority groups. Like all of Hiroshima's cuts, it blended the sounds of Japanese instruments (taiko drums and koto) with conventions of black and Latino popular music. "It's natural for us to make this combination," Kuramoto remarked, "because that's what we [the band members] listened to when we were growing up. Cross-culturalization is part of our lifestyle."[46]

Hiroshima's sound grew out of the youth movement. In 1973 Kuramoto described Hiroshima as "the spirit of all people who have suffered . . . injustices and inhumanity." The group's goal, he continued, was to "develop the understanding that is necessary for peace and harmony in the world" by communicating "those elements of our heritages that best express the reality of the lives of Asians in America."[47] But car cruising, according to Warren Furutani, did not best reflect the reality of all Japanese American youth. He asserted that gang members within the ethnic community were not interested in car cruising and, if they were, did not identify with the "Buddhahead" style of middle-class, suburban youth.

Because they "could not afford to drive a BMW 320I or Datsun 280ZX like those rich Buddhaheads," the gangsters bought used Chevrolets and turned them into low-riders as a way of identifying with the gang culture of Chicano youth.[48]

Furutani's observations revealed the transformation of student radicalism. Although the youth movement addressed both the identity of the ethnic group and the predicaments of its internal others, the culture of car cruising was predicated on only the former concern. Nor did it reflect the conception of Japanese Americans as part of national and international forces of racial domination. Although groups like Hiroshima emphasized the linkages between ethnic group and other racial minorities, the car cruisers themselves replicated the kind of parochialism the student radicals opposed within the ethnic community. For the typical Japanese American youth, the new cosmopolitanism was reduced to the assertion of ethnic pride. This appropriation underscored not only the elite position of student intellectuals but also the class differences between them and the majority of the ethnic community.

QUEENS AND SISTERS

The same tension between student radicals and the Japanese American mainstream was evident in the renewed protest of the Nisei Week beauty contest. In spring 1985, a group of JACLers known as the Women's Concerns Committee (WCC) encouraged the local chapters of their organization to stop sponsoring queen candidates. Beauty contests, asserted WCC leader Mei Nakano, "by their very nature promote the notion of physical attributes as being a women's most desirable feature."[49] Despite the lip service about the importance of a candidate's personality and intelligence, Nakano insisted that at Nisei Week "you don't get a foot in the door if you happen to be dumpy or homely, though you may have an IQ of 140 and a personality a yard wide" (Nakano, *Pacific Citizen,* April 12, 1985). In proposing a JACL resolution that called upon the organization's chapters to boycott beauty pageants, the WCC identified the harmful effects of such seemingly innocuous spectacles. The problem with glorifying women's bodies in this way, the WCC proposal read, was that it "tends to diminish her worth as a whole human being, relegating to the status of secondary importance her accomplishments, potential, intelligence, and nurturing qualities" (ibid., March 11, 1983).

The WCC attack against the Nisei Week pageant was based on a critique of male domination within the ethnic community. "Sexism,"

Nakano explained in 1983, "like its demon twin racism, operates on the assumption that one group is superior to another. The group that considers itself superior puts all sorts of complex machinations into play in order to hold sway: benevolent paternalism, tokenism, job discrimination, use of 'biological inferiority' as a rationale, biased language, ad infinitum" (ibid.). In other words, Japanese American men were reproducing the types of discrimination they faced from white America in subordinating Japanese American women. What made matters worse, she added, was that no one was really aware that Japanese American women were victims of sexual discrimination. "We Japanese Americans know all about racism," Nakano continued, but sexism was a problem that escaped even the "most enlightened of us." But this misrecognition, she concluded, should not hide the fact that the ethnic community

> is a sexist society, *more so even than the larger society within which it exists.*
> With us, it's more deeply ingrained, more pervasive, more subtle, and therefore more pernicious and difficult to root out.... As a microcosm of middle-class Nikkei society, JACL has unremittingly perpetuated the notions of male superiority and dominance, making believers out of almost everybody, including women. It has nurtured an atmosphere within its body which is, if not hostile, certainly not conducive to developing and sustaining creative participation by women. (ibid.)

Nakano's plea was for Japanese American women to see themselves in a "different light" in order to gain equal opportunity and the "same freedom historically accorded to men" (ibid., June 7, 1985). The WCC's attempt to raise the ethnic community's and JACL's gender consciousness was reminiscent of the Asian American movement's earlier efforts to instill a radical awareness within the ethnic community. Both the WCC and the movement activists expressed a combination of pity and contempt for an ethnic group that apparently needed to be led out of the darkness of its own ignorance. As had always been the hallmark of Japanese American cosmopolitanism, Nakano blamed the false consciousness of Japanese Americans (in this case their misunderstanding of sexism) on "our cultural heritage." To be sure, attitude about gender inheritance that many women would (and did) find objectionable was passed on from Japan through the Issei and Nisei. But Nakano was loath to understand the ethnic community's gender roles and relations on their own terms, preferring, instead, to hold Japanese Americans up to the "more liberated" standards of white America. Although movement activists would have been more comfortable comparing Japanese Americans to the "more liberated" standards of black America, they, like Nakano, were equally dismissive of Japanese American conservatism. Consequently, both sets of protesters were reluctant to compromise their utopian visions of the ethnic community. For movement activists, this eventually meant turning away from the JACL and Nisei Week as vehicles of radical social change. And for the WCC, it meant the resounding defeat of its proposed JACL resolution to boycott beauty contests.

Given the conservative nature of Japanese Americans, it was easy to see why Nakano claimed that the protest against the Nisei Week beauty contest was "doomed from the start" (ibid., April 19, 1985). But a close look at the JACL debate shows the ethnic community itself in quite a different light. One man's response to the "liberal elements" of the WCC suggested that Japanese American beauty contests played an important role in racial uplift. Given that Asians were so often portrayed as weird and unattractive, he maintained that "it doesn't hurt to let the country know that Japanese or mix-race women of Japanese extraction are beautiful . . . regardless of their personal traits, education, physical attributes and/or image." [50] In this sense, the WCC's call to ban beauty contests failed to grasp their significance as mechanisms for resisting racialized standards of beauty, and, as such, the WCC's struggle could be seen as tantamount to embracing racism.

After all, Japanese Americans had long asserted ethnic pride through the bodies of beautiful women. Ever since the Nisei Week pageant began in 1935, the festival queen was said to symbolize the ethnic community's vitality and reigning ethnic orthodoxy. This community significance was paramount to Stella Nakadate, who entered the contest in 1955 to serve as a bridge between whites and Japanese Americans. As a student of modern dance, Nakadate had spent most of her young life in "mixed groups" and thus saw the Nisei Week contest as a way of getting more involved in the ethnic community by encouraging Japanese Americans to expand their racial horizons. Raised in Idaho, Carol Itatani, Nisei Week queen in 1965, had even less contact with Japanese Americans than Nakadate. Before she entered the contest, Itatani saw herself as "strictly American" and consciously sought to overcome her shyness, reticence, and other qualities she associated with the "typical Japanese American woman." Although she was excited to learn about the ethnic community, what ultimately drew her to Nisei Week was the idea of becoming a goodwill ambassador between whites and Japanese Americans.

In the 1970s, Nisei Week queens continued to see the pageant as a form of community service, but they emphasized even more the importance of learning about their ethnic heritage. In her trip to Japan as Nisei

Week queen, Joyce Kikuchi experienced the dilemmas of Sansei assimilation when she was mistaken for a Japanese national. "It was then," she
revealed, "that I realized how close I am in some ways to my ancestors
and yet how far removed in others."[51] This was a conversion narrative
often expressed by those queens who were able to visit Japan. For many
of them, like Sandra Toshiyuki, going to Japan was their first chance to
meet distant relatives, thus forging personal connections to the old country. Yet equally important to Toshiyuki was becoming aware of the history of Japanese in the United States. Before her entrance in Nisei Week's
pageant, Toshiyuki paid little attention to being Japanese American and,
despite her parents having been raised in Little Tokyo, was largely unfamiliar with the downtown ethnic enclave. Consequently, the festival
taught her about the Japanese American experience and afforded her a
greater appreciation of her own parents and grandparents. In a similar
way, JoAnn Yamashiro appreciated Nisei Week for encouraging her to
recognize and appreciate her ethnicity. "I realized that my heritage was
rich with qualities other than what I [had] seen portrayed here in the
United States. . . . The qualities that many younger Japanese people dis-
like are the ones that give us the foundation strength" such as having
"integrity, working hard, expecting nothing from others but yourself,
being truthful, respecting others, and working out problems rather than
being the problems."

   If the Nisei Week contest encouraged its participants to appreciate themselves as Japanese Americans, it also enabled them to appreciate
themselves as women. In 1973, columnist Ellen Endo opposed the movement activists' opposition to the festival pageant, arguing that such contests instilled a positive sense of self for young Japanese American women
living amidst the hegemony of white standards of beauty. Thus the Nisei
Week pageant had a psychological imperative "as long as greater America's idea of perfect womanhood is a 5 ft. 10 in. blonde with blue eyes, a 38-
inch bust and legs that won't quit."[52] Nearly twenty years later, Nisei Week
queen Jane Nakamura also testified to the need for competing ideals of
American beauty. Although she thought the Nisei Week pageant's "aesthetic component" should be "downplayed," Nakamura opposed those
who would do away with it completely. "I think one of the reasons I don't
denigrate pageants altogether," she asserted, "is that it is an important
thing for women of color to have a forum in which they can feel really
attractive, because most of these girls could not—simply could not—
compete as models or in other contests whether it is because of racial
prejudice or facial image or [their] lacking the 'beauty-pageant body.' "

The gender consciousness of Nisei Week beauty contestants stood in stark contrast to the WCC's portrayal of them as merely victims of male privilege and sexual inequality. As a result, the debate to ban beauty contests hinged on two different strategies for equalizing the sexes. The Nisei Week leadership posed the main opposition to the WCC campaign, countering it with an equally strong appeal to self-improvement. Given that JACL chapters sponsored seven of the eight queen candidates in 1985, Douglas Masuda, responsible for that year's coronation ball, took the lead in saving his event. He assured JACLers that "all candidates have had the opportunity to expand their horizons" by having the opportunity to meet people, travel around the world on "goodwill missions," develop poise and confidence, and "most of all to be damn proud of being Japanese Americans!"[53] If this were not enough to shoot down the idea of banning beauty pageant sponsorships, then the corroboration of Masuda's points by past Nisei Week queens proved the death knell for the WCC proposal. These women denied the charge that beauty pageants subordinated them by claiming that beauty was a "competitive asset" enabling them to better appreciate their own identity and serve the ethnic community.[54]

The Nisei Week beauty contestants articulated a different, softer version of feminism than did the WCC, and, in the end, this view proved more acceptable to the ethnic community. In interviewing Nisei Week queens and pageant organizers from the 1950s to the 1990s, I found that the contestants were hardly willing to become the playthings of Japanese American men. In fact, their concerns about their treatment as women provided the foundations for changing the pageant in ways mirroring the WCC critique of sexism within the ethnic community.

Despite the idea that beauty was a "competitive asset," women involved in the queen contest objected to the focus on the candidates' bodies. The contestants in her day, noted one past queen and pageant organizer in the early 1950s, opposed being judged in swimsuits because their bodies failed to meet the standards of white beauty. In the 1970s, another Nisei Week official claimed that the women found it simply exploitative to appear in public in revealing swimsuits. Columnist Ellen Endo gave voice to such complaints in 1972 by asserting that becoming Nisei Week queen was not "worth the humiliation of parading bare-legged in front of a small cocktail-hour crowd."[55] Equally disturbing was the comparison made by a male columnist of the beauty contestants to entrants in a horserace. From the 1950s to the early 1970s, George Yoshinaga delighted in handicapping the queen contest. But all the queens I interviewed shuddered at the memory of his listing their body measurements, identifying favorable traits and characteristics, and laying down odds as to their chances of winning the pageant. Ellen Endo was one woman who chastised Yoshinaga for portraying candidates as horses and not humans and for treating them like "meat to be poked and prodded."[56] Yoshinaga himself admitted being persuaded to end his annual ritual not by his colleague Endo but by women connected with the queen pageant itself.

The beauty queens were also sensitive to the male chauvinism of festival officials. "What I enjoyed least about being a candidate and member of a Nisei Week court," Faye Hirata contended, "was the outdated notions . . . that we were just fluff-props to be placed next to their favorite politicians and businessmen for photo opportunities." Excited about the chance to represent the ethnic community, Judy Sugita de Queiroz at the same time remembered that being the queen was a "big let down." Festival organizers instructed her not to speak when being introduced to foreign dignitaries and kept her from any decision making. According to Sandra Toshiyuki, only demure smiles and waves were required of queens. Festival planners modeled them after the Japanese Princess Michiko, an ideal of traditional Japanese women's grace and etiquette. No wonder, as Toshiyuki was pained to remember, a "well meaning [Los Angeles City] councilperson would refer to us as his 'little Japanese dolls.'" The image of a demure, passive Japanese woman also did not sit well with Carol Itatani, who was uncomfortable with being treated like "decoration." She, too, was told by festival representatives not to speak upon meeting dignitaries and celebrities, but beyond this she felt besieged by the queen's many community obligations, which often interfered with her college studies and reinforced her title's superficiality.

Part of the problem was that, until the 1970s, men largely ran the festival's beauty pageant and assumed full responsibility for the contestants' activities, clothes, and overall well-being. The absence of women in Nisei Week leadership was typical for, as Christine Naito remarked, the festival "had been a very male-dominated organization." Naito was one leader who insisted that women be immediately responsible for the queen contest and contestants. As a result of urgings like hers, queen candidates since the late 1970s interacted primary with women leaders. Faye Hirata was one queen who felt reassured by this change in beauty pageant leadership. "It made me feel comfortable," she noted, "because I knew they were the type who would respect us as women." From 1970 to 1994, women would move into more leadership positions with four of them breaking the barriers of gender to lead Nisei Week as general chair.

Perhaps the most revealing change initiated by the women in the Nisei Week leadership was the establishment of a reunion for past queens as part of the festival's official program. The impetus for this event came from the former queens themselves. Beauty pageant coordinator Christine Naito decided to pursue the idea of a reunion after listening to a former queen complain about her disconnection from other contest winners. Naito then impressed the idea of a reunion upon former queen Emiko Kato, who proceeded to organize the event for the next ten years. Attending the former queens' luncheon differed markedly from participating in the beauty pageant. Most obviously, the event was not predicated on women's competition, nor was there a hint of inequality among the former beauty contestants. Many queens shared Judy Sugita de Queiroz's opinion that at the reunion "everyone is equal and the same." If there was distinction at the event, it was a reverence for age. On one occasion the former queens countered an effort to rank them by order of beauty. Festival parade leaders one year created a float reportedly intended to showcase younger queens while marginalizing older ones. But the queens bonded together in their insistence that they be presented equally and fairly. The former queens showed no interest in reliving their past beauty competition.

Indeed, attendees at the queens' reunion challenged indignities they suffered as pageant winners. Reportedly, one year the former queens bonded in their criticism against columnist George Yoshinaga, known for his handicapping of candidates. The women at the reunion reveled in recounting numerous "horror stories" involving the controversial columnist. This exemplified the freedom with which attendees spoke at the queens' reunion. Because it was an all-female event organized by the queens themselves, the reunion promoted what attendees called "sisterhood." Faye Hirata appreciated the event as Nisei Week's only sanctioned space for women's culture. She particularly enjoyed the woman-centered atmosphere, generational bonding between older and younger queens, and celebration of "girl talk." Seemingly without exception, former queens enjoyed uniting with their peers at the queens' reunion. "Even though I have this animosity towards the way Nisei Week treats me," said Jane Nakamura, "I'll probably go to the queens' reunion . . ." for "there is a certain sense of bonding because on some level we've all gone through the same thing."

Did former queens participate in the women's resistance? Certainly, most of them embraced the idea of Nisei Week as a community institution and, unlike the WCC protesters, saw nothing wrong with Japanese American women vying to represent the ethnic community. But their criticism of the festival and behavior at the queens' reunions exposed limits to their acceptance of traditional gender roles. They consistently rejected festival conventions that they believed humiliated or exploited women. Moreover, they planned and attended an event that contradicted their treatment as beauty contestants. Although hardly subversive, the queens' reunion emerged as a counterritual within Nisei Week proper. It was planned by the former queens themselves, while the queen pageant was run by Nisei Week leaders; the former event enabled women to speak and act freely, while the latter circumscribed women's speech and behavior; and most importantly the reunion united women in "sisterhood," while the beauty contest divided them in competition. Despite disagreement about the beauty pageant's value, former queens and JACL feminists like Mei Nakano denounced Nisei Week's reproduction of women's inequality and indignity. The queens generally did not share the feminists' gender ideology or critique of American society, but they did exhibit a local knowledge of women's subordination. Their involvement with Nisei Week did not evidence a "false consciousness" supporting male domination. Rather, it revealed a particular response to Japanese American male authority, a soft variety of women's resistance that, while critical of gender inequality, moved with, not against, Nisei Week orthodoxy.

THE END OF INTEGRATION

While the Nisei Week leaders were wrestling with the long-standing problems of gender within the ethnic community, they also had to contend with the new and pressing issue of race. This centered on the participation of racially mixed women in the festival beauty pageant. For all the years since World War II that Japanese American leaders had touted the ideals of integration, Japanese Americans remained uncomfortable with the ultimate end of integration: miscegenation. This was nowhere more apparent than in the ensuing debates about the racial qualifications for contestants in the Nisei Week beauty contest. Elisa Akemi Cuthbert, the daughter of a white father and Japanese mother, began the controversy in 1974 by becoming the first Nisei Week queen of mixed ancestry. Although Eurasians, commonly known as *hapas,* deriving from the Hawaii term *hapa-haole* or "half-white," had competed in the festival pageant before Cuthbert, she was the first winner, and her victory marked a growing trend in Japanese American beauty pageants.[57] Never one to mince words, columnist George Yoshinaga frowned upon the increase of hapa contestants. In 1976 he complained, "It's getting so that 'pure bred' Japanese American candidates are things of the past. Two years ago we had Elisa Cuthbert as the Nisei Week queen. Up in San Francisco a girl by the name of Anna Przybyiski won the Miss Cherry Blossom crown. In fact, there were five entries in the San Francisco contest with non-Japanese names. . . . Will we have another queen named simply 'Midori Tanaka' in our lifetime?"[58]

According to Yoshinaga, Eurasian contestants were unfairly privileged because "the facial difference of a half Japanese, half non-Japanese [white] is an advantage." He added that while "all the other candidates look 'alike' by their Japanese facial feature, the Junko Hutchins and Anna Przybyiskis and Elisa Cuthberts stand out." Because of this "unfair advantage," Yoshinaga asserted that the rules for judging the queen contest should be changed to penalize hapa candidates, if not to ban them altogether from competition.[59] It is difficult to say how much of the ethnic community supported Yoshinaga's antihapa stance. When interviewed in 1993, the columnist intimated that he had received many letters supporting his position, enabling him to speculate that most Nisei had agreed with him. If he were correct, then this could explain Akiko Posey's surprise when her daughter Hedy Ann became Nisei Week queen in 1980. Because Hedy Ann was only half-Japanese and had a Western surname, her mother warned her that she did not have a chance of winning.[60]

The hapa controversy erupted into a full-blown debate after Janet Barnes claimed the Nisei Week title in 1982. That year apparently four of the nine candidates, including the queen, were Eurasian. In a letter to the *Rafu Shimpo,* Linden Nishinaga voiced his discontent about the increasing number of hapa candidates. "This disproportionate selection and seeming infatuation with the Eurasian looks," he wrote, "not only runs counter to what I consider pride in our Japanese ancestry but also to the very idea of the Nisei Week queen tradition itself." Nishinaga criticized Nisei Week leaders for favoring Western beauty standards. To him, Eurasian features did not make women prettier than Japanese women. "But in order to appreciate the particular Japanese beauty one must look through a different set of glasses and discover the many other special qualities, features and mannerisms one normally wouldn't be looking for in our often superficial commercialized Hollywood glamour-model

Hedy Ann Posey, Nisei Week queen in 1980, became part of the controversy surrounding racially mixed beauty contestants that would transform the language of radical protest. *Courtesy Toyo Miyatake Studios.*

environment." Because hapas constituted a small proportion of southern California Japanese Americans, Nishinaga concluded they were an inappropriate choice for a Nisei Week queen who was "supposed to represent our Nikkei community[,] which is still large, viable and strongly identifiable[;] our beauty representatives should at least be representative." To Nishinaga, the increase in hapa candidates was correlated with Japanese American low self-esteem or, in other words, their sense of ethnic inadequacy to white Americans. He suggested that festival organizers "stop playing games and start becoming truly proud of being just what we really are, Japanese Americans," for "their lack of judgment tends not only to hurt the self-image of the Nikkei, or overseas Japanese, community but also gives the general public a distorted picture of what we are all about."[61]

Nishinaga's letter sparked a heated and protracted exchange about the politics of hapa beauty contestants. Most of the respondents supported Nishinaga's opposition to hapa candidates. One noted that "I had questioned the wisdom and had felt unhappy about the continued choice of a Eurasian to represent a community which is not majority Eurasian."[62] Another respondent echoed the point about hapa contestants' "unfair advantage." "Full-blooded" Japanese women, he remarked, may be unwilling to compete with perceived "superior physical features of those of mixed ancestry." But more disturbing to him was that "younger Japanese in general are beginning to lose their sense of pride and identity with the rich cultural and ethnic qualities of the Japanese."[63]

The antihapa camp's rather sad and pathetic depiction of cultureless Japanese Americans was lifted straight out of the Asian American movement. Recall that Amy Uyematsu's yellow power manifesto more than a decade earlier had derided Japanese Americans for rejecting their ethnic heritage by wanting to look and be like whites. In similar fashion, the 1980s sentiment against hapa beauty contestants rehashed the student radicals' charge that the Nisei Week beauty contest epitomized the ethnic community's internalization of racist beauty standards. But there was a difference; the antihapa campaign became a central issue within the ethnic community, whereas the earlier criticisms of movement activists was usually ignored by the larger community. The strong demand for racial purity, in this sense, testified to the popularization of the movement's radical cosmopolitanism.

Curiously, the defense of hapa beauty queens also drew upon the language of anti-integrationism and ethnic pride. Eurasians, it was argued, could celebrate Japanese American ethnicity and community as much as anyone. "Who is Mr. Nishinaga to say," wrote one respondent, "that because my parents were not both Japanese I should be less proud of being Japanese American than he is, or that I am less a representative of the Nikkei [Japanese living outside Japan] population than he is?"[64] Cindy Miller insisted that being Japanese American is a "feeling of pride of your heritage and culture," and so if a Nisei Week queen is "half Caucasian, I feel that she shows her strength, love and pride of the Japanese culture just as much as a full-blooded Japanese who [has] not realized the struggles and meaning of what Japan is."[65] Former Nisei Week queen Hedy Ann Posey questioned why she had to fight for acceptance as a Japanese American. "Who's to say that I'm not as 'Japanese' as any other Nisei, Sansei, or Yonsei?" she asked. "What is the definition of a Japanese American anyway? I know a lot of full-blooded Japanese Americans who know a lot less about their heritage than some of my Eurasian friends." At the most poignant moment in the debate, Posey confessed that it "breaks my heart to think that the very people that I have been so proud to represent aren't proud that I'm representing them."[66]

The supporters of hapa beauty contestants also emphasized themes of victimization that had punctuated Asian American movement writings.

Cindy Miller addressed the stigmas and discrimination Eurasians faced in Japan and the United States. "Nishinaga," she interjected, "makes it sound as though Eurasians are impure and are not worthy of representing the Japanese community." Miller suggested that Nishinaga not only consider the self-image of the Japanese American community, but that of "some Eurasian children who are not accepted as [w]hite or Japanese."[67] Hedy Ann Posey claimed that these stigmas made it more difficult for hapa candidates to become Nisei Week queen. "Being half and half," she revealed, "I knew I would have a hard time because it generally means that I don't belong to any group."[68] In her retort to Nishinaga, Posey said that within the ethnic community she sometimes feels "like a drop of oil in a glass of water." Perhaps the most interesting defense of hapa candidates evoked the memory of the wartime internment, which was particularly timely given that, in the early 1980s, the movement to make the government redress this injustice was in full swing. Eurasians should be considered fully Japanese American, one respondent contended, because they too were interned during World War II and thus shared the predicament of anti-Japanese racism.[69]

In addition to opposing Nisei Week's beauty pageant on gender grounds, the WCC also criticized its use of "racial purity tests." This charge referred to a rule, in existence since at least 1981, stipulating that eligibility required at least one "full-blooded" Japanese parent.[70] JACLer Raymond Okamura maintained that pageants such as Nisei Week designed ancestral prerequisites to "keep out the increasing number of biracial and multiracial women who were entering and winning the contests. Entries are strictly limited to women possessing the required percentage of Japanese ancestry; and no amount of superior qualifications such as fluency and literacy in Japanese, understanding of Japanese culture, proficiency in Japanese art, knowledge of Japanese American history, service to the Japanese American community, etc., can be used to overcome the pedigree requirement."[71] Mei Nakano charged that barring a candidate on the basis of racial purity violated her civil rights. Okamura concurred that it was ironic for JACL to support this kind of ethnic segregation. "As a civil rights organization, dedicated to the principle of equal opportunities for all regardless of race or ancestry," he argued, "the JACL cannot with good conscience support an activity which discriminates on basis of ancestry." Okamura favored an open competition based on cultural consciousness, not genetic constitution.[72]

Debate over the eligibility of beauty contestants renegotiated ethnic group boundaries. Supporters of hapa candidates sought to get beyond Nisei society's ambivalence about miscegenation. Their arguments were aimed at supplanting a group construction based on phenotype parentage and heredity with one based on identity, culture, and interest. But Nisei Week leaders did not honor the WCC's call to abandon queen candidates' ancestral prerequisites. Nor did they follow the other extreme of restricting participation to only full-blooded candidates. Festival officials took a middle road by making the requirement 50 percent Japanese parentage, which meant one "full-blooded" parent (and not two hapa parents). Interestingly, the increasing number of mixed-Asian contestants (for example, half-Japanese and half-Chinese) was not controversial. Despite her mixed Korean-Japanese parentage, Jennifer Kusumoto-Ahn reigned as the 1986 Nisei Week queen with none of the criticism Eurasian queens had evoked. Another racial combination that was ignored was Afroasian. That there has never been a half-black contestant in the Nisei Week contest suggests that Japanese Americans have continued to subscribe to a notion of racial hierarchy in which whites and Asians were clearly above African Americans.

The beauty-pageant controversy revealed that Nisei Week organizers had not come to terms with interracial relationships. Unlike national JACLers, southern California Nisei leaders reconstituted forms and ideologies of ethnic cohesion. As argued in chapter 4, Nisei society combined the ideal of integration with the practice of self-segregation. Nisei Week officials at best marginalized interracial couples and their children. Thus Nisei Week regulated both hapa contestants and the boundaries of Japanese American ethnicity. Eurasians were allowed to participate in the queen pageant and therefore were included in the festival's official ethnic definition but not without risking community disapproval, jealousy, and stigmatization. Beauty contest regulations reflected a guarded expansion of group parameters.

The Eurasian controversy also exposed an expanded Nisei conception of American beauty. Neither the hapa candidates' supporters nor detractors idealized Western standards of beauty. In fact, both sides had denounced Nisei Week for allegedly denigrating Japanese female characteristics. Curiously, the feminist Mei Nakano and the WCC shared this position with the conservative columnist George Yoshinaga. Since the 1960s Yoshinaga repeatedly criticized, to little avail, the queen contest for relying on white judges and rewarding Western features. Yet by the 1970s, the push for ethnic standards gained momentum. Since that time, the beauty pageant had featured just as many—if not more—Asian judges as white ones. Questions asked of queen candidates at the coronation ball often centered on themes of ethnic identity and service to the Japanese American community. And there was an overwhelming increase in Asian American performers and emcees at the balls. The ethnic influence in the queen contest grew so much that officials had to disallow contestants' speeches in Japanese because such speeches allegedly gave unfair advantage to bilingual contestants.

The centrality of ethnic identity and pride in the Nisei Week beauty contest would have been a familiar theme to Asian American movement activists, who had good reason to take credit for much of the resurgence of ethnicity among Japanese Americans in the 1970s and 1980s. In assessing the larger significance of movement activism, Candice Ota maintained that the "development of a new Asian American identity had paved the way into the '80s with a stronger and more focused community." [73] Ota herself mirrored this connection between student radicalism and the larger ethnic community. In the early 1970s, she was part of the antiwar protest that had disrupted the Nisei Week parade, and by 1990, she had become part of the festival leadership, responsible for putting together the festival's souvenir booklet and making sure that the "radical awakening" of her generation was remembered as an integral part of the Japanese American experience. This was not always an easy task as the movement in the late 1970s had lost its cohesiveness, splintering into a number of directions and, in many ways, reaching dead ends. Some say that the movement lost its urgency after American troops were pulled out of Vietnam; others maintain, more grimly, that student radicalism was snuffed out by the FBI's offensive against radical leaders and organizations. Still others blame the activists for abandoning their once-lofty ideals in search of money and power in the Reagan-Bush years. There seem to be grains of truth to each of these perspectives, but what they each overlook is the possibility that the Asian American movement suffered from its own success at transforming the identity of Japanese Americans.

In the end, the more acceptable the Asian American movement became in the ethnic community, the more blurred became the line between student radicalism and ethnic orthodoxy. Historian John Higham described this blending of alternative and mainstream perspectives by commenting on the larger significance of the ethnic revival throughout the United States. He argued that in the early 1970s the alternative vision of American society as maintaining its ethnic pluralism had supplanted the mainstream notion of a uniform culture and national identity: "Patriotism had gone out of fashion; the melting pot was a subject of mockery."[74] In short, he observed that pluralism, which had been a central tenet of the Asian American movement, had supplanted integration as the new orthodoxy of ethnicity. For Japanese Americans, this meant adopting the rhetoric of the student radicalism, while scaling back and softening its overtly political message. In this way, Japanese American youth rebelled through the creation of a distinct and extralegal car culture rather than through antiwar protests that directly challenged American policy and institutions. In addition, reformers changed the Nisei Week beauty pageant into a "competitive asset" for women rather than dismissing it entirely as a sexist tool. And in the end, the popular debate about hapa beauty contestants, in which both sides stood in favor of ethnic pride and against racial victimization, revealed the ultimate triumph of the new pluralist orthodoxy.

The hapa controversy smoldered throughout the 1980s. In 1983, columnist Yoshinaga delighted that all queen candidates had Japanese surnames and that the contest was starting to be reclaimed by "pure" Japanese Americans, but three years later he again railed against the hegemony of Western standards at Nisei Week.[75] In that same year, the writings of another columnist revealed that the hapa issue was more than just a question of American race relations. Takeshi Nakayama insisted that the beauty contest be reserved for "pure-blooded" candidates because they best symbolized the blood ties between Japanese Americans and the people of Japan. This trans-Pacific alliance, he maintained, was a critical defense against the "Japan-bashing racists" who were spurred on by rising U.S.-Japan tensions.[76] In the 1980s, as Japan rapidly challenged America's global economic hegemony, such internationalist appeals would return Nisei Week to its original discourse about bridging the United States and Japan.

SIX

Nationalism and Internationalism

New Left, Ethnic Rights, and Shopping Centers

By 1974, the name "Nisei Week festival" was coming under attack. Critics of Nisei Week claimed that it discouraged the participation of Sansei and succeeding generations, but they were even more concerned about its exclusion of groups beyond the ethnic community. Columnist George Yoshinaga, who launched an editorial campaign to preserve the name "Nisei Week festival," explained that the effort to broaden the celebration's title to "Japanese festival" marked a showdown between two parties: those seeking to maintain Little Tokyo's immigrant heritage and those catering to the foreign investors driving the enclave's dramatic redevelopment. Although the columnist applauded the building of new hotels and shopping centers by Japanese corporations, he drew the line at Nisei Week. "We can't control the big money from Japan," he allowed, "but let's not lose our identity. At least, let's not help them take our identity away."[1]

The naming controversy revealed the direct relationship between urban renewal and the formation of Japanese American ethnicity in the 1970s and 1980s. Beginning in the early 1960s, Little Tokyo leaders had sought to address the enclave's alarming decline in business and blighted physical and social environment. Their plans to redevelop the historic area attracted interest from Japanese firms seeking to expand into the American market and from the city of Los Angeles, which sought to capitalize on this growing trade from Japan. Nisei Week, in turn, welcomed foreign investment by moving away from integration toward a pluralist identity bridging the United States with Japan. Yet by the mid-1970s, the construction of shopping centers catering especially to Japanese-speaking clientele provoked a native backlash from an unlikely collection of ethnic leaders, student radicals, and self-styled conservatives like George Yoshinaga, who came together under the banner of self-determination for racial minorities. Together they opposed outside plans for redevelopment while proposing a vision based on the preservation of Japanese American culture and history. Here was perhaps the most telling instance in which student radicalism was transformed into the pluralist orthodoxy of ethnic rights.

THE "MIRACLE" ON FIRST STREET

In May 1963 Reverend Howard Toriumi traveled the short distance to Little Tokyo from Los Angeles City Hall, where he inquired about purchasing a city-owned lot adjacent to his church. Toriumi was told that his plan to expand Union church might be facilitated if Little Tokyo had a representative body with which the city could negotiate. Wasting no time, Toriumi organized a meeting to discuss community revitalization to which he invited Japanese American leaders, as well as Little Tokyo businesspersons, property owners, and residents. Within two months this group formed the Little Tokyo Redevelopment Association (LTRA), which called upon the city to study the area's land use. LTRA's reported goal was to "build a more beautiful and prosperous Japantown as a cultural and business center of Japanese Americans in southern California."[2] Redevelopment organizer Kango Kunitsugu characterized this goal as a "return to the halcyon days of the 1920s and 1930s, but in a slightly different form." That prewar period, he explained, was the "golden age of Little Tokyo" when the enclave "had large department stores, hotels, bath houses, drug stores, restaurants and other amenities of a complete community. The large farming populations made their weekly trip to Little Tokyo to do their shopping . . . [along with] those living in the 'suburbs' like West Los Angeles, Boyle Heights, Uptown, and Southwest Los Angeles."[3] Despite its nostalgic ambitions, the original redevelopment plan, according to Little Tokyo historian Ichiro Mike Murase, was actually quite "modest." It rested upon widening an alley into a "full-fledged street," as well as planting trees and modernizing streetlights.[4]

If Murase was correct, then LTRA's proposals did not begin to address Little Tokyo's urban problems. The Japanese quarter had never been a model community. Even during its so-called heyday in the 1930s, Little Tokyo possessed the characteristics of an inner-city ghetto. Historian John Modell found that in 1940, the district remained one of the poorest sections in Los Angeles, with about 20 percent of its Japanese population residing in substandard housing.[5] Over the next three decades, Little Tokyo's structural dilapidation worsened while its residential population dwindled. A late 1960s study identified eight of ten enclave buildings as, at best, "structurally substandard." Further examination documented the decline in the number of Japanese American residents from more than seven thousand in 1940 to fewer than four hundred in 1969.

Little Tokyo decay was bad enough, but hungry land predators worsened the situation and hastened redevelopment timing. If they underestimated the community's blight, Japanese American leaders certainly did not discount the city's appetite for Japantown property. Los Angeles officials taught southern California Japanese Americans a hard lesson in 1947 when they invoked the right of "eminent domain" to replace a quarter of Little Tokyo with a police headquarters.[6] Twenty years later the community feared losing even more property to the city. Indeed, a common argument for redevelopment in the 1960s held that if Japantown structures remained substandard, "the city will eventually condemn the area[,] and in all probability . . . Little Tokyo will never be the same again."[7] Such concern was not unwarranted, for encroachment into the Japanese district reflected the rapid expansion of the Los Angeles civic center, which by the late 1960s had become the largest complex of government buildings outside the nation's capital. A redevelopment study flagged the area's "inevitable" growth as a continuing threat to Little Tokyo. The report not only noted that expansion potentially generated thousands of customers for nearby Japanese businesses but it also warned that "Little Tokyo's very existence may be threatened by the Civic Center's insatiable demand for land."[8] Redevelopment leader George Umezawa articulated community mistrust of this city expansion. He gave two reasons for suspicion: first, the city's appropriation of Little Tokyo land in the 1940s, and, second, its recent campaigns to widen Japantown's main thoroughfare. Reconstructing First Street, Umezawa reported, would remove 68 Japanese businesses and 150 residents.[9] Thus from the community's perspective, one benefit of redevelopment was that it might strengthen Little Tokyo's infrastructure so it could better resist external land grabbing.

Indeed, despite Little Tokyo's dilapidation, the future of the community was a matter of great concern. Many Japanese Americans felt emotionally tied to the historic community. Kango Kunitsugu listed keeping a Japanese presence in Little Tokyo as one of the redevelopment campaign's primary goals. If nothing were done to save the area, he stated, "the place will just collapse and everybody will go." [10] Kunitsugu appreciated redevelopment as a means for keeping Japanese cultural groups downtown, thus ensuring the continuation of Little Tokyo's community and social events. Redevelopment plans balanced an appreciation for the area's historic and artistic significance with pragmatic concern for its economic well-being. While increasing inner-city blight and flight may have tarnished Little Tokyo's image, they did not ruin its economy. The area remained a functioning Japanese business community. Indeed, as Kunitsugu suggested, Little Tokyo was "more than meets the eye." [11] A 1969 survey showed that the area contained 433 businesses, mostly commercial establishments including 34 medical, 13 accounting, 10 law, 11 insurance, 32 retail, 30 auto service/parking, 27 restaurants, 27 cultural activities, 17 barber/beauty shops, 16 bars, and 14 news/printing services. The survey estimated that Little Tokyo possessed a workforce of 1,761 strong. [12] Another study found that this business district maintained a healthy attraction to outlying Japanese American communities. A survey of fifteen hundred Japanese American households in southern California reported that half of the ethnic population visited Little Tokyo two or more times a month and that almost all the other half went once a month or less to the district. Only 4 percent of those questioned had never visited the historic community. The study added that Little Tokyo also attracted a significant influx of out-of-town Japanese Americans, who often ventured downtown with southland Japanese American hosts, friends, and relatives. Researchers projected that for at least the next five years Japanese Americans would remain an important market for Little Tokyo. The study further ascertained strong Japanese American support for redevelopment. Most desired were an improved commercial and physical atmosphere, increased parking, a community center, and a hotel. A significant number of Japanese Americans even considered themselves potential Little Tokyo residents, provided that new housing facilities were built. [13]

The community's redevelopment interest exhibited its softening commitment to integration. Kango Kunitsugu directly addressed Nisei concerns about a self-segregated Little Tokyo. "Protests of creating another 'ghetto' may be forthcoming," he predicted, "but in this day and age, integration for the sake of integration appears to be not everybody's bag." To encourage Japanese Americans to consider returning to live in Little

Tokyo, Kunitsugu assured that "there is nothing wrong with people wanting to live among their own people. Whether one does or does not live among members of their own race is no longer important. You live where you want to live and let it go at that." [14] Plans to recenter Little Tokyo as an ethnic community not only romanticized the "halcyon days" of the immigrant enclave but also reinvigorated the ideal of Japanese American self-segregation. In this way, redevelopment rejected the fantasy of complete and irreversible integration into white America.

As an ethnic island, Little Tokyo also appealed to newcomers from Japan. After World War II, the enclave continued to serve as a way station, easing the transition for Japanese immigrants and visitors. From 1924 to 1952, restrictionist American laws had all but excluded Japanese American immigration, but in 1952 Congress had ended race-based immigration exclusion by accepting a small quota of migrants from Japan. A few hundred or so Japanese newcomers were joined by thousands of compatriots entering the country as wives of U.S. servicemen. War brides initially swelled the ranks of *shin-Issei*, translated literally as "new Japanese immigrants." But as their numbers declined, they were replaced by other compatriots willing to move overseas. From 1952 to 1980, more than 135,000 Japanese immigrants entered the United States, an average of about 4,500 each year. The total of postwar immigration amounted to a little more than half the number of the Issei who had entered the United States from 1900 to 1924, the peak years of Japanese immigration. By 1980, shin-Issei constituted roughly 22 percent of Japanese Americans in the Los Angeles area (approximately 26,000 out of a population of 117,190). Like the original Issei, many of the new immigrants relied on Little Tokyo's Japanese-speaking businesses for employment and cultural sustenance. [15]

Despite its community support and its fast start in the early 1960s, the redevelopment campaign foundered for want of funds and experience. If not for the introduction of outside players, redevelopment would probably have been impossible. The first to express interest in Little Tokyo redevelopment was the city of Los Angeles. Its plans for a civic center expansion into Japantown were curbed by the opportunities generated by increasing U.S.-Japan trade. In 1968, Los Angeles had received a record high number of imports from Japan, so many that Japanese goods made up more than 20 percent of the city's international trade. [16] Partly on the basis of these figures, city planners observed that Los Angeles–area trade with Japan had increased at a rate greater than any other and that this trade would continue to contribute substantially to the city's business visitors.[17] Indeed, by the late 1960s, the growing strength of Japan's economy had become apparent in the United States. The smaller nation's power could be gauged not only by commercial but also by human exports. From 1975 to 1990, Japan posted spectacular growth in its citizens' overseas travel. Japan sent to the United States a staggering number of so-called "nonimmigrants," an Immigration and Naturalization Service category identifying foreigners entering the country on a temporary basis for a number of reasons, including schooling, travel, business, and diplomacy. Tourists made up the majority of nonimmigrants from Japan. Since the 1960s, Japanese tourism rose so sharply that in 1982 Japan sent more visitors to the United States than any other nation. In that year more than 1.2 million Japanese tourists entered the country. Eight years later the number of tourists from Japan had nearly doubled that of the United Kingdom, the second largest source of U.S. tourism. Throughout the 1980s, only the U.K. sent more business visitors to the United States than Japan. Students represented the third largest category of Japanese nonimmigrants to the United States. In 1982 and again in 1990, Japanese students were the most numerous of all foreigners studying at American schools.[18]

The rise of Japan's economy and U.S.-Japan trade convinced Los Angeles officials to support Little Tokyo redevelopment. To city planners, redevelopment in Little Tokyo was perfectly suited to meet the growing needs of Los Angeles trade with Japan. The rapid influx of Japanese tourists, businesspersons, and students to southern California, they contended, could provide a critical market for Little Tokyo that could complement its stable Japanese American clientele. In other words, the city projected a reinvigorated Japantown that would attract Japanese nationals seeking familiar foods, services, or products. It became an official player in Little Tokyo redevelopment in early 1969 when the Los Angeles city council authorized the application for federal funds to restore Little Tokyo. A month later the U.S. Department of Housing and Urban Development approved the city's request and appropriated monies for planning purposes. The Los Angeles mayor delegated authority for the Little Tokyo project to a committee representing a cross section of Japanese Americans and the Community Redevelopment Agency (CRA), a quasi-civic body responsible for much of the city's urban renewal. In May 1969, the community committee was established, and the CRA opened an office in Japantown. Thus the city that had once taken away a key tract of Little Tokyo was now poised to give land back to the Japanese enclave. City leadership breathed new life into the community's dormant redevelopment campaign.[19]

Support from Los Angeles officials spurred the initiation of a comprehensive program of Little Tokyo renewal, far exceeding the original redevelopment conception. More than expanding an alley and planting trees, the new blueprints envisaged a radical restructuring of Little Tokyo's physical landscape and community function. The participation of outside players enabled ethnic leaders to look beyond improving Japantown's immediate business climate and thus renewed ambitions to recenter Japanese Americans around the downtown enclave. After all, it was redevelopment that brought to fruition the old prewar Nisei dream of a community center. Redevelopment leaders turned the dream into reality by planning the construction of the Japanese American Cultural and Community Center (JACCC). Such a place, the leaders argued, would prove essential to bringing Japanese Americans back to Little Tokyo. In addition to the community center project, redevelopment organizers believed that new, affordable housing would repopulate the area with more desirable Japanese American residents. The construction of a federally subsidized high-rise apartment complex targeted older Japanese Americans, some of whom were eager to live in the old Japanese enclave, and thus rejuvenated Little Tokyo's marginal residential community.

The introduction of new players also introduced a new redevelopment agenda. Two goals marked the opening stages of Little Tokyo construction: one, as discussed, was to attract southern California Japanese Americans to the old enclave; the other was to facilitate overseas Japanese business in Los Angeles. The CRA broadened Little Tokyo revitalization to buttress the city's hopes of boosting U.S.-Japan trade. Initially this goal centered on erecting a first-class luxury hotel catering to Japanese business travelers. A CRA report identified a great demand for "transient commercial facilities to serve the Japanese business market."[20] Its survey of 187 Little Tokyo businesses suggested that the idea of building a "modern" hotel received strong community support. CRA plans also received a warm welcome from Japanese American leaders, who agreed that Japantown fortunes were linked integrally with the strength of U.S.-Japan trade.

But it soon became apparent that outside economic interests were not always in line with the ethnic concerns. The two redevelopment goals—rebuilding the community and promoting trade—coexisted in projects such as the Japanese American Cultural and Community Center. Although the idea for JACCC had, as mentioned, originated within the Japanese American community, overseas corporations contributed substantially to its construction. Reported to be the largest American ethnic institution of its kind, the center would not have been possible without Japanese money. If Japanese Americans saw JACCC as a place to showcase the ethnic community, Japanese corporations viewed it as a site for negotiations of U.S.-Japan cultural and commercial trade. A representative from Kajima International, a major foreign investor in Little Tokyo redevelopment, revealed the corporation's vision for the proposed JACCC. "We think in terms of propagating, introducing what Japan is all about," he stated. "We don't think about this cultural center in narrow perspectives. We are talking about the wide spectrum of things that truly represent Japan. . . . *Little Tokyo Cultural Center is not going to be one in which Japanese American history is portrayed*" (emphasis added).[21] Indeed, Japanese corporations often neglected the area's humble immigrant origins, and their drive for profit clashed with community concerns. The creation of an upscale shopping mall further evidenced a split between the redevelopment interests of Japanese Americans and foreign investors. Matsuzakaya, an exclusive Japanese department store, anchored the new Little Tokyo mall. The new store's targeted clientele, Matsuzakaya executive Katsuhiko Kobayashi claimed, would be overseas Japanese followed by what he called "non-Oriental Americans." Kobayashi expected that despite the fact that parts of Little Tokyo remained a "dirty slum," Matsuzakaya and redevelopment in general would attract high-class shoppers from places like Rodeo Drive in Beverly Hills to the downtown enclave. According to him, the store considered Japanese and other Asian Americans of tertiary concern, at best.[22]

Nisei Week leaders also hoped to attract overseas Japanese to its annual festivities. Since the late 1950s, the celebration had commingled trade and ethnic concerns. Redevelopment, however, heightened the event's Japanese corporate influence. Nisei Week rewarded foreign businesspersons for improving U.S.-Japan trade. Japanese industrialist Konosuke Matsushita returned as a Nisei Week honoree in 1976, America's bicentennial year. The chair of the committee that selected Matsushita likened his achievements of rebuilding Japan's war-torn economy with the Issei's pioneering spirit that built Japanese American communities. Nisei Week leader Mitsuhiko Shimizu asserted that "the Bicentennial is a time for us to reflect on the spirit of America's founders—the same spirit that impelled Issei pioneers to seek their future in a new land, the same spirit or 'konjo' which Mr. Matsushita embodies, that enabled Japan to make such an amazing recovery from the ashes of World War II." [23] Not coincidentally, some Nisei Week honorees were also redevelopment benefactors. For example, Japanese newspaper publisher Shintaro Fukushima helped raise over four million dollars for JACCC construction and subsequently served as Nisei Week's honorary grand marshal in 1984. [24] Further, Japanese corporate influence became more noticeable in the festival parade and beauty pageant. By the 1970s, foreign corporations sponsored nearly all the parade floats and provided the bulk of prizes awarded to the Nisei Week queen. In 1977, the queen's "treasure chest" included gifts from such Japanese firms as Matsushita Electric, Japan Airlines, Sumitomo Bank, California First Bank (formerly Bank of Tokyo), Tokai Bank, Mitsubishi, and Anshindo Jewelers. [25]

Japanese corporations also proved an increasing source of Nisei Week funding. Until the late 1970s, monies had been generated primarily within the Japanese American community. As the festival's general chairman in 1969, Koshiro Torii hoped to raise funds for the event from outside Little Tokyo. A press release, issued by the leading organization for Little Tokyo businesses, heralded that "[t]he new chairman's ambition is to introduce Nisei Week Festival to powerful Japanese professional groups who were always [bystanders] but never have become participants of the community festivity." [26] Torii's fund-raising tactics became legendary among Nisei Week leaders. He is reported to have journeyed to the southern California offices of leading Japanese corporations accompanied by Nisei Week queen candidates. In meeting with foreign businessmen, Torii would mention the contributions made by other Japanese firms. The only way corporate leaders could save face in front of Torii and the queen candidates would be to donate to Nisei Week. Although such maneuvering increased overall support from Japanese firms, it was not until the late 1970s that these businesses composed the leading source of Nisei Week funds. In 1977, contributions from Japanese businesses equaled more than half the festival's revenues, twice as much as the sum total contributed by Japanese American merchants. [27] From then to at least the mid-1990s, foreign firms remained the festival's leading benefactors, as the event's budget climbed well into six figures. [28]

Such contributions were bound to shape Nisei Week. Japanese corporations influenced the selection of the Nisei Week queen and, symbolically, the aesthetic standard for Japanese American women. Because they provided most of the queen's awards, foreign businessmen procured a standing seat as beauty contest judges. Some of the recent queens and those close to the beauty pageant viewed the businessmen as having a significant impact on the contest. It has been argued that Japanese money redirected the pageant toward a bicultural beauty standard that appreciates traditional Japanese charms and Japanese language skills, as well as more quintessentially American qualities. That Nisei Week queens were presented, and presented themselves, more and more as authorities of Japanese culture, style, and traditions became increasingly obvious during the coronation ball. Gone were the days when a queen candidate boldly asserted ignorance of her ancestral homeland and indifference to identifying with it. Moreover, gone were the days when the festival featured primarily American cultural forms and activities, such as the Nisei talent revue. Since the 1960s the number of exhibits showcasing flower arrangement, calligraphy, bonsai, water painting, martial arts, cooking, dolls, plants, and other Japanese cultural expression had expanded significantly. Finally, in the early 1990s, the Nisei Week booklet's inclusion of topics related to overseas Japanese nationals and of Japanese translations of articles written in English further evidenced the festival's "Japanization."

The wave of foreign investment associated with Little Tokyo redevelopment began to erode the indigenous base of Japanese American ethnicity. Japan's postwar resurgence as an American trading partner made possible the re-creation of a bicultural identity linking Japanese Americans' birth nation and their ancestral homeland. During this age of redevelopment, the reconstruction of a bridge mentality, an ethnicity predicated on favorable U.S.-Japan relations, was particularly visible. As in the 1930s, biculturalism stressed the liaison benefits of hyphenated ethnicity. The common rationale for redevelopment heralded Japanese Americans as go-betweens facilitating the harmonious flow of international commerce. Nisei Week's prewar biculturalism not only spoke to opportunities and responsibilities in the so-called Pacific Era, but it also addressed the enclave's growing Issei-Nisei rift. The bridge mentality, as it was originally articulated during Nisei Week, sought first to solidify ethnic generations and second to mollify concerns about international trade. Prewar festival organizers focused on the ethnic enclave; they hoped that Nisei Week would benefit immigrant enterprise and secure the future of the ethnic community. But during the era of redevelopment, Nisei Week leaders reversed these bicultural priorities: Japanese American hybridity first addressed issues of international trade and second attended to community issues. Lucrative redevelopment politics transformed Little Tokyo into a superhighway speeding corporate capital back and forth across the Pacific. The bridge of ethnicity initially designed to unite Japanese Americans was transformed into a wedge that increased divisions within Japantown. Foreign investors and the ethnic community had maintained conflicted notions of Japanese American identity. The redevelopment of Little Tokyo and the reestablishment of a thriving economic base for ethnic solidarity did not signify a concomitant return to prewar ethnicity. On the contrary, Nisei Week's renewed biculturalism exhibited declining Japanese American authority to shape their historic community and to define their ethnic identity. Ironically, redevelopment often marginalized rather than centralized southern California Nisei society.

PROFIT MARGINS

Ideally, redevelopment's two goals of stimulating U.S.-Japan trade and serving the ethnic community complemented each other. At first, all parties—Japanese Americans, Los Angeles officials, and foreign investors —were convinced that a buoyant Little Tokyo economy would satisfy its ambitions, and therefore each approved CRA plans to renew the downtown enclave. Yet inevitably redevelopment rhetoric and blueprints were confronted by the hard facts of urban renewal. Local businesses were relocated or closed; residents were evicted; commercial leases inflated; and workers lost jobs. The CRA made way for an upscale Little Tokyo by clearing out the area's blight, decay, and working-class immigrant roots. Businesses, residents, and employees once centered in the heart of Little Tokyo found themselves pushed to the community's margins, castaways in the quest for Pacific Rim profit. Redevelopment threatened not only Japantown's weak but also its leaders. Declining Japanese American authority over the renewal process upset many who believed that the CRA was sacrificing ethnic community to international commerce. The struggle to control Nisei Week epitomized the community's mixed reaction to redevelopment. While some festival leaders welcomed outside influence, at the same time others fought to maintain the celebration's community roots. Japanese corporations enjoyed increasing power to shape Nisei Week and Little Tokyo, but those marginal to Pacific Rim profit resisted the ethnic community's "Japanization."

George Yoshinaga's vernacular press column became a stronghold against Little Tokyo foreign authority. A community newspaperman since the early 1950s, Yoshinaga was intimately acquainted with Japantown politics and considered himself a voice for those Nisei raised before World War II. His background followed a familiar second-generation pattern. Born a son of sharecroppers in Redwood City, Yoshinaga grew up in nearby northern California farming communities. He joined the U.S. Army while imprisoned in a WRA internment camp. After his tour of duty, Yoshinaga returned to Los Angeles (where he had lived for a short while before the war) and "hung out" in Little Tokyo with other *yogore* or what he called "shiftless young men." The ex-GI then studied at the University of Southern California but left college to take a job in the Japanese American press. Yoshinaga worked for almost forty years at various community newspapers, spending most of his time as the *Kashu Mainichi*'s English-language editor. Like many other older and middle-aged Nisei, the columnist remained tied to Japanese American communities and institutions throughout his life. More importantly, he maintained a steadfast commitment to countering anti-Japanese prejudice by proving that the Nisei were legitimate and trustworthy Americans. It was this commitment, in fact, that generated his mistrust of foreign investment in Little Tokyo. Yoshinaga opposed redevelopment because he believed it jeopardized the image of Nisei as all-American. A self-professed conservative, his antagonism to redevelopment spoke more of restoring the glory of the Nisei than to opposing social inequities of urban renewal.[29] Yoshinaga, perhaps like most Nisei, resisted redevelopment's challenge to the Little Tokyo status quo.

To this end, the columnist tirelessly denounced the transformation of Nisei Week. His criticism of changing the celebration's name from "Nisei Week" to "Japanese Festival" established the tone for all his redevelopment commentary. From the mid-1970s on, Yoshinaga pinpointed the close relationship between the festival and redevelopment. The columnist predicted that "as more and more Japanese nationals move in to Little Tokyo with the redevelopment project, it [Nisei Week] will become more and more a showcase for these people rather than for the Nisei."[30] In 1974, he observed a dearth of Japanese American influence throughout the celebration. "No longer are there street dances for young folks," he lamented. "In its place we talk about the culture of Japan and have all sorts of exotic exhibits from Japan. All these things are fine but I think there should be more added to the program where the youngsters can participate" (*Kashu Mainichi*, August 26, 1974). That same year, Yoshinaga reported that Japanese firms had donated all the prizes to the Nisei Week queen. The columnist viewed this and beauty contest judging by Japanese businessmen as signs of Nisei Week's foreign "take over" (ibid., August 19, 1974). When a foreign company published the Nisei Week booklet, Yoshinaga criticized festival chair George Saiki, reportedly an executive with a Japanese bank. "Let's give Nisei Week back to the people," the columnist wrote (ibid., August 19, 1976). "Isn't it [Nisei Week] held to recognize the fact that we are Americans of Japanese ancestry and [N]isei [W]eek makes us think about our heritage," he later mused rhetorically (ibid., July 20, 1982). Redevelopment proceeded to bear out Yoshinaga's projections for Nisei Week; as Little Tokyo attracted more and more foreign businesses, the festival became less and less connected to Japanese American sensibilities. "If we don't watch out (perhaps it's too late already)," the columnist warned, "there will be nary a Nisei businessman left in Little Tokyo. It will become an all-Japan operation" (ibid., July 7, 1981).

Yoshinaga's contempt for Little Tokyo's foreign corporations went beyond politics and economics. Not only did he criticize Japanese firms for "taking over" Nisei Week, but he also chided them for their token financial commitment to the festival and to Japanese Americans in general. What irked him was the firms' willingness to spend millions for a Super Bowl television commercial but to then donate only ten thousand dollars for Nisei Week. This, the columnist surmised, was because the foreign businessmen played down ethnic ties to Japanese Americans in favor of appearing more mainstream American. In short, he chastised the Japanese companies for forgetting their roots in Little Tokyo and the critical support they had received from Japanese Americans (ibid., July 11, 1984). Yoshinaga implicitly launched the same criticism against the Nisei Week leaders he thought had led the festival astray from its original—and still necessary—intention. He recalled that Nisei Week originally was "a public relations vehicle to sell our position to the [American] community at large, because there was a time when we felt we were not Japanese and we wanted people to recognize . . . that we were Americans." The festival's increasing attention to Japanese culture, Yoshinaga maintained, moved it away from the community's best interests and toward those of foreign businesses. "We are not Japanese," he declared. "That's not my culture. I'm American." [31]

Yoshinaga proved equally critical of newer—as opposed to older—Japanese corporations in United States. His hostility to recently arrived Japanese firms was apparent in a controversy over renaming a Little Tokyo street. In 1986 the community supported changing Weller Street to Onizuka Street. The latter name was intended as a posthumous tribute to astronaut Ellison Onizuka, the first Japanese American to fly in space. Foreign merchants on Weller Street rejected the new name, supposedly because it would require costly changes in advertising.[32] Yoshinaga, however, was unsympathetic to their financial concerns. "It's time these merchants realize and other people from Japan realize," he protested, "that it were [sic] men like Onizuka and members of the 442d Regimental Combat Team who gave their lives for this glorious country of ours, [and] that hastened the acceptance of Japanese Americans back into the mainstream of American life." Yoshinaga turned the controversy into a showdown between the foreign firms and the Japanese American community. "If these merchants have their way and defeat the plan to rename Weller Street in honor of Onizuka," he maintained, "the rest of us in the Los Angeles Japanese American community should hang our heads in shame. Many of us have been complaining both silently and vocally about the infiltration of Japanese-owned businesses in Little Tokyo, which have literally taken control of our town."[33] Undergirding Yoshinaga's fear of foreign invasion was a refined sense of class conflict. He considered many of the Weller Street merchants to be consumer snobs. When Japanese Americans shop at "one of these stores," he claimed, "they are always ignored because these merchants have a very low opinion of the Japanese Americans." According to Yoshinaga, they catered mostly to Japanese tourists, who were believed to have more money and to be more avid consumers.[34] In the end, he blamed foreign Japanese for erecting a wall between themselves and Japanese Americans.[35]

Mistrust against foreign businesses in Little Tokyo was not limited to one outspoken Nisei. A number of Japanese Americans wrote in support of Yoshinaga's pro-Onizuka Street campaign. One person suggested a boycott and lawsuit against the Weller Street merchants for refusing the name change. The letter distinguished between Japanese Americans and Japanese nationals: "We Nisei look like the Japanese but we are very different in our thinking."[36] Little Tokyo leaders also expressed mixed reactions to the large Japanese corporations of the Japanese Business Association (JBA).[37] When some proposed a merger between JBA and the community's leading commercial organization, the Japanese Chamber of Commerce, others countered the attempt—and won. Former chamber of commerce president and Nisei lawyer Kenji Ito opposed the merger because he thought it would forfeit community leadership to foreign businesses. The "Japanese Chamber of Commerce," he explained, "is essentially an organization of Japanese American citizens. It is not a business organization, but rather [a] Japanese American Association. Therefore, it cannot merge with JBA. If merged, it will be controlled by the big businesses from Japan."[38] Similarly, Japanese Americans echoed Yoshinaga's Nisei Week criticism. Fellow *Kashu Mainichi* columnist and community leader Katsumi Kunitsugu wrote repeatedly about the festival's "crass commercialism" detracting from a cultural and community focus. Although diplomatic toward Japanese firms, Kunitsugu nevertheless opposed their turning the celebration "into a glossy commercial venture, all shine and no substance."[39] A *Rafu Shimpo* writer also condemned "the quiet take over of the nearly four-decade-old event by overseas Japanese interests." Her outlook for Nisei Week, however, proved more optimistic than Yoshinaga's. In 1979 she observed, "The parade and related events, although still not totally open to . . . community input, showed definite signs of a re-discovery of its roots." The *Rafu Shimpo* writer considered promising the "young voices in the community clamoring for more social and historical relevance to be incorporated into the festival."[40]

Sansei activists joined older Japanese Americans in opposing Little Tokyo's corporate control. Youth protesters had initially envisioned redevelopment as a golden opportunity to strengthen ethnic solidarity, consciousness, and social services. Like their Nisei counterparts, they supported restoring and recentering the historic Japanese American community. But they also insisted on ethnic leadership, or self-determination, in Japantown, and they struggled against outside authority. As redevelopment proceeded, Asian American movement leaders mistrusted foreign investment in Little Tokyo. "The philosophy of 'survival of the fittest' that Japan-based firms espouse," the leftist *Gidra* warned, "chooses to ignore the long history of Japanese Americans. Long and arduous struggles of our forefathers are about to be cast aside brutally by the profit[-]seeking newcomers from Japan."[41] Movement activists countered outside influence in their community by committing themselves to a self-determined Little Tokyo. Poetically this translated into putting "People in Command."

> The rich have dreams of tourist-towns
> to occupy the land,
> alliances of capital
> from here and from Japan,
> But we have dreams more powerful
> on which we take our stand
> a thriving Little Tokyo with
> the people in command . . . [42]

In addition to poetry, activists used humor to empower Japanese Americans to withstand corporate invasion. Dedicated to Little Tokyo redevelopment, *Gidra*'s August 1973 issue contained two graphics that parodied the quest for Pacific Rim riches. One presented pot-bellied, camera- and golf bag–toting Japanese businessmen posed as the famous Iwo Jima photo of victorious soldiers raising an American flag. But in the drawing the caricatured executives raise a yen-symboled flag in a ground littered with garbage and degenerated Little Tokyo landmarks. The ironic message of Japan's postwar recovery was clear: Japanese corporations had grown fat with economic success and were bent on conquering Little Tokyo. The cover of the August edition waved another flag against foreign investment. The picture portrays Japantown as an urban theme park—a dystopic Disneyland—cluttered with Japanese corporate advertisements and featuring ghoulishly tacky Japanese tourists. The foreign visitors relax atop Little Tokyo skyscrapers and watch masses of faceless bodies tumble to their death. Like the first drawing, this one portrays opposition to Japanese investment. In both pictures, the fantasy of redevelopment appears as a dark and vicious harbinger of crass commercialism and reckless indifference to human life.[43]

Activists who observed the redevelopment of San Francisco's Japantown found reason to be pessimistic. The lesson learned from up north was bleak, *Gidra* reported, for the newly constructed "Japan Trade Center" wiped out the entire history of the area's Japanese American community. Activists considered the San Francisco case a complete loss to overseas capital and held Japanese American leaders partly responsible for the abandonment of Japantown.[44] "Japan Week," a San Francisco festival, provided an occasion to criticize the ethnic leadership's alleged complicity with foreign corporations. *Gidra* viewed the event as a prostitution of Japanese American interests and linked it to Japanese American complicity with government authorities during World War II evacuation and relocation:

> The local Japanese-American community is an important part of any tribute to the Japanese economy, oops culture, for any tribute would ring hollow if they did not lend their support. And who else could supply the knowledge and manpower to put on the show? The Japanese-American community is, as it was in 1942, a pawn in the struggle for economic aggrandizement. The gun in the back used 27 years ago has been replaced by the carrot, or rather the dollar, dangled in front of the nose. And for $350,000 . . . and a pat on the head, the victim of rape in 1942 has become a prostitute in 1969.[45]

In southern California a vital part of the Asian American movement fought to save Japantown from outside influence. One of the first organizations of its kind, the Little Tokyo Redevelopment Task Force assembled workers, students, teachers, and community activists to champion the needs of the area's more marginal constituents. The task force articulated three major concerns. First, it sought "equal replacement housing for resident tenants, small businesspersons, and community organizations presently in the redevelopment area." Second, the task force opposed evictions of residents. Finally, it argued against the construction of a new luxury hotel that would increase foreign ownership in Little Tokyo. The task force disfavored Japanese corporations because with foreign investment "the needs and priorities of the Japanese American community and our development, identity and future will be subservient to the needs of the people who do not identify with or are not interested in our . . . community." Furthermore, "with large capital, there is always a reordering of priorities which puts the interests of the resident, tenants and workers below the pursuit of profits."⁴⁶ Like their Nisei counterparts, Sansei protesters welcomed urban renewal in Little Tokyo but not at any cost. "We want the community to be rebuilt," claimed youth activists, "but redevelopment in the hands of the CRA and monopoly capitalists interests has only meant hardship and dispersal of . . . Japanese Americans, and other minorities and other working people who live and work in Little Tokyo." Before they would support CRA's actions, the activists argued that "[r]edevelopment must meet the needs of the local residents, workers, small businesses, and community and cultural groups. It should not enable any large corporations to grab control of Little Tokyo to serve their own profit needs."⁴⁷ These redevelopment standards contrasted sharply with the CRA's fundamentally profit-driven objectives. Consequently, the activist vision for the community remained fugitive.

Movement organizers defended Little Tokyo's disempowered through words and deeds, in newspapers and on picket lines. One major campaign was the effort to ensure that the JACCC remained, as originally intended, an ethnic community institution. Redevelopment leader Kango Kunitsugu characterized the center as Japantown's "heart and soul," the key element to restore the enclave to its prewar heyday.⁴⁸ But more conservative Japanese American leaders, redevelopment resisters cautioned, sought to transform the building into a vehicle promoting U.S.-Japan trade similar to New York City's Japan House, an institution near the United Nations that promoted Japanese fine arts and international business. "Some people," they reported, "hold that the Japanese Cultural and Community Center should be an elite institution, providing upperclass Japanese culture to wealthy patrons. This [position] is held by Japanese corporate-types (and the Japanese government) and the local heavyweight corporation representatives, who feel that the JACCC's role should be to serve the 'Japan House of the West', and help cement relations between business and government leaders of both nations."[49] In this way, youth activists fought against JACCC's class bias. "We in Los Angeles," they asserted, "need to insure that the 'community' aspect of the Cultural Community Center is not forgotten. We need and want a real center in Little Tokyo that can provide for the daily cultural and social service needs of the people here."[50] Through their dogged insistence, community activists managed to maintain JACCC's openness to Japanese American groups, artists, social services, and history. Although some doubtlessly considered it the "Japan House West," the center became known to many Japanese Americans as the fulfillment of a more-than-forty-year community aspiration.

Movement activists also struggled to maintain Nisei Week's ties to the historic ethnic community. "Nisei Week," they noted, "is only a microcosm of the internal struggles in the community."[51] At the festival's carnival in 1974, youth activists created a slogan for the antiredevelopment campaign in the form of buttons reading in English and Japanese, "Defend Little Tokyo." Similar to Nisei protests, activists frowned upon the celebration's increasingly foreign leadership. "Nisei Week," the youth proclaimed in 1976, "has always been a time for the Japanese American community in southern California to come together. But today the emphasis is changing from a community celebration to a testimonial for Japanese corporate interests. Parade floats advertise Kirin Beer. Banners stress 'Japanese Festival' instead of the Japanese American community. This year's honorary grand marshal is Konosuke Matsushita, leader of one of Japan's largest corporate monopolies."[52] A year later, activists contended that "Nisei Week is not just for entertainment. The sponsors of Nisei Week use it to promote their political views, and so we get a celebration of corporate greed and big business politicians." Again parade floats symbolized to the youth the loss of community leadership. "In this year's parade," they complained, "it seemed that nearly every float was an advertisement for a Japanese corporation. The Nisei Week Queen and her court rode the Tokai Bank float. Sumitomo, East-West Development and New Otani Hotel, Mitsui Bank, and Horikawa restaurant all bought floats emblazoned with their names."[53]

Although they could not match this corporate marketing, movement activists argued against Nisei Week's commercialization and blamed foreign businesses for violating a time-honored Japanese American tradition. Activists framed Nisei Week as an occasion for working people,

Activists protest the planned demolition of the Sun Building in Little Tokyo, where many Asian American movement organizations were headquartered. *Courtesy Visual Communications Archives.*

attaching it to the long history of folk festivals where "Japanese Americans would come together to celebrate their hard work, and the products of their labor." In this vision, corporate influence was seen as the bastardization of an authentic working-class ritual. "Whereas in past parades we might have seen farm wagons and cars decorated by church groups, community service organizations and prefectural associations; this year, large self-propelled floats will carry the banners of the Bank of Tokyo, Toyota Motors, and many other corporate sponsors which are eager to make inroads in Little Tokyo." [54] According to the activists, corporate newcomers uprooted Little Tokyo and Nisei Week from their historic role in the "struggle of Japanese Americans and other minorities against oppression. . . . What should Nisei Week represent," they added, "the proud history of struggle and perseverance of Japanese people in America, or the glorification of corporate wealth?" [55]

Twenty years of redevelopment in Little Tokyo offered no clear answer to this question. During that period, 46 buildings were rehabilitated and 568 housing units built, along with the nation's largest ethnic cultural and community center, a theater, a Christian church, a Buddhist temple, luxury hotels, specialty shopping centers, and office space. Furthermore, Little Tokyo received an overall face-lift, part of it was deemed a historic district, and plans were on the drawing board for the restoration of historic buildings and the construction of new ones.[56] In short, redevelopment projects embodied commitments to promoting both U.S.-Japan trade and ethnic community. Whether godsend or gift from hell, the phenomenal growth of foreign businesses in Little Tokyo introduced new constituents to the Japanese American community and consequently restructured its indigenous power relations and ethnic construction. Foreign businesses and city planners reinserted economic power as the baseline for Japanese American ethnicity. They portrayed the community and Nisei Week as bridges uniting Japanese and American markets and rebuilt Japantown as a center for U.S.-Japan business and cultural relations. On the margins of this quest for Pacific Rim profit, many Japanese Americans decried the changes to their historic community. While they could not resist the onslaught of overseas capital, they struggled against redevelopment to maintain a viable Japanese American presence in Little Tokyo. Although forging affiliations with Japanese capital, Los Angeles redevelopment retained an ethnic community where San Francisco's renewal eliminated most of its historic Japantown. Also, although in one sense threatening the community's future, Little Tokyo redevelopment helped increase generational solidarity and cooperation. Opposition to Little Tokyo's "Japanization" partly bridged cultural, political, and social gaps separating Nisei leaders and Sansei activists. As was the case in Nisei Week's beginning, Japanese American generations came together when confronted with an external threat to the community's livelihood. In the age of redevelopment, however, ethnic leadership enjoyed less power to shape ethnic cohesiveness. Like Little Tokyo itself, Nisei Week was bowing to outside authority.

HISTORY IN THE PRESENT TENSE

In the 1980s and early 1990s, southern California Japanese Americans once again debated the fate of their community. As in the 1930s, they feared encroachment from outside forces ready to take over Japanese American enterprises and to deny Japanese American authority to govern Little Tokyo and to construct their ethnicity. The opening stage of redevelopment did not appease these fears as originally had been hoped. In the end, Little Tokyo's renewal exacerbated Japanese American despair about the ethnic community's future. Columnist George Yoshinaga continued to denounce Nisei Week's foreign influence and community neglect. As late as 1994, he refused to share the faith of one festival leader who declared that the celebration would always be titled "Nisei Week."[57] Yoshinaga viewed the renaming of "Nisei Week" to "Japanese Festival" as inevitable as Little Tokyo's colonization by outside corporations. Perhaps more forcefully than any public figure, the columnist questioned the value of a foreign-dominated Nisei Week (or Little Tokyo) for Japanese Americans. "If we never had another Nisei Week," he asked, "would our community come tumbling down?"[58]

Yoshinaga's doubts about the future of Nisei Week exposed uneasiness about ending Japanese American traditions. Not only did he blame Japanese corporations for appropriating the celebration, but the columnist also held ethnic leaders accountable for allowing Nisei Week's "Japanization." The foreign investors, he surmised, did not receive support from most Japanese Americans, "except those who are standing in the wings hoping some of the affluent ones will throw some crumbs their way." Yoshinaga further observed that "many people in Little Tokyo are tied to Japanese money so they are going to sway with the tide of the almighty yen. These people certainly do not want to rub the [Japanese] nationals [the] wrong way."[59] Little Tokyo activist Mo Nishida launched a similar criticism against the community's redevelopment leaders, who, he declared, stressed commercial development and cultural hype without meeting the needs of "the little guy." A former member of the mayor's Little Tokyo Community Development Advisory Committee (LTCDAC), Nishida condemned it as unrepresentative of the ethnic community, as a "self-serving group of bankers, developers, and architects, with no momma/poppa small shop owners, workers, and few actual residents."[60] Another examination of redevelopment made the same claim about the community committee. "A major portion of the members of the LTCDAC," one university student found, "are upper[-]class businessmen who have direct investment interests in the redevelopment of Little Tokyo. They include your wealthy property owners and more influential Japanese businesses who have allegedly been known to practice class discrimination within their own community." Although he recognized its class bias, the student's conclusion about the committee was conditional. "[W]hether the LTCDAC is a true representative of the Little Tokyo community," he observed, "remains to be seen."[61] Along with redevelopment, Nisei Week leaders also were accused of being elitist. Dwight Chuman, *Rafu Shimpo*'s English-language editor, reported hearing much talk attributing Nisei Week's diminishing community support to its leaders' class bias. Chuman speculated that "the whole Nisei Week Festival has turned into a great big ego trip for a few honchos and has alienated itself from the community."[62] While outside interests were buying Little Tokyo, some within the community were selling property, businesses, and Nisei Week.

Yet not even critics of redevelopment blamed Nisei Week's declining community support entirely on outside influence or inside collaboration. Yoshinaga included younger Japanese Americans among those culpable for the festival's "Japanization." The role played by Sansei and subsequent generations in supporting the ethnic community particularly upset him. Nisei Week, he maintained, was betrayed not only by Japanese corporations and ethnic leaders but also by a loss of Japanese American voluntarism. In Yoshinaga's estimation, the festival would barely last into the twenty-first century because newer Japanese American generations, unlike their Nisei relatives, were unwilling to volunteer support for the ethnic community.[63] A number of Nisei Week leaders echoed his concern regarding the younger generations' estrangement from the festival, Little Tokyo, and Japanese American identity. They often referred to younger generations as "spoiled," "selfish," "assimilated," or preoccupied with work and private life. Like their Issei parents, Nisei fretted over their children's (and grandchildren's) unwillingness to sustain the ethnic community and wondered if Little Tokyo would die with them.

Little Tokyo CRA director Gloria Uchida contended that Japantown had outgrown its original purpose as a segregated ethnic neighborhood. She noted that out-marriage rates for younger Japanese Americans, found to be as high 50 percent, evidenced their assimilation and diminished ties to Japanese American culture and community.[64]

The path of redevelopment, however, eventually provided some hope to proponents of the Japanese American community. In the first stage of Little Tokyo renewal, the driving impulse was to replace old with new— to supplant historic buildings, institutions, and traditions with modern, economically efficient counterparts. But in the mid-1980s, according to Uchida, this emphasis changed to a commitment to renovate and re-store, rather than remove, blighted areas. The maintenance of Little Tokyo's past, she implied, better served the community's expanding role as a national symbol and center for Japanese American history, arts, and service organizations.[65] Museums and memory became part of CRA's strategy to attract further funds for Little Tokyo redevelopment, for by at least the late 1980s, Japanese corporations began to curtail overseas investment. Concerned by "Japan-bashing" incidents abroad and re-strained by recession at home, Japanese companies developed a new style of American investment. Gone were the days of unmindful specu-lation and foreign investment without much thought to the social and cultural ramifications of U.S.-Japan trade. In their place emerged a pe-riod in which Japanese firms endeavored to acculturate to American so-ciety in order to soften anti-Japanese hostility and economic reprisals. Foreign corporations, often seen as cutthroat competitors, fostered an image of being community-minded, pro-American, local businesses. Consequently, the notion of rebuilding the Japanese American past, of constructing a historical "bridge of understanding" between Japan and the United States, began to interest them.

Memorializing Japanese American history also served as a prologue to maintaining ethnic community and solidarity. Beginning around 1980, a series of exhibitions and discussions began paying tribute to Japanese American history. As one of the community's main functions, Nisei Week was connected to at least two of these events. First, the Japanese American Historical Society of southern California's inaugural research project was to document the festival's beginning.[66] Second, Nisei Week was the occasion when community leaders planned the Los Angeles opening of an exhibition honoring Nisei soldiers during World War II. Originating in San Francisco, this "Go for Broke" program made quite an impression on George Yoshinaga, who outlined the benefits that such displays could have for the ethnic community. The columnist suggested highlighting the Nisei war record to combat heightened anti-Japanese prejudice resulting from U.S.-Japan trade friction. He understood all too clearly that many Americans blurred the distinction between Japan and Japanese America and that Japanese Americans (and other Asian Americans) suffered assaults and insults for being confused with Japanese nationals.[67] "With all the flack that the Japanese Americans have been getting lately," he wrote, "it's time to start boosting our image again. And what could be better than to have a permanent display showing the role the Nisei played during World War II." After all, as Yoshinaga maintained, "[i]t was the courage and the accomplishments of the Nisei GIs which did more than any other contribution to re-establish the Japanese Americans in the United States." In his mind, remembering Japanese American loyalty and service to American democracy, to him, would help counter the "growing trend toward anti-Japanese feelings in America." Moreover, glorifying the heroism of Nisei soldiers underscored the ethnic community's importance, the Japanese American legacy that Japanese corporations often dismissed as economically irrelevant. Indeed, Yoshinaga boasted that "the war record of the Nisei GIs is the one thing which all the money from Japan can't take away from us."[68]

The most extravagant site of memory construction became Little Tokyo's Japanese American National Museum (JANM). Begun in 1984 as a joint venture between Nisei veterans and businessmen, the museum initially showcased Japanese American soldiers during World War II. As the JANM grew and found a home in Japantown, it attracted the same outside sources behind Little Tokyo redevelopment. Although Japanese American community groups established, administered, and raised funds for the JANM, the city of Los Angeles, through the CRA, provided the museum with its permanent site, and Japanese multinational corporations pledged generous financial contributions. Despite the JANM's backing, its development differed from that of earlier redevelopment projects, namely the JACCC, the development of which was marred by conflict. The community, the city, and corporations all cooperated on the JANM. The CRA backed the JANM because the museum fit perfectly into the new plan to restore—rather than raze—old structures. Housed in a revitalized Buddhist temple, the museum was to anchor the restoration of a historic Little Tokyo block known as North First Street. The ethnic community, for its part, generally approved of the CRA's new redevelopment agenda, and previously conflicted community groups united in support of the JANM. Almost everyone agreed that the

Nisei Week ondo dancers in 1981 parade against the backdrop of the New Otani hotel and Weller Court shopping complex, cornerstones of redevelopment designs seeking to enhance Little Tokyo's appeal to Japanese businesspeople and tourists. These two structures replaced the Sun Building that previously housed several Asian American movement organizations. *Courtesy Toyo Miyatake Studios.*

museum could raise awareness of Japanese American concerns and in this way counteract anti-Japanese discrimination and prejudice. Sansei activists viewed the museum as an institutional legacy of the Asian American movement, the social protests that powerfully reclaimed Japanese American history and transformed it into a vehicle for developing ethnic identity and political consciousness. The Nisei who made up most of the JANM's authorities and volunteers looked upon the museum as an homage to their extraordinary lives and those of their parents—the hardships they endured and the achievements they made as an American racial minority. Moreover, as many Nisei reached their seventies in the 1990s, the JANM offered them a chance to reconstruct their past while also providing them with a memorial.

Thus the museum's creation witnessed a rare convergence of community interests. A study of North First Street restoration, conducted by UCLA graduate students, commented upon this alliance between Nisei leaders and Sansei activists. Examining past redevelopment controversies between supporters of community and defenders of corporations, the study team found remarkable the North First Street project's easy approval. "The early '80s," they argued, "were a time of community . . . solidarity and the . . . strengthening of ties between groups that had at one time been antagonistic." The basis for solidarity was a common interest in historic preservation and appreciation for the Japanese American past. Furthermore, the study team noted that ethnic unity was made possible through Japanese corporations' salutary neglect of Little Tokyo preservation: "Because there was no outside interests such as Japanese capital, the idea of cultural preservation could serve as the common goal of all these [community] groups." Moreover, CRA's proposals for other outside interests to invest in the North First Street project further galvanized the Japanese American community.[69] While Japanese Americans disagreed about the acceptability of Japanese businesses in Little Tokyo, they often bonded in their rejection of non-Japanese (almost always white) or city attempts to appropriate the ethnic district.

Indeed, as the museum grew in scale and ambition, its backers were not shy about soliciting support from Japanese corporations. The JANM expanded well beyond its inaugural mission to exhibit the heroism of southern California Nisei soldiers. Instead the museum became a national center for Japanese American culture and history, an ethnic version of the Smithsonian's Museum of American history. The radical change in scope required additional funding beyond the means of the ethnic community and foundation grants. Hence JANM officials turned to Japanese corporations for help. The firms, in turn, responded to the opportunity to support Japanese American history. Their support for the JANM reinvoked the notion of Japanese Americans as a "bridge of understanding" between the United States and Japan. But more important to the foreign businesses, the museum enabled them to embrace the pro-American patriotism of Nisei soldiers. Undoubtedly, Japanese corporations perceived the JANM as a bulwark against any form of anti-Japanese action or suspicion. Beyond notions of blood ties between Japanese nationals and Japanese Americans, they sponsored awareness of Japanese American history to serve their economic interests. This motivation partly explained why large firms such as Sony (among many others) contributed generously to the JANM and why the Japanese emperor and empress included a visit to this museum on their rare U.S. tour.

The creation of memory on the scale envisioned by Nisei leaders went beyond the community's resources. Once again, extravagant dreams of reclaiming the community's past, redeveloping its historical image, and securing its place in southern California and the broader American society compromised the ability of Japanese Americans to define themselves and to withstand outside ethnic descriptions and prescriptions. Throughout the redevelopment era, internal responsibilities toward the community and external enticements offered by the corporations placed a heavy burden on the Japanese American leadership. They did not always represent the community. Their influence in the making of the JANM's first exhibit revealed their privileged position. The glorification of Nisei soldiers and military service as the ultimate patriotic expression excluded other Nisei patriots. Such a representation failed to mention, for example, those who resisted the draft to protest Japanese American internment and to defend American civil liberties. Caught between corporations and community, the JANM supported a version of history that played down the fractured community politics of the war era. The museum's policies and exhibits revealed the intention of its directors to please its constituents, while disguising its salient contribution to the process of identity formation.

Conclusion

A perusal of the anniversary booklet of the fiftieth Nisei Week festival in 1990 shows the historical transformation of an ethnic community. The young, fresh faces at the front of booklet are old and weathered by the end. The discussion of economic and racial problems that provided the original impetus for Nisei Week is supplanted by narratives of Japanese American successes—on the battlefield and the playing fields and ultimately in redressing the wartime internment. Old-timers look back wistfully to the festival's beginnings as a time when there were no commercial floats or corporate sponsorships; everyone was welcome to dance the ondo (not just professionals and their students); and the beauty pageant's goal was to benefit the enclave first and contestants second. They recalled an ethnic neighborhood in Little Tokyo; streets and parking lots that have since given way to shopping malls, gang fights that were fought with fists, not guns; and a cohort of Nisei leaders now almost entirely deceased.

The booklet's impression of the past also reveals the contemporary state of Japanese America. Animating the nostalgic reflections are fears that the ethnic community is dying. The Nisei are passing on, while the majority of their children and grandchildren seem to distance themselves from their roots as they continue to assimilate and marry outside the ethnic group. Meanwhile the historic and symbolic center of the ethnic community, Little Tokyo, seems to keep falling into the hands of foreigners and foreign corporations. It remains a desperate situation for ethnic leaders, who now look to the past to build consensus within the current competition of Japanese American identities.

One result has been an official history of Nisei Week that emphasizes the common ground of racism and achievement. In the pages of the anniversary booklet, the distinction between Meiji-era intellectuals and the immigrants from Japan's farming classes is reduced to the celebration of Issei pioneers. The booklet ignores the failure to bridge the gap between Japan and the United States and the bitter clashes at Manzanar and other internment camps in favor of the heroism of Nisei veterans. And the "radical awakening" of Japanese American youth in the 1960s and 1970s is cast as a successful mechanism for strengthening the ethnic community rather than an aborted attempt to deconstruct it and reformulate it in a revolutionary new cosmopolitanism. Although the booklet acknowledges generous monetary support from Japanese corporations, its version of history diplomatically ignores concerns about the Japanization of Little Tokyo.

Such a glossy vision of Japanese American history fits with the celebration that has been Nisei Week. Festivals, by their nature, do not concentrate on imperfections but celebrate idealized notions of past and present. By portraying all Japanese Americans as inherently cosmopolitan, law-abiding, and (potentially) good citizens, Nisei Week has rearticulated pejorative stereotypes. It has blended the best parts of Japanese and American cultures. Yet the image of Japanese Americans as a phoenix rising from the ashes of racial hostility conceals the consequences of discrimination within the ethnic community against women, blue-collar workers, disadvantaged youth, the less educated, and other disadvantaged groups. The vision of a harmoniously united ethnic community has legitimized the authority and identity conceptions of the ethnic leadership. By their nature, festivals are also inherently political acts.

This historical examination of Nisei Week's micropolitics has revealed a pattern of class conflict shaping, and shaped by, conceptions and contestations of anti-Japanese racism. Of the many factors contributing to class distinctions among Japanese Americans perhaps the foundational element was educational attainment. Although Meiji Japan witnessed a historic flowering of public education (the average Issei had gone to school for ten years), it was exceedingly rare for individuals to have gone to college in either Japan or the United States. The select few who did were much more likely to have learned English and become ethnic leaders as a result of their education and bilingualism. In the two decades before World War II, the JACLers, replicating the pattern established by the Issei leadership, emerged as the college-educated Nisei elite. Both generations of leaders sought to modernize the ethnic community by insisting that Japanese Americans adapt felicitously to the cosmopolitanism of American life. The internment emboldened the less educated to eschew such Anglo conformity and the leaders who advocated it in the name of a salutary separation from white America (either by returning to Japan or remaining insulated in internee/ethnic communities).

Freer access to higher education after the war equalized power relations among Japanese Americans. Although a discernible Nisei elite persisted (especially concentrated in regions outside the West Coast), the status of typical Japanese Americans improved so that they were able to attend college and thus enter the cosmopolitan world of middle-class professionals. By the late 1960s, what distinguished a new generation of ethnic leaders was not simply a college degree but a combination of high educational achievement and an interracial political vision. The student radicals of the Asian American movement represented an intellectual vanguard vying for the loyalty of the ethnic community, which they both dismissed as politically "backward" and yet idealized as culturally authentic. Their revolutionary vision and the conservatism of the average Japanese American were brought together in confronting the growing Little Tokyo authority of Japanese corporations, whose status derived from neither education nor ideology but from a more Marxian notion of class privilege. It remains to be seen whether the importation of Japan's economic "miracle" will transform the class dynamics internal to Japanese America and thus the ways in which the ethnic community understands and negotiates American race relations.

The cracks in the mold of apparent group solidarity are hidden stakes in the game of racial rearticulation. In encountering anti-Japanese racism, Meiji intellectuals, JACLers, Manzanar protesters, student radicals, feminists, and corporate businessmen in their own ways reproduced unequal power relations inside the ethnic community. Analyzing these political orchestrations is one way to understand the barriers separating racial minorities from themselves and to come to terms with the shifting and porous boundaries between seemingly clear-cut ethnic and racial groups.

Notes

PREFACE

1. The festival was seen as a coming-out ritual for children of Japanese immigrants. In Japanese, *Nisei* means "second generation" and conforms to a practice of naming successive generations of overseas Japanese, beginning with the immigrants. The first through fourth generations are the Issei, Nisei, Sansei, and Yonsei.

2. David A. Hollinger, *Postethnic America: Beyond Multiculturalism* (New York: Basic Books, 1995), 6–7. For an incisive critique of *Postethnic America*, see Gary Gerstle, "The Power of Nations," *Journal of American History* 84, no. 2 (Sept. 1997): 576–79.

3. For the origins of *obon*, see Kunio Yanagita, *About Our Ancestors—The Japanese Family System*, trans. Fanny Hagin Mayer and Ishiwara Yasuyo (Japan: Ministry of Education, 1970; reprint, New York: Greenwood Press, 1988), 44–45, 55–56.

INTRODUCTION

1. The best-known statement of the model minority thesis for Japanese Americans is William Petersen's "Success Story: Japanese American Style," *New York Times Magazine* (Jan. 9, 1966): 19–43. Petersen, a sociologist, based his praise of Japanese American acculturation and social mobility on an implicit comparison to the predicament of urban blacks in the wake of the Watts riots. This article was indicative of a movement in American sociology that sought answers to the persistent plight of black America in the cultural retention of Asian Americans. Such works include William Petersen's *Japanese Americans: Oppression and Success* (New York: Random House, 1971); Harry H. L. Kitano's *Japa-*

nese Americans: Evolution of a Subculture (Englewood Cliffs, N.J.: Prentice-Hall, 1969); and Ivan H. Light's *Ethnic Enterprise in America: Business and Welfare among Chinese, Japanese, and Blacks* (Berkeley: University of California Press, 1972).

2. The most cited works that criticized model minority studies and popular rhetoric include those of Bob H. Suzuki, "Education and Socialization of Asian Americans: A Revisionist Analysis of the 'Model Minority' Thesis," *Amerasia Journal* 4, no. 2 (1977): 23–51; Ki-Taek Chun, "The Myth of Asian American Success and Its Educational Ramifications," *IRCD Bulletin* (Teacher's College, Columbia University) 15, nos. 1–2 (winter/spring 1980): 1–12; Paul Takagi, "The Myth of Assimilation in American Life," *Amerasia Journal* 1, no. 2 (1973): 149–57; and Amy Uyematsu, "The Emergence of Yellow Power in America," in *Roots: An Asian American Reader*, ed. Amy Tachiki et al. (Los Angeles: UCLA Asian American Studies Center, 1971), 9–13. Analyses that concentrate on the resurgence of model minority discourse in the 1980s include those of Thomas K. Nakayama, "'Model Minority' and the Media: Discourse on Asian America," *Journal of Communication Inquiry* 12, no. 1 (1988): 65–73; and Ronald Takaki, *Strangers from a Different Shore: A History of Asian Americans* (Boston: Little, Brown, 1989), 474–84. For a comparison of earlier and later model minority formulations, see Keith Osajima, "Asian Americans as the Model Minority: An Analysis of the Popular Press Image in the 1960s and 1980s," in *Reflections on Shattered Windows: Promises and Prospectus for Asian American Studies*, ed. Gary Okihiro et al. (Pullman: Washington State University Press, 1988), 165–74.

3. Gary Y. Okihiro, *Margins and Mainstreams: Asians in American History and Culture* (Seattle: University of Washington Press, 1994), 34.

4. Sylvia Yanagisako, "Transforming Orientalism: Gender, Nationality, and Class in Asian American Studies," in *Naturalizing Power: Essays in Feminist Cultural Analysis*, ed. Sylvia Yanagisako and Carol Delaney (New York: Routledge, 1995), 285.

5. The "marginal man" was coined by University of Chicago sociologist Robert E. Park; see Robert E. Park, "Human Migration and the Marginal Man," *American Journal of Sociology* 33 (May 1928): 881–93. Everett V. Stonequist, Park's student, applied it to Asian Americans in this way: "He belongs neither to America nor to the Orient. Culturally he is an American; racially he is of the Orient. He cannot identify himself completely with either civilization." See Everett V. Stonequist, *The Marginal Man: A Study in Personality and Culture Conflict* (1937; reprint, New York: Russell and Russell, 1961), 105. For specific uses of the marginal man thesis to understand the Nisei, see, for example, Edward K. Strong Jr., *The Second Generation Japanese Problem* (Stanford: Stanford University Press, 1934); William Caudill, "Japanese-American Personality and Acculturation," *Genetic Psychology Monographs* 1 (1952): 3–102; and George DeVos, "A Quantitative Rorschach Assessment of Maladjustment and Rigidity in Acculturation of Japanese Americans," *Genetic Psychology Monographs* 52 (1955): 51–87. Model minority studies contrasted the marginal identity of Japanese Americans before and during World War II with their successful

social and cultural adjustment after the war. See Petersen, *Japanese Americans*, and Kitano, *Japanese Americans*. Other historical studies, too, have taken the "marginal man" as their starting point in tracing a rather whiggish progression of Americanization. Bill Hosokawa, *Nisei: The Quiet Americans* (New York: William Morrow, 1969) and, to a lesser degree, Robert A. Wilson and Bill Hosokawa, *East to America: The History of Japanese in the United States* (New York: William Morrow, 1980) put forth the most triumphalist narratives. More critical, yet still tied to a linear process of cultural adaptation, is Roger Daniels, *Asian America: Chinese and Japanese in the United States since 1850* (Seattle: William Morrow, 1988).

6. Daniels, *Asian America*, 5–8. For the argument about the basic similarity (notwithstanding race) between Asian and European immigrants, see also Daniels's earlier and later essays: "Westerners from the East: Oriental Immigrants Reappraised," *Pacific Historical Review* 35, no. 4 (1966): 373–84, and "No Lamps Were Lit for Them: Angel Island and the Historiography of Asian American Immigration," *Journal of American Ethnic History* 17 (fall 1997): 3–18.

7. See Brian Masaru Hayashi, *"For the Sake of Our Japanese Brethren": Assimilation, Nationalism, and Protestantism among the Japanese of Los Angeles, 1895–1942* (Stanford: Stanford University Press, 1995), 119–26, and *Governing Japanese: Internees, Social Scientists, and Administrators in the Making of America's Concentration Camps, 1942–1945* (Princeton, forthcoming); Jere Takahashi, *Nisei/Sansei: Shifting Japanese American Identities and Politics* (Philadelphia: Temple University Press, 1997), 48–84; Yuji Ichioka, "A Study of Dualism: James Yoshinori Sakamoto and the Japanese American Courier, 1928–1942," *Amerasia Journal* 13, no. 2 (1986–87): 49–81. Other works that focus on the retention (or assertion) of ethnic and national identity before World War II include John J. Stephan, *Hawaii under the Rising Son: Japan's Plan for Conquest after Pearl Harbor* (Honolulu: University of Hawaii Press, 1984); Yuji Ichioka, "Japanese Immigrant Nationalism: The Issei and the Sino-Japanese War, 1937–1941," *California History* 69, no. 3 (fall 1990): 260–75, 310–11; Eiichiro Azuma, "Racial Struggle, Immigrant Nationalism, and Ethnic Identity: Japanese and Filipinos in the California Delta," *Pacific Historical Review* 67 (May 1998): 163–99; and David Yoo, *Growing Up Nisei: Race, Generation, and Culture among Japanese Americans of California, 1924–49* (Urbana: University of Illinois Press, 2000).

8. The beginnings of this debate in American historiography are found in Rudolf Vecoli, "Contadini in Chicago: A Critique of the Uprooted," *Journal of American History* 51 (Dec. 1964): 404–17. For analysis of the subsequent debate, see John Higham, "Current Trends in the Study of Ethnicity in the United States," *Journal of American Ethnic History* (fall 1982): 5–15, and the forum centering on Olivier Zunz, "American History and the Changing Meaning of Assimilation," *Journal of American Ethnic History* 4 (1985): 53–84.

9. George J. Sánchez, *Becoming Mexican American: Ethnicity, Culture, and Identity in Chicano Los Angeles, 1900–1945* (New York: Oxford University Press, 1993), 13.

10. For a thoughtful discussion of different types of constructionism, see

Dana Y. Takagi, *The Retreat from Race: Asian American Admissions and Racial Politics* (New Brunswick, N.J.: Rutgers University Press, 1992), 12–16.

11. Omi and Winant define racial rearticulation as a "practice of discursive reorganization or reinterpretation of ideological themes and interests already present in the subjects' consciousness, such that these elements obtain new meanings or coherence. This practice is ordinarily the work of 'intellectuals.' Those whose role is to interpret the social world for given subjects—religious leaders, entertainers, schoolteachers, etc.—may on this account be 'intellectuals' ": Michael Omi and Howard Winant, *Racial Formation in the United States: From the 1960s to the 1980s* (New York: Routledge and Kegan Paul, 1986), 173, n. 11.

12. Ibid., 93–95.

13. See Lawrence W. Levine, *Black Culture and Black Consciousness: Afro-American Folk Thought from Slavery to Freedom* (New York: Oxford University Press, 1977).

14. Evelyn Brooks Higginbotham, "African-American Women's History and the Metalanguage of Race," *Signs* 17 (winter 1992): 267.

15. Ibid., 255.

16. Levine, *Black Culture*, 420.

17. Bourdieu defines the concept of habitus as follows: "The structures constitutive of a particular type of environment (e.g., the material conditions of existence characteristic of a class condition) produce habitus, systems of durable and transposable dispositions, structured structures predisposed to function as structuring structures, that is, as principles of the generation and structuring of practices and representations which can be objectively 'regulated' and 'regular' without in any way being the product of obedience to rules, objectively adapted to their goals without presupposing a conscious aiming at ends or an express mastery of the operations necessary to attain them and, being all this, collectively orchestrated without being the product of the orchestrating action of a conductor." Pierre Bourdieu, *Outline of a Theory of Practice*, trans. Richard Nice (Cambridge: Cambridge University Press, 1977), 72.

Bourdieu is a name not as familiar to American social historians as it is in sociology, anthropology, and educational studies. For informed introductions to Bourdieu's work, including his concepts of habitus and capital, see Michael Grenfell and David James, eds., *Bourdieu and Education: Acts of Practical Theory* (London: Falmer Press, 1998); and Pierre Bourdieu and Loïc J. D. Wacquant, *An Invitation to Reflexive Sociology* (Chicago: University of Chicago Press, 1992). A very useful discussion of the significance of habitus for the ethnography of ethnicity and the study of microlevel ethnic identity is G. Carter Bentley's "Ethnicity and Practice," *Comparative Studies in Society and History* 29, no. 1 (Jan. 29, 1987): 24–55.

18. Kitano, *Japanese Americans*, 5; Milton M. Gordon, *Assimilation in American Life: The Role of Race, Religion, and National Origins* (New York: Oxford University Press, 1964), 51–54; William Julius Wilson, *The Declining Significance of Race: Blacks and Changing American Institutions* (Chicago: University of Chicago Press, 1980); William Julius Wilson, *The Truly Disadvantaged: The Inner City, the Underclass, and Public Policy* (Chicago: University of

Chicago Press, 1987); and Peter Kwong, *The New Chinatown* (New York: Noonday Press, 1987).

19. Eric Hobsbawn, "Introduction: Inventing Traditions," in *The Invention of Tradition*, ed. Eric Hobsbawn and Terence Ranger (Cambridge: Cambridge University Press, 1983), 1.

20. John J. MacAloon, "Introduction: Cultural Performances, Cultural Theory," in *Rite, Drama, Festival, Spectacle: Rehearsal toward a Theory of Cultural Performance*, ed. John J. MacAloon (Philadelphia: Institute for the Study of Human Issues, 1984), 1. The scholarly literature on festivals is extensive, particularly within the disciplines of anthropology and folklore. For discussion of festivals (and rituals in general) as agents of cultural reproduction and transformation see MacAloon, ed., *Rite, Drama, Festival, Spectacle*; Clifford Geertz, "Religion as a Cultural System," in Geertz, *The Interpretation of Cultures*, 112; Roger D. Abrahams, "Toward an Enactment-Centered Theory of Folklore," in *Frontiers of Folklore*, ed. William R. Bascom (Boulder, Colo.: Westview Press, 1977), and "Shouting Match at the Border: The Folklore of Display Events," in *"And Other Neighborly Names": Social Process and Cultural Image in Texas Folklore*, ed. Richard Bauman and Roger D. Abrahams (Austin: University of Texas Press, 1981), 319–20; Catherine Bell, *Ritual Theory, Ritual Practice* (New York: Oxford University Press, 1992), 74, 197–223; M. M. Bakhtin, *Rabelais and His World*, trans. Helene Iswolsky (Cambridge, Mass.: MIT Press, 1968); and Victor Turner, ed., *Celebration: Studies in Festivity and Ritual* (Washington, D.C.: Smithsonian Institution, 1982).

21. Mona Ozouf, *Festivals and the French Revolution*, trans. Alan Sheridan (Cambridge, Mass.: Harvard University Press, 1988); Takashi Fujitani, *Splendid Monarchy: Power and Pageantry in Modern Japan* (Berkeley: University of California Press, 1996); John Bodnar, *Remaking America: Public Memory, Commemoration, and Patriotism in the Twentieth Century* (Princeton: Princeton University Press, 1992); and Robert Anthony Orsi, *The Madonna on 115th Street: Faith and Community in Italian Harlem, 1880–1950* (New Haven: Yale University Press, 1985). The significance of festivals in American history is also discussed in April Schultz, " 'The Pride of the Race Has Been Touched': The 1925 Norse-American Immigration Centennial and Ethnic Identity," *Journal of American History* 77, no. 4 (Mar. 1991): 1265–95; Susan G. Davis, *Parades and Power: Street Theatre in Nineteenth-Century Philadelphia* (Berkeley: University of California Press, 1986); Matthew Frye Jacobson, *Special Sorrows: The Diasporic Imagination of Irish, Polish, and Jewish Immigrants in the United States* (Cambridge, Mass.: Harvard University Press, 1995); and George Lipsitz, *Time Passages: Collective Memory and American Popular Culture* (Minneapolis: University of Minnesota Press, 1990).

CHAPTER 1. SUCCEEDING IMMIGRANTS

1. As quoted in Akira Iriye, *Pacific Estrangement: Japanese and American Expansion, 1897–1911* (Cambridge, Mass.: Harvard University Press, 1972), 109.

2. Dorothy Swaine Thomas, with Charles Kikuchi and James Sakoda, *The Salvage* (Berkeley: University of California Press, 1952), 12–13. Analysis of the

political campaigns to exclude Japanese immigration can be found in Roger Daniels, *The Politics of Prejudice: The Anti-Japanese Movement in California and the Struggle for Japanese Exclusion* (1962; reprint, New York: Atheneum, 1968). For the Gentlemen's Agreement in particular, see Thomas A. Bailey, *Theodore Roosevelt and the Japanese-American Crisis* (Stanford: Stanford University Press, 1934); and Charles E. Neu, *An Uncertain Friendship: Theodore Roosevelt and Japan, 1906–1909* (Cambridge, Mass.: Harvard University Press, 1967).

3. Fifteenth Census of the United States, Population, vol. 3, pt. 1, California, table 15, 260; Sixteenth Census of the United States, Population, vol. 2, California, tables 4 and B-36, 516, 630.

4. For a recent study of the Immigration Act that concentrates on its racial dimension, see Mae M. Ngai, "The Architecture of Race in American Immigration Law: A Reexamination of the Immigration Act of 1924," *Journal of American History* 86 (June 1999): 67–92. In a larger work, Ngai extends the narrative of Progressive Era immigration politics through to the Immigration Act of 1965. See Mae M. Ngai, "Illegal Aliens and Alien Citizens: United States Immigration Policy and Racial Formation, 1924–1945" (Ph.D. diss., Columbia University, 1998). The classic study of the politics leading up to the Immigration Act of 1924 is John Higham's *Strangers in the Land: Problems of American Nativism* (New Brunswick, N.J.: Rutgers University Press, 1955). For Japanese American exclusion, see also Daniels, *Politics of Prejudice,* 92–105; and Yuji Ichioka, *The Issei: The World of the First Generation Japanese Immigrants, 1885–1924* (New York: The Free Press, 1988), 244–54.

5. For the remigration of Japanese immigrants from the United States, see Masao Suzuki, "Success Story? Japanese Immigrant Economic Achievement and Return Migration, 1920–1930," *Journal of Economic History* 55 (Dec. 1995): 889–901. In separate studies, Dorothy Swaine Thomas and Imre Ferenczi touch upon the issue of Japanese remigration; see Thomas, *The Salvage,* 15–17; and Imre Ferenczi, *International Migrations,* vol. 1, *Statistics* (New York: National Bureau of Economic Research, 1929), 166. Relevant statistics can also be found in two other publications: Yamato Ichihashi, *Japanese in the United States* (Stanford: Stanford University Press, 1932), 401–8; and Thomas J. Archdeacon, *Becoming American: An Ethnic History* (New York: The Free Press, 1983), table V-3, 118–19. By dividing the average annual in-migration by the average annual out-migration, Archdeacon calculates that roughly 26 percent of Japanese immigrants left the United States from 1908 to 1924. This rate compares to 133 percent for Chinese, 46 percent for Italians, 33 percent for Poles, and 4 percent for "Hebrews."

6. Yuji Ichioka, "Japanese Immigrant Nationalism: The Issei and the Sino-Japanese War, 1937–1941," *California History* 69, no. 3 (1990): 274.

7. John Modell, *The Economics and Politics of Racial Accommodation: The Japanese of Los Angeles, 1900–1942* (Urbana: University of Illinois Press, 1977), 99.

8. Ibid., 103–4. For opposing views, see Ichioka, *Issei,* 234–43; and Masakazu Iwata, "The Japanese Immigrants in California Agriculture," *Agri-*

cultural History 36 (1962): 25–37, and *Planted in Good Soil: A History of the Issei in the United States Agriculture*, American University Studies, ser. 9, History, vol. 1 (New York: Peter Lang, 1992), 280–88. For the larger debate about Issei economic achievement, contrast Suzuki, "Success Story?" to Robert Higgs, "Landless by Law: Japanese Immigrants in California Agriculture to 1941," *Journal of Economic History* 38 (Mar. 1978): 205–25.

9. Nishimoto reports the growth of commercial and personal trade businesses among Japanese Americans in Los Angeles as follows: 1904: 160; 1909: 495; 1915: 750. See Richard Nishimoto, "Japanese in Personal Services and Urban Trade," manuscript, n.d., pp. 3, 29, 35–6, folder W 1.90, Japanese American Evacuation Resettlement Records (hereafter referred to as JAERR), BANC MSS 67/14 C (Bancroft Library, University of California, Berkeley) (numbers, such as "W 1.90," in later references indicate this collection of designated folders).

10. Ibid., 4–34 (quotation, 33).

11. Stanford M. Lyman, "The Significance of Asians in American Society," in *The Asian in North America* (Santa Barbara, Calif.: ABC-Clio, 1970), 25–37.

12. Modell, *Economics and Politics,* 102–3.

13. For recent studies of Chinese exclusion, see Sucheng Chan, ed., *Entry Denied: Exclusion and the Chinese Community in America, 1882–1943* (Philadelphia: Temple University Press, 1991); George Anthony Peffer, *If They Don't Bring Their Women Here: Chinese Female Immigration before Exclusion* (Urbana: University of Illinois Press, 1999); and Andrew Gyory, *Closing the Gate: Race, Politics, and the Chinese Exclusion Act* (Chapel Hill: University of North Carolina Press, 1998).

14. Iriye, *Pacific Estrangement,* 84–85. A useful analysis of Meiji immigration policy concerning Hawaii is Alan Takeo Moriyama, *Imingaisha: Japanese Emigration Companies and Hawaii, 1894–1908* (Honolulu: University of Hawaii Press, 1985).

15. Modell, *Economics and Politics,* 94.

16. For labor conflict between Japanese growers and Mexican and Filipino pickers, see Modell, *Economics and Politics,* 122–24; and Eiichiro Azuma, "Racial Struggle, Immigrant Nationalism, and Ethnic Identity: Japanese and Filipinos in the California Delta," *Pacific Historical Review* 67 (May 1998): 163–99.

17. Modell, *Economics and Politics,* 104, 113.

18. Ibid., 113.

19. Akira Iriye, *After Imperialism: The Search for a New Order in the Far East, 1921–1931* (Cambridge, Mass.: Harvard University Press, 1965), 278–83.

20. Sei Fujii, *Kashu Mainichi,* May 23, 1934, August 16, 1939.

21. Ibid., July 12, 1935; Meeting Minutes, Japanese Association of Los Angeles, May 22, 1934, Box 238, Japanese American Research Project (Special Collections, University of California, Los Angeles).

22. *Rafu Shimpo,* June 13, 26, 27, 1934 (Japanese language section, hereafter cited as "Jpn."), June 25, 26, 30, and July 2, 1924; *Kashu Mainichi,* May 23, 1934. For the origins and function of Japanese associations, see Ichioka, *Issei,* 156–64; and S. Frank Miyamoto, *Social Solidarity among the Japanese in*

Seattle (1939; reprint, Seattle: University of Washington Press in cooperation with the Asian American Studies Program, University of Washington, 1981), 58–63.

23. *Rafu Shimpo* (Jpn.), July 28, 1934.

24. Yuji Ichioka, "A Study of Dualism: James Yoshinori Sakamoto and the Japanese American Courier, 1928–1942," *Amerasia Journal* 13, no. 2 (1986–87): 57–58; Iriye, *Pacific Estrangement*, 85. See also Jere Takahashi, "Japanese American Responses to Race Relations: The Formation of Nisei Perspectives," *Amerasia Journal* 9, no. 1 (June 1982): 59–87; and David Yoo, "'Read All about It': Race, Generation, and the Japanese American Ethnic Press, 1925–41," *Amerasia Journal* 19, no. 1 (1993): 69–92.

25. For Abiko's life, see Valerie Matsumoto, *Farming the Home Place: A Japanese American Community in California, 1919–1982* (Ithaca: Cornell University Press, 1993); Ichioka, *Issei*, 60–61; Seizo Oka, "Biography of Kyutaro Abiko: Issei Pioneer with a Dream," *Pacific Citizen*, Holiday Issue (Dec. 19–26, 1980): 65.

26. Katsuma Mukaeda, interview, April 27, 1966, oral history tapes, Japanese American Research Project (Special Collections, UCLA); Katsuma Mukaeda, interview with author, February 3, 1993.

27. *Japanese Who's Who in America* (San Francisco: Japanese American News, 1922), 123. This information was translated for the author by Seizo Oka.

28. Fujii, *Kashu Mainichi*, August 17, 1934.

29. *Kashu Mainichi*, July 20, 1934.

30. For discussion of the "Nisei dilemma," see Modell, 127–72; Ichioka, "Study of Dualism," 49–81.

31. Modell, *Economics and Politics*, 127–28; *Rafu Shimpo*, July 23 1938, June 17, 1934.

32. Modell, *Economics and Politics*, 138.

33. Richard Nishimoto, "Personal Services and Urban Trade," 65–74 (quotation is on p. 71), W 1.90, JAERR.

34. Strong's findings are presented in Paul R. Spickard, *Japanese Americans: The Formation and Transformations of an Ethnic Group* (New York: Twayne, 1996), 86–87 (table 5.2); *Rafu Shimpo*, June 17, 1934; "Data from WRA Form 26: Evacuee Summary Data ('Locator Index')," electronic dataset, 1942, U.S. Department of the Interior, War Relocation Authority, RG 210 (Washington, D.C.: National Archives). "WRA Form 26" is an electronic dataset containing census-like information for 109,358 Japanese Americans who completed form 26 upon entering the War Relocation Authority's internment camps in 1942.

35. This paragraph is derived from Togo Tanaka, "History of the JACL," unpublished manuscript, n.d., T 6.25, JAERR. For the early history of JACL, see chaps. 2–4. A more celebratory history of JACL is Bill Hosokawa, *JACL in Quest of Justice: The History of the Japanese American Citizens League* (New York: William Morrow, 1982).

36. Shinoda, *Rafu Shimpo*, August 10, 1934. For JACL exclusiveness, see also *Rafu Shimpo*, August 2, 1936.

37. Kango Kunitsugu, "Grand Marshall Kay Sugahara," Nisei Week sou-

venir booklet, 1983 (official publication of Nisei Week Japanese Festival), Japanese American National Museum, Los Angeles, Calif., 56–57, 103; Kay Sugahara personal record, "WRA form 26."

38. Patrick Kiyoshi Okura, phone interview with author, November 17, 1992.

39. Togo Tanaka, "How to Survive Racism in America's Free Society," in *Voices Long Silent: An Oral Inquiry into the Japanese American Evacuation,* ed. Arthur A. Hansen and Betty E. Mitson, Oral History Program (Fullerton: California State University, 1974), 83–109; Togo Tanaka, interview with author, October 20, 1992; Togo Tanaka personal record, "WRA form 26."

40. Togo Tanaka, "Report on the Manzanar Riot: Personality Sketches of Principals Involved," unpublished manuscript, n.d., pp. 1–8, folder 1, O 10.12, JAERR; Fred Tayama personal record, "WRA form 26."

41. Kurt Lewin, "The Problem of Minority Leadership," in *Studies in Leadership: Leadership and Democratic Action,* ed. Alvin W. Gouldner (1950; reprint, New York: Russell and Russell, 1965), 193; see also John Higham, ed., *Ethnic Leadership in America* (Baltimore: Johns Hopkins University Press, 1978), 193.

42. Roger Daniels, "The Japanese," in Higham, *Ethnic Leadership,* 49.

43. Yasuo Wakatsuki, "Japanese Emigration to the United States, 1866–1924: A Monograph," *Perspectives in American History* 12 (1979): 439–40.

44. Iriye, *Pacific Estrangement,* 89. For the adulation of the West by certain Japanese intellectuals, see Kenneth Pyle, *The New Generation in Meiji Japan: Problems of Cultural Identity, 1885–1895* (Stanford: Stanford University Press, 1969), 19; and Mitziko Sawada, "Culprits and Gentlemen: Meiji Japan's Restrictions of Emigrants to the United States, 1891–1909," *Pacific Historical Review* 60, no. 3 (1991): 339–59. An interesting comparison with Chinese immigrants can be found in K. Scott Wong, "Liang Qichao and the Chinese of America: A Re-evaluation of His *Selected Memoir of Travels in the New World,*" *Journal of American Ethnic History* 11, no. 4 (summer 1992): 3–24.

45. Pyle, *New Generation,* 86–89.

46. Wakatsuki, "Japanese Emigration," 460.

47. Ibid., 459–60.

48. Iriye, *Pacific Estrangement,* 143.

49. Ibid., 143–44.

50. Shinoda, *Rafu Shimpo,* June 10, 1934.

51. Matsumoto, *Rafu Shimpo,* August 12, 1935.

52. *Rafu Shimpo,* August 19, 1934.

53. *Kashu Mainichi,* July 26, 1936.

54. Letter responding to Walter Cribbens editorial *(Kashu Mainichi),* July 3, 1936; *Kashu Mainichi,* July 19, 1936.

55. Masao Satow, *Kashu Mainichi,* July 8, 1934.

56. Shinoda, *Rafu Shimpo,* June 3, 1934.

57. "WRA form 26." WRA data reveal that 16 percent of Nisei women in Los Angeles attended at least one year of college, compared to 23 percent of Nisei men. For Issei in Los Angeles, the numbers were 3 percent of women compared to 6 percent of men.

58. "WRA form 26." WRA data indicate that 93 percent of Issei older than twenty-one years of age in Los Angeles had not attended even one year of college.
59. Modell, *Economics and Politics*, 71–72.
60. "WRA form 26." WRA data show 20 percent of Nisei to have attended at least one year of college, 6 percent of whom completed four or more years.
61. Isami Arifuku Waugh, "Hidden Crimes and Deviance in the Japanese-American Community" (Ph.D. diss., University of California, Berkeley, 1978), 135–39; "Olivers: Since 1917," souvenir booklet for Oliver Club's eighty-third anniversary, 1990, Japanese American National Museum, Los Angeles, Calif., collection 91.15.1.
62. Waugh, "Hidden Crimes and Deviance," 143.
63. Ibid., 148.
64. James Sakoda, "Personal Adjustment," unpublished manuscript, January 12, 1943, pp. 17–18, folder 11, James Sakoda Reports on Tule Lake, R 20.86, JAERR.
65. Wakatsuki, "Japanese Emigration," 461–62.
66. Ibid., 463–64; Iriye, *Pacific Estrangement*, 102; Moriyama, *Imingaisha*, 24–26.
67. H. K. Misaki, "Delinquency and Crime," in *Vocational Attitudes of Second-Generation Japanese in the United States*, ed. Edward K. Strong Jr. (Stanford: Stanford University Press, 1933), 160–61.
68. "Racial uplift" is borrowed from Kevin K. Gaines's discussion of elite ideologies within black America. See Kevin K. Gaines, *Uplifting the Race: Black Leadership, Politics, and Culture in the Twentieth Century* (Chapel Hill: University of North Carolina Press, 1996).
69. Mikhail Bakhtin, *Rabelais and His World*, trans. Helen Jowolsky (Cambridge, Mass.: MIT Press, 1968), 7.

CHAPTER 2. RISE AND FALL OF BICULTURALISM

1. *Rafu Shimpo*, August 20, 1934; the quotation is from *Kashu Mainichi*, August 20, 1934.
2. Charles Chaplin, *My Autobiography* (New York: Simon and Schuster, 1964), 377. Chaplin's relationship to the Japanese (and Japanese Americans) is better documented in Gerith von Ulm's unauthorized biography *Charlie Chaplin: King of Tragedy* (Caldwell, Idaho: Caxton Printers, 1940), 19–28, 347–66, and is also referred to in David Robinson, *Chaplin: His Life and Art* (New York: McGraw-Hill, 1985), 188. A study of Lafcadio Hearn and other Westerners who lived in turn-of-the-century Japan is Robert A. Rosenstone's *Mirror in the Shrine: American Encounters with Meiji Japan* (Cambridge, Mass.: Harvard University Press, 1988). Chaplin's passion for Japan, like that of his predecessor Hearn, is consistent with Edward Said's notion of "Orientalism," which Said defines as a ruling style of thought that shaped and was shaped by Western colonialism in the Near East. Edward W. Said, *Orientalism* (New York: Vintage, 1978). For the persistence of Orientalism in studies of East Asia and the United States, see, respectively, Rey Chow, *Writing Diaspora: Tactics of Intervention in Contemporary Cultural Studies* (Bloomington: University of Indiana Press,

1993), 1–26; and Henry Yu, *Thinking Orientals: Migration, Contact, and Exoticism in Modern America* (New York: Oxford University Press, 2001).

3. *Rafu Shimpo*, August 10, 1934; *Kashu Mainichi*, August 5, 1934, August 18, 1939.

4. *Rafu Shimpo*, August 19, 1934. Not much is known about this employment bureau, except that it was informally connected to the JACL and was criticized as being biased toward members of that organization. See *Rafu Shimpo*, August 7, 1938. The broader context of Japanese American unemployment is addressed in John Modell, *The Economics and Politics of Racial Accommodation: The Japanese of Los Angeles, 1900–1942* (Urbana: University of Illinois Press, 1977), 138–39. He claims that the low rate of unemployment for Japanese Americans in the retail and sales trade reported by the 1940 census was deceptive. Only two-thirds of these workers were employed for the full year in 1939, and many unskilled Japanese Americans found no work at all. Yet the Japanese compared favorably with "other races" in the retail and sales trade, whose unemployment rate was more than twice theirs.

5. *Kashu Mainichi*, August 16, 1936.

6. Roku Sugahara, *Kashu Mainichi*, August 5, 1934.

7. Warren Tsuneishi, *Kashu Mainichi*, August 28, 1938.

8. Ibid.

9. George Yamada, *Kashu Mainichi*, August 28, 1938.

10. Sugahara, *Kashu Mainichi*, August 5, 1934.

11. *Rafu Shimpo*, August 29, 1938; Sugahara, *Kashu Mainichi*, August 5, 1934.

12. Isami Suzukawa, *Kashu Mainichi*, August 12, 1935.

13. Carl Kondo, *Kashu Mainichi*, August 12, 1935; Suzukawa, *Kashu Mainichi*, August 12, 1935.

14. *Kashu Mainichi*, August 15, 1937.

15. *Manzanar Free Press* (internee newspaper at the Manzanar internment camp for Japanese Americans during World War II), November 30, 1942.

16. Nisei Week souvenir booklet, 1936, n.p. (in author's possession); *Kashu Mainichi*, July 24, 1937.

17. *Kashu Mainichi*, July 11, 1940; Nisei Week souvenir booklet, 1940, n.p. (in author's possession).

18. *Rafu Shimpo*, August 27, 1939.

19. Sei Fujii, *Kashu Mainichi*, August 4, 19, 1934 (Jpn.).

20. Joseph Shinoda, *Rafu Shimpo*, August 19, 1934.

21. Yoshiko Mori (pseudonym), interview with author, Los Angeles County, Calif., May 20, 1993 (audiotape in author's possession).

22. Chiye Nagano (pseudonym), interview with author, Los Angeles County, Calif., April 19, 1993 (audiotape in author's possession).

23. *Kashu Mainichi*, July 9, 1935.

24. Ibid., August 4, 1935; *Rafu Shimpo*, July 19, 1935; August 14, 1935.

25. Tsuyoshi Matsumoto, *Rafu Shimpo*, August 3, 1941. See also Tsuyoshi Matsumoto, "History of the Resident Japanese in Southern California," manuscript (in English and Japanese), 1941, "Togo Tanaka Journal," folder 3, A 17.06, JAERR.

26. *Rafu Shimpo*, June 17, 1934.

27. Nisei Week souvenir booklet, 1940, n.p. (in author's possession).

28. John Kitahara, *Doho*, July 1, 1940.

29. *Doho*, June 10, 1938; James Sakoda, "Personal Adjustment," manuscript, January 12, 1943, 11–12, 17–18, file 11, "James Sakoda Reports on Tule Lake," R 20.86, JAERR.

30. For other criticisms of Nisei Week, see *Kashu Mainichi*, August 8, 1937, and *Rafu Shimpo*, August 18, July 28, 1935.

31. *Doho*, June 10, 1938; Togo Tanaka, "Report on the Manzanar Riot," 1–5, O 10.12, JAERR.

32. *Rafu Shimpo*, August 6, 1939. For attendance figures, see *Kashu Mainichi*, August 29, 1938, and *Rafu Shimpo*, August 29, 1938.

33. *Kashu Mainichi*, August 18, 1936.

34. *Rafu Shimpo*, July 30, 1939.

35. May Sakurai response to author's questionnaire, April 1993 (in author's possession).

36. *Rafu Shimpo*, June 26, 1938, August 17, 1941; *Kashu Mainichi*, August 11, 1940.

37. Sandra Sakai (pseudonym), interview with author, Los Angeles County, Calif., January 28, 1993 (audiotape in author's possession).

38. Martha Kaihatsu, *Rafu Shimpo*, August 31, 1938.

39. "WRA Form 26" data show occupations (other than homemaker) for 63 percent of Japanese American women age sixteen and older. Yet their employment outside the home did not diminish gender differences; in the workplace, Issei women clustered in domestic service and agricultural labor, while the Nisei, because of their English-language skills, became typists, secretaries, and general office clerks. Managerial jobs were almost the exclusive domain of Japanese American men. "WRA Form 26: Evacuee Summary Data ('Locator Index'), electronic dataset, 1942, U.S. Department of the Interior, War Relocation Authority, RG 210 (Washington, D.C.: National Archives).

40. Sylvia Junko Yanagisako, *Transforming the Past: Tradition and Kinship among Japanese Americans* (Stanford: Stanford University Press, 1985), 98; *Doho*, March 15, 1941.

41. Takeno, *Kashu Mainichi*, July 17, 1938.

42. *Kashu Mainichi*, July 7, 1940.

43. Nisei Week souvenir booklet, 1936, n.p. (in author's possession). For the history of the flora-dora number, see Lois W. Banner, *American Beauty* (New York: Knopf, 1983), 181–82.

44. Patrick Kiyoshi Okura, phone interview, September 3, 1997, notes (in author's possession). For biographical information on Okura, see *JACL Reporter*, 4 (Sept. 1948), FF 870 J3 J222 (Bancroft Library, University of California, Berkeley).

45. Modell, *Racial Accommodation*, 174; Togo Tanaka, "Pre-Evacuation Pressure Group Activity in Southern California: Personality Sketches," May 30, 1943, 68, A 16.260, JAERR.

46. Nisei Week souvenir booklet, 1936, n.p. (in author's possession); *Kashu Mainichi*, July 18, 1940.

47. James Sakoda, "Personal Adjustment," manuscript, January 12, 1943, 15–16, file 11, "James Sakoda Reports on Tule Lake," R 20.86, JAERR.

48. *Rafu Shimpo,* July 25, 1940.

49. "Chico," *Kashu Mainichi,* August 18, 1940.

50. Roger D. Abrahams, "Shouting Match at the Border: The Folklore of Display Events," in *"And Other Neighborly Names": Social Process and Cultural Image in Texas Folklore,* ed. Richard Bauman and Roger D. Abrahams (Austin: University of Texas Press, 1981), 319–20.

51. The quotations are from Isami Arufuku Waugh, "Hidden Crimes and Deviance in the Japanese-American Community" (Ph.D. diss., University of California, Berkeley, 1978), 135; *Rafu Shimpo,* September 6, 1938.

52. Waugh, "Hidden Crimes and Deviance," 135.

53. Ibid., 151.

54. Ibid., 146.

55. *Rafu Shimpo,* June 30, 1940; February 11, 12, and September 7, 1941.

56. *Sangyo Nippo,* July 18, 1940; *Kashu Mainichi,* August 4, 1940, August 24, 1941; Waugh, "Hidden Crimes and Deviance," 152.

57. Louise Suski, *Rafu Shimpo,* July 27, 1941; Louise Suski, interview with author, Cerritos, Calif., October 5, 1992, audiotape (in author's possession). On Suski's father, see Louise Suski, "Biography of Father," August 25, 1945, T 1.8682, JAERR.

58. *Pacific Citizen,* August 1, 1931, quoted in H. K. Misaki, "Delinquency and Crime," in *Vocational Aptitudes of Second-Generation Japanese in the United States,* ed. Edward K. Strong Jr. et al. (Stanford: Stanford University Publications, Educational Psychology, no. 1, 1933), 172.

59. Ibid.

60. Waugh, "Hidden Crimes and Deviance," 135.

61. Nisei Week souvenir booklet, 1936, n.p. (in author's possession); *Kashu Mainichi,* August 10, 1936; John Maeno, interview with author, Los Angeles, Calif., September 2, 1991, audiotape (in author's possession).

62. Nisei Week souvenir booklet, 1940 and 1941, n.p. (in author's possession).

63. *Rafu Shimpo,* August 20, 1934.

64. *Kashu Mainichi,* August 11, 1936; Nisei Week souvenir booklet, 1936, n.p. (in author's possession).

65. Isamu Masuda, *Kashu Mainichi,* September 11, 1938.

66. Asayo Kuraya, *Pacific Citizen,* November 1936 (vol. 4, no. 60).

67. Shinoda, *Rafu Shimpo,* August 4, 1935; August 5, 1934.

68. Togo Tanaka, "The Vernacular Newspapers," 18–19, 38. For discussion of Japanese nationalism in the ethnic community in the 1930s, see also Brian Masaru Hayashi, *"For the Sake of Our Japanese Brethren": Assimilation, Nationalism, and Protestantism among the Japanese of Los Angeles, 1895–1942* (Stanford: Stanford University Press, 1995); Yuji Ichioka, "Japanese Immigrant Nationalism: The Issei and the Sino-Japanese War, 1937–1941," *California History* 69, no. 3 (1990): 260–75, 310–11; and James Sakoda, "Reports on Tule Lake," 11.

69. Togo Tanaka, "History of the JACL," chap. 3, p. 5, T 6.25, JAERR.

70. Tanaka, "Pre-evacuation Pressure Group Activity in Southern California," 10–11, JAERR; Nishimoto, "Personal Service and Urban Trade," 38–39, 73–74, JAERR; Tanaka, "History of the JACL," chap. 3, p. 12, JAERR.

71. Tanaka, "History of the JACL," chap. 3, p. 17, JAERR.

72. Tanaka, "Political Organizations," 6–7, JAERR; Tanaka, "Vernacular Newspapers," 8, 9, 17, 38–39; JAERR; Minutes of Rafu Shimpo's Board of Editorial Counsellors Meeting, July 14, 1941, folder 2, Togo Tanaka "Journal," A 17.06, JAERR.

73. Rafu Shimpo press release, March 20, 1941, folder 2, Togo Tanaka "Journal," A 17.06, JAERR.

74. Kashu Mainichi, August 4, 1940.

75. Nisei Week souvenir booklet, 1941, n.p. (in author's possession).

76. Sangyo Nippo, July 19, 30, 1941; Rafu Shimpo, August 10, 2, 1941.

77. Doho, July 1, 1938.

78. "Whose Talking for Whom?" Sam Hohri, Sangyo Nippo, August 14, 1941.

79. Lieutenant Commander Ringle's Confidential Intelligence Report to Chief of Naval Operations (c. Jan. 20–Mar. 27, 1942), A 5.01, p. 3, JAERR. For a fascinating analysis of Ringle's and other intelligence activity in southern California, see two articles by Pedro Lourerio, "Japanese Espionage and American Countermeasures in Pre-Pearl Harbor California," Journal of American-East Asian Relations 3 (fall 1994): 197–210, and "The Imperial Japanese Navy and Espionage: The Itaru Tachibana Case," International Journal of Intelligence and Counterintelligence 3 (spring 1989): 105–21. See also Bob Kumamoto, "The Search for Spies: American Counterintelligence and the Japanese American Community, 1931–1942," Amerasia Journal 6, no. 2 (1979): 45–75; and Michi Weglyn, Years of Infamy: The Untold Story of America's Concentration Camps (New York: Morrow Quill, 1976), 33–53.

80. Togo Tanaka, "Pre-Evacuation Pressure Group Activity in Southern California," May 30, 1943, 1–39, JAERR; Lieutenant Commander Ringle's Confidential Intelligence Report to Chief of Naval Operations (c. Jan. 20–Mar. 27, 1942), A 5.01, JAERR; Los Angeles Times as quoted in Kashu Mainichi, August 25, 1941; Rafu Shimpo, August 25, 1941.

81. Lieutenant Commander Ringle's Confidential Intelligence Report to Chief of Naval Operations (c. Jan. 20–Mar. 27, 1942), A 5.01, JAERR.

82. Tanaka, "Pre-evacuation Pressure Group Activity in Southern California," 28, JAERR.

83. Fletcher Bowron, radio address on KECA (Los Angeles), transcript, February 5, 1942 (6:30 P.M.); Fletcher Bowron correspondence, A 15.14, JAERR.

84. Morris Edward Opler, "The Repatriate-Expatriate Group of Manzanar," manuscript, August 4, 1944, 20, O 3.03, JAERR.

85. The number of internees housed in each internment camp is contained in War Relocation Authority, The Evacuated People: A Quantitative Description (1946; New York: AMS Press, 1975), table 19, 61. For the physical environment of the Manzanar camp, see War Relocation Authority, "Manzanar Final Report," vol. 1, 1946, Reel 76, microform of National Archives records, BANC FILM 1932 (Bancroft Library, University of California, Berkeley).

CHAPTER 3. WAR AND THE AMERICAN FRONT

1. The narrative of the Manzanar protest is described in Togo Tanaka, "Report on the Manzanar Riot," manuscript, 1943, 9–11, 33–40, O 10.12, JAERR; Arthur A. Hansen and David A. Hacker, "The Manzanar Riot: An Ethnic Perspective," *Amerasia Journal* 2, no. 2 (fall 1974): 113–15.

2. The terminology of the internment has been part and parcel of its changing historical interpretation. The reference to "internment camps" in this chapter reflects an uneasiness with both the government's formal term *(relocation centers)* and the revisionists preference for using *concentration camps*. For the same reason, I have deviated from the existing terminology to describe differences among the internees. By *protester*, I mean individuals who for a wide variety of reasons, many of which had nothing to do with loyalty, found themselves part of Manzanar unrest. While *collaborator* can have pejorative connotations, I use it simply to describe the tight, but by no means uncomplicated, bonds between a small group of internees and the government officials running the internment.

3. Lieutenant Commander Ringle's Confidential Intelligence Report to Chief of Naval Operations (c. Jan. 20–Mar. 27, 1942), A 5.01, JAERR, 5.

4. *Rafu Shimpo*, December 9, 1941, as quoted in Paul R. Spickard, "The Nisei Assume Power: The Japanese American Citizens League, 1941–1942," *Pacific Historical Review* 52, no. 2 (May 1983): 161. For the JACL's role in the arrest of Issei leaders, see also Lieutenant Commander Ringle's Confidential Intelligence Report to Chief of Naval Operations, JAERR; Togo Tanaka, "History of the JACL," chap. 3, T 6.25, JAERR, 13–14; and Bob Kumamoto, "The Search for Spies: American Counterintelligence and the Japanese American Community, 1931–1942," *Amerasia Journal* 6, no. 2 (1979): 57–58.

5. Spickard, "Nisei Assume Power," 158–61 (quotation is on p. 161); see also JACL's "Anti-Axis Committee" Records in *American Concentration Camps*, ed. Roger Daniels, vol. 2 (New York: Garland Publishing, 1989).

6. Tanaka, "History of JACL," chap. 4, JAERR, 54; JACL, "Meeting Minutes from Special National Council Meetings," March 10, 1942, T 5.12, JAERR.

7. Kenneth D. Ringle, "The Japanese Question in the United States: A Compilation of Memoranda," n.d., A 5.01, JAERR, 15.

8. Tanaka, "Manzanar Riot," 9–10.

9. Togo Tanaka, journal entry, January 11, 1942, and Togo Tanaka "Journal," A 17.07, JAERR.

10. Ibid.

11. *Rafu Shimpo*, December 23, 28, 1941; for Tanaka's meeting with the first lady and attorney general and more on his imprisonment, see Tanaka, "How to Survive Racism in America's Free Society," in *Voices Long Silent: A Oral Inquiry into the Japanese-American Evacuation*, ed. Arthur A. Hansen and Betty E. Mitson (Fullerton: California State University, 1974), 91–94, 102.

12. Figures based on a prewar estimate by the *Rafu Shimpo*. For JACL membership, see Tanaka, "Manzanar Riot," JAERR, 9. At the national level, Tanaka reported that JACL membership reached twenty thousand in February 1942: Tanaka, "History of JACL," chap. 4, JAERR, 5, 42–44.

13. Tanaka, "History of JACL," chap. 4, JAERR, 27–30; Togo Tanaka and Joe Grant Masaoka, "Documentary Report 91," manuscript, January 25, 1943, O 10.06, JAERR, 408–12.

14. Nisei Writers' and Artists' Mobilization for Democracy, "Alternative Evacuation and Resettlement Plans: Farm Cooperatives, and Post-war Los Angeles Financial Survey," manuscript, n.d., A 16.259, JAERR.

15. Tanaka, "Manzanar Riot," 14–15; United Citizens Federation Meeting Minutes, February 19, 1942; Togo Tanaka, "Journal," A 17.01, JAERR; United Citizens Federation, "Report on Resettlement," manuscript, n.d., T 1.78, JAERR; Ringle, "Japanese Question," 25–26.

16. Joseph Yoshisuke Kurihara, "Autobiography," manuscript, 1946, 38–39, R 30.00, JAERR.

17. Ibid., 51.

18. Tanaka, "Manzanar Riot," 8.

19. Ibid., 11–15. For the general antagonism against the JACL, see Tanaka, "JACL History," chap. 4, JAERR, 40–41; Tanaka, "Journal," January 9, 1942; and letter to editor of the *Sangyo Nippo,* March 2, 1942, JAERR.

20. Tanaka, "History of JACL," chap. 4, JAERR, 55–56.

21. Ibid., 56–57.

22. Commission on Wartime Relocation and Internment of Civilians, *Personal Justice Denied* (1982, 1983; reprint, Seattle: University of Washington Press, 1997), 154, 178.

23. Spickard, "Nisei Assume Power," 172; Togo W. Tanaka interview with Betty Mitson and David A. Hacker, May 19, 1973, 12, O.H. 1271a, Oral History Program (Fullerton: California State University).

24. Morton Grodzins, "The Manzanar Shooting," manuscript, January 10, 1943, 15, O 10.04, JAERR.

25. Tanaka, "Manzanar Riot," 69–70; Grodzins, "Manzanar Shooting," 15.

26. Tanaka, "Manzanar Riot," 69–70, 72–75.

27. Janet Goldberg, "The Manzanar 'Incident': December 5 to December 19, 1942," n.d., 2, miscellaneous documents on Manzanar Riot, 1942–43, O 7.00, JAERR.

28. Morris Edward Opler, "A History of Internal Government at Manzanar, March 1942 to December 6, 1942," July 15, 1944, O 3.02, 84–85, JAERR.

29. Tanaka and Masaoka, "Documentary Report 87," December 1, 1942.

30. Ibid., "Report 31," July 21, 1942, and "Report 36," July 29, 1942, JAERR.

31. Joseph Yoshisuke Kurihara, "Speech #1," manuscript, n.d., R 30.00, 2–3, JAERR.

32. Hansen and Hacker, "Manzanar Riot," 142.

33. Tanaka, "Manzanar Riot," 15–20.

34. Ibid., 80.

35. Hansen and Hacker, 149–50 n. 59.

36. The social profile of protesters was derived by cross-checking "WRA Form 26" data with the names of sixty-three internees imprisoned in a special "troublemaker" camp at Leupp, Arizona. The findings show that 18 percent of the protesters had attended at least one year of college but only 3 percent were

professionals: "WRA Form 26"; WRA, "Registration Summary for Inmates of WRA Isolation Center at Leupp, Arizona," July 31, 1943, reprinted in Sue Kunitomi Embrey et al., eds., *Manzanar Martyr: An Interview with Harry Y. Ueno* (Fullerton: California State University, 1986), appendix 32, 201–2.

37. Opler, "History of Internal Government," 85, JAERR; "The Repatriate-Expatriate Group of Manzanar," manuscript, August 4, 1944, O 3.03, 26, 29, JAERR.

38. Biographical descriptions of Togo Tanaka are drawn largely from three oral interviews: Togo W. Tanaka, interview with author, Los Angeles, Calif., February 18, 1999, transcript (in author's possession); Togo Tanaka, "How to Survive Racism in America's Free Society," in *Voices Long Silent: An Oral Inquiry into the Japanese American Evacuation*, ed. Arthur A. Hansen and Betty E. Mitson (Fullerton: California State University, 1974), 83–110; and Togo Tanaka, interview with Betty E. Mitson and David A. Hacker. For a critical view of Tanaka and other collaborators, see Spickard, "Nisei Assume Power." Roger Daniels portrays the sort of cooperation Tanaka espoused as "frantic and often pitiful": Roger Daniels, *Concentration Camps, USA: Japanese Americans and World War II* (New York: Holt, Rinehart and Winston, 1971), 40–41, 80. While agreeing that Tanaka's "patriotic boosterism sometimes included a repudiation of the Issei leadership," Hansen and Hacker reveal evidence to the contrary: Hansen and Hacker, "Manzanar Riot," 124, 147 n. 45.

39. Embrey et al., *Manzanar Martyr*, 40.

40. Ibid., 4–6.

41. Ibid., 8–9, 16–18.

42. Togo Tanaka, interview with author, Los Angeles, Calif., February 18, 1999, transcript (in author's possession).

43. For gender conflicts among Japanese Americans, see Sylvia Junko Yanagisako, *Transforming the Past: Tradition and Kinship among Japanese Americans* (Stanford: Stanford University Press, 1985), 97–105.

44. Valerie Matsumoto, "Japanese American Women during World War II," in *Unequal Sisters: A Multicultural Reader in U.S. Women's History*, ed. Ellen Carol Dubois and Vicki L. Ruiz (New York: Routledge, 1990), 385. For other discussions of family relations during the internment, see Leonard Bloom, "Familiar Adjustment of Japanese-Americans to Relocation," *American Sociological Review* 8, no. 5 (Oct. 1943): 551–60; Leonard Bloom, "Transitional Adjustments of Japanese-American Families to Relocation," *American Sociological Review* 12, no. 2 (Apr. 1947): 201–9; and Leonard Bloom and John Kitsuse, *The Managed Casualty: The Japanese-American Family in World War II* (Berkeley: University of California Press, 1956). For broader studies of Japanese American gender and family, consult Evelyn Nakano Glenn, *Issei, Nisei, War Bride: Three Generations of Japanese American Women in Domestic Service* (Philadelphia: Temple University Press, 1986); Yanagisako, *Transforming the Past;* and these works by Valerie Matsumoto: *Farming the Home Place: A Japanese American Community in California, 1919–1982* (Ithaca: Cornell University Press, 1993); "Desperately Seeking 'Diedre': Gender Roles, Multicultural Relations, and Nisei Women Writers of the 1930s," *Frontiers* 12, no. 1 (1991): 19–32; "Redefining Expectations: Nisei Women in the 1930s," *California History* 73 (spring 1994):

44–53; and "Japanese American Women and the Creation of Urban Nisei Culture in the 1930s," in *Over the Edge: Remapping the American West*, ed. Valerie J. Matsumoto and Blake Allmendinger (Berkeley: University of California Press, 1999), 291–306.

45. Susan Jeffords, *The Remasculinization of America: Gender and the Vietnam War* (Bloomington: Indiana University Press, 1989), especially 54–86.

46. Jeanne Wakatsuki Houston and James D. Houston, *Farewell to Manzanar: A True Story of Japanese American Experience during and after the World War II Internment* (Boston: Houghton Mifflin, 1973), 39, 58–59.

47. Jack Shimatsu, "Report by Investigator," Manzanar Internal Police, Letters 2, 8, and 3, September 25, 1942, O 2.52, JAERR.

48. Ibid., Letters 6, 7, and 8, JAERR.

49. Ibid., Letters 6, 10, 3, and 8.

50. Joseph Kurihara, "speech #1," 5, JAERR. For a slightly different version of this speech, see Joseph Kurihara, notebook, 10, 93.3.1, Dr. Charles and Lois Ferguson collection (Japanese American National Museum, Los Angeles, California).

51. Embrey et al., *Manzanar Martyr*, 30, 36. For Tanaka's position, see the report of his exchange with an Issei leader on the question of self-government: Tanaka and Masaoka, "Documentary Report 87," December 1, 1942, JAERR.

52. Joseph Kurihara, "Murder in Camp Manzanar," manuscript, n.d., 10, 4, 28, miscellaneous materials on Manzanar Riot, 1942–1943, O 7.00, JAERR.

53. Kurihara, "Murder in Camp Manzanar," 12–14; Opler, "History of Internal Government," 50, JAERR.

54. Kurihara, "Murder at Camp Manzanar," 26; Kurihara, "Autobiography," 50. For a contrary view of Raymond R. Best, the camp director Kurihara praised when he directed the Tule Lake segregation center, see Minoru Kiyota, *Beyond Loyalty: The Story of a Kibei*, trans. Linda Klepinger Keenan (Honolulu: University of Hawaii Press, 1997), 104, 124.

55. Embrey et al., *Manzanar Martyr*, 40–41.

56. Tanaka, "Manzanar Riot," 9–10.

57. Tanaka and Masaoka, "Documentary Report 91," January 25, 1943, JAERR; Tanaka, "Manzanar Riot," 15–20, 65–66, 81; Hansen and Hacker, "Manzanar Riot," 134.

58. E. R. Fryer (deputy directory) and Lewis A. Sigler (assistant solicitor) with assistance from Robert B. Throckmorton, "Report Concerning the Incident at the Manzanar Relocation Center on December 5 and December 6, 1942," manuscript, December 16, 1942, 75, Manzanar Incident Material Folder, Reel 75, BANC 1932 (Bancroft Library, University of California, Berkeley).

59. Commission on Wartime Relocation and Internment, *Personal Justice Denied*, 234; Dillon S. Myer, *Uprooted Americans: The Japanese Americans and the War Relocation Authority during World War II* (Tucson: University of Arizona Press, 1971), 168.

60. Myer, *Uprooted Americans*, 131–34.

61. Commission on Wartime Relocation and Internment, *Personal Justice Denied*, 191–92.

62. The original response to Question 28 in February and March 1943 was more negative. Almost 25 percent of Nisei men at Manzanar refused to answer "yes." But this number lessened to 12 percent as these men were allowed to change their minds: WRA, *Evacuated People*, tables 73 and 74, 164–65. The same was true for those requested to give up American citizenship. Morris Opler noted a significant number of cancellations, especially when expatriation no longer was a means to avoid the draft; see Morris Edward Opler, "The Repatriate-Expatriate Group of Manzanar," manuscript, August 4, 1944, 7–8, O 3.03, JAERR.

63. WRA, *Evacuated People*, table 14, 50.

64. WRA, press release, May 12, 1944, "Press Releases Folder," Reel 76, BANC 1932 (Bancroft Library, University of California, Berkeley).

65. Carl Kondo, "Eastern Impressions," June 9, 1944, Evacuee Attitudes Folder, Reel 75, BANC 1932 (Bancroft Library, University of California, Berkeley).

66. Dorothy Swaine Thomas, with Charles Kikuchi and James Sakoda, *The Salvage* (Berkeley: University of California Press, 1952), 125, 128. Thomas's claims about resettlers were based on sample data from three WRA camps: Poston I in Arizona, Minidoka in Wyoming, and Tule Lake in northern California. For an important analysis and assessment of Thomas's work, and the larger research project she led during World War II, see essays in Yuji Ichioka, ed., *Views from Within: The Japanese American Evacuation and Resettlement Study* (Los Angeles: UCLA Asian American Studies Center, 1989).

67. Togo Tanaka, interview with author, Los Angeles, Calif., October 20, 1992, audiotape (in author's possession).

68. Ibid.

69. Ibid.

70. Patrick (Kiyoshi) Okura, phone interview with author, November 17, 1992, notes (in author's possession); Kango Kunitsugu, "Grand Marshall Kay Sugahara," Nisei Week souvenir booklet, 1983, official publication of Nisei Week Japanese Festival, Los Angeles, Calif. (Los Angeles: Japanese American National Museum); Teru Kanazawa, "Kay Sugahara–'Nisei Onassis,'" *Tozai Times* 1 (Aug. 1985): 1, 10–11, 20. For Sugahara's postwar experience, see also Bill Hosokawa, *JACL in Quest of Justice: The History of the Japanese American Citizens League* (New York: William Morrow, 1982).

71. Thomas, "Japanese Americans," in *Understanding Minority Groups*, ed. Joseph B. Gittler (New York: John Wiley, 1956), 101–8. Survey data from a national study conducted on three generations of Japanese Americans in the 1960s also revealed that the adult Nisei who stayed in the East and Midwest made up a primarily white-collar population that was twice as likely to have completed college than those who returned to Los Angeles; data compiled by author from Gene N. Levine, *Japanese-American Research Project: A Three-Generation Study, 1890–1966* (computer file), 2d ed. (Los Angeles: UCLA, Institute for Social Science Research), and Chicago: National Opinion Research Center (producers), 1985, Ann Arbor, Mich.: Interuniversity Consortium for Political and Social Research (distributor), 1992.

72. Thomas, "Japanese Americans," 95–102. A more thorough analysis of the segregants at Tule Lake can be found in Dorothy Swaine Thomas and Richard S. Nishimoto, *The Spoilage* (Berkeley: University of California Press, 1946).

73. Compare, for example, tables 25 and 78 in WRA, *Evacuated People*, 80, 175.

74. Opler, "Studies of Segregants," 8, JAERR.

75. Ibid.

76. Ibid., 74, 76.

77. Roy Takeno, "Project Report 79," manuscript, February 22, 1943, "Manzanar Project Reports Folder," Reel 76, BANC 1932 (Bancroft Library, University of California, Berkeley).

78. Takeno, "Project Report 92," January 7, 1944, BANC 1932 (Bancroft Library, University of California, Berkeley).

79. Thomas, *Salvage*, 115, 86–87.

80. Compare, for example, tables 37g and 47b(6) in WRA, *Evacuated People*, 102, 113.

81. Chokichi Nakano to Dillon S. Myer, February 27, 1945, Manzanar Community Government Section, Memos and Correspondence, O 2.93, JAERR.

82. Allan Markley, "Special Field Reports to Dillon S. Myer," n.d., T 1.79, 1–3, JAERR.

83. James L. Shelly, "Final Report: Southern California Area," February 28, 1946, F 3.64, 55–109, JAERR. See also Audrie Girdner and Anne Loftis, *The Great Betrayal: The Evacuation of Japanese Americans during World War II* (London: Macmillan, 1969), 399–400.

84. Henry Mori, *Rafu Shimpo*, June 24, 1946.

85. Girdner and Loftis, *Great Betrayal*, 396.

86. Frank F. Chuman, *The Bamboo People: The Law and Japanese-Americans* (Del Mar, Calif.: Publisher's Inc., 1976), 201. Although Nisei legally could own land, because of the amendments to the 1913 Alien Land Act, they could not do so if they were merely holding title to land controlled by their parents.

87. Ibid., 203.

88. Roger Daniels, *Prisoners without a Trial: Japanese Americans in World War II* (New York: Hill and Wang, 1993), 86.

89. Toshio Yatsuhiro, Iwao Ishino, and Yoshiharu Matsumoto, "The Japanese American Looks at Resettlement," *The Public Opinion Quarterly* 8 (summer 1944): 193–95.

90. Bill Hosokawa, *Pacific Citizen*, January 4, 1947.

91. Tanaka, *Pacific Citizen*, July 19, 1947.

92. Sue Takimoto, *Rafu Shimpo*, June 24, 1947. For the other cities, see *Pacific Citizen*, February 15, 1947, August 13, 1949; and *Rafu Shimpo*, July 11, 1947.

93. Mary Oyama, *Rafu Shimpo*, July 11, 1947. See also *Rafu Shimpo* columns on May 31, June 7, 14, and 26, and July 5, 1947.

94. Ibid., June 26, 1947.

95. As quoted in T. Sasaki, "Daily Report 27," August 7, 1946, Los Angeles, Calif., W 2.11, JAERR.

96. As quoted in Sasaki, "Report 29," August 9, 1946, W 2.11, JAERR.

97. John Kitasako, *Pacific Citizen*, January 4, 1947.

98. *Pacific Citizen*, February 22, 1947.

99. Kango Kunitsugu, interview with David Biniasz, November 28, 1973, O.H. 1334, Oral History Program (Fullerton: California State University).

100. As reported in *Pacific Citizen*, February 1, 1947.

101. For black–Japanese American conflicts, see *Pacific Citizen*, March 8, 1947; Sasaki, "Report 1," June 24, 1946, JAERR; and Taro Kawa, interview with author, Pasadena, Calif., March 4, 1994 (audiotape in author's possession).

102. Sasaki, "Report 1," June 24, 1946, W 2.11, JAERR.

103. Taro Kawa, interview with author, Pasadena, Calif., March 4, 1994, audiotape (in author's possession).

104. Tanaka, *Pacific Citizen*, March 22, 1947.

105. As quoted in Sasaki, "Report 115," October 21, 1946, W 2.11, JAERR.

106. As quoted in Sasaki, "Report 44," August 22, 1946.

107. Yasuko I. Takezawa, *Breaking the Silence: Redress and Japanese American Ethnicity* (Ithaca: Cornell University Press, 1995).

108. Sasaki, "Report 19," August 1, 1946.

109. Ibid., "Report 24," August 4, 1946. Other informants' statements opposing the JACL can be found in "Report 59," August 9, 1946 and "Report 44," August 22, 1946.

110. Ibid., "Report 53," August 27, 1946.

111. Ibid., "Report 44," August 22, 1946.

112. *Rafu Shimpo*, August 30, 1946.

113. Fred Fertig, *Los Angeles Vanguard* 1, no. 2 (Sept. 1947), Los Angeles, Calif., fF 870 J3L6, Bancroft Library, University of California, Berkeley.

114. Frank Chuman, *Los Angeles Vanguard* 1, no. 2 (Sept. 1947), Los Angeles, Calif., fF 870 J3L6, Bancroft Library, University of California, Berkeley.

CHAPTER 4. DEFINING INTEGRATION

1. Taro Kawa, interview with author, Pasadena, Calif., March 4, 1994, audiotape (in author's possession); "History of Nisei Week," Nisei Week souvenir booklet, 1949, n.p. (in author's possession).

2. *Pacific Citizen*, August 20, 1949.

3. *Rafu Shimpo*, June 1, July 27, August 8, 1949.

4. "The Years Between," Nisei Week souvenir booklet, 1949, n.p. (in author's possession).

5. *Santa Ana Register*, October 5, 1945, Box 304, William Carr Scrapbook, Special Collections, University of California, Los Angeles.

6. Ibid., October 11, 1945.

7. WRA, press release, August 14, 1945, Box 304, William Carr Scrapbook.

8. See Audrie Girdner and Anne Loftis, *The Great Betrayal: The Evacuation of the Japanese-Americans during World War II* (London: Macmillan, 1969), 404–5, 421; Fletcher Bowron testimony, House Subcommittee No. 5 of the Committee on the Judiciary, *Hearings to Amend H.R. 7435, the Japanese-American Evacuation Claims Act of 1948*, 83d Cong., 2d sess., 1954, 232.

9. Frank Chuman, *The Bamboo People: The Law and Japanese-Americans* (Del Mar, Calif.: Publisher's Inc., 1976), 204–6.

10. Larry Tajiri, *Pacific Citizen,* January 18, 1947.

11. For *Oyama v. California* and other cases concerning the elimination of the Alien Land Law, see Chuman, *Bamboo People,* 203–14.

12. John Dower, *War without Mercy: Race and Power in the Pacific War* (New York: Pantheon Books, 1986), 311.

13. Brenda Gayle Plummer, *Rising Wind: Black Americans and U.S. Foreign Affairs* (Chapel Hill: University of North Carolina Press, 1996); Gerald Horne, *Black and Red: W. E. B. DuBois and the Afro-American Response to the Cold War* (Albany: State University of New York Press, 1986); Mary L. Dudziak, *Cold War Civil Rights* (Princeton: Princeton University Press, 2000). See also Richard Polenberg, *One Nation Divisible: Class, Race, and Ethnicity in the United States since 1938* (New York: Viking Press, 1980), 126.

14. Demaree Bess, "California's Amazing Japanese," *Saturday Evening Post,* April 30, 1955, 38–39.

15. Ibid., 80, 83.

16. Gina Marchetti, *Romance and the "Yellow Peril": Race, Sex, and Discursive Strategies in Hollywood Fiction* (Berkeley: University of California Press, 1993), 137, 144.

17. Ibid., 144.

18. Harry Honda, "Your Community Center," Nisei Week souvenir booklet, 1950, n.p., Japanese American National Museum, Los Angeles, Calif.

19. *Rafu Shimpo,* August 2, 1949.

20. Taro Kawa, interview with author, Pasadena, Calif., March 4, 1994, audiotape (in author's possession).

21. Leonard Broom and Ruth Riemer, *Removal and Return: The Socio-Economic Effects of the War on Japanese Americans* (Berkeley: University of California Press, 1949), 64.

22. Ibid., 66–67.

23. Ibid., 52, 63–64.

24. Midori Nishi, "Japanese Settlement in the Los Angeles Area," *Association of Pacific Coast Geographers Yearbook* 20 (1958): 47; see also Midori Nishi, "Changing Occupance of Japanese in Los Angeles County, 1940–1950" (Ph.D. diss., University of Washington, 1955).

25. Nishi, "Japanese Settlement," 45, 47.

26. Harry Honda, *Rafu Shimpo,* August 30, 1950.

27. Ibid., July 25, 1951.

28. Carl Kondo, *Rafu Shimpo,* August 16, 1951.

29. Honda, *Rafu Shimpo,* August 3, 1949.

30. *Rafu Shimpo,* July 22, August 15, 1953.

31. Ibid., July 7, 1956. For lackluster businessmen's support for Nisei Week, see Honda's column from July 25, 1951.

32. Midori Nishi and Young Il Kim, "Recent Japanese Settlement Changes in the Los Angeles Area," *Association of Pacific Coast Geographers Yearbook* 26 (1964): 24–32.

33. Kango Kunitsugu, *Little Tokyo Magazine* 2, no. 1 (1970): 14.

34. Joe Ishikawa, *Kashu Mainichi*, September 28, 1957.

35. "Nisei in Community Affairs," Nisei Week souvenir booklet, 1958, n.p., Japanese American National Museum, Los Angeles, Calif.

36. For an overview of the postwar migration and settlement of Japanese Americans in southern California, see William Halford Warren, "Asian Populations in Los Angeles County: A Focus on the Development of Japanese Communities from a Cartographic and Landscape Perspective" (Master's thesis, UCLA, 1985); and Nishi and Kim, "Recent Japanese Settlement Changes."

37. *Kashu Mainichi*, August 5, 1960.

38. "Story of Nisei Week," Nisei Week souvenir booklet, 1949, n.p. (in author's possession).

39. John Modell and Edna Bonacich, *The Economic Basis of Ethnic Solidarity: Small Business in the Japanese American Community* (Berkeley: University of California Press, 1980), 181. For a comparison of the Los Angeles community to national patterns, see ibid., 155, table 10:1.

40. Ibid., 136.

41. Ibid., 104.

42. Alva J. Fleming, speech for the 25th anniversary of Sacramento Nisei VFW Post 8985, 1972, notes (in author's possession); Sixth National Nisei Veterans' Reunion souvenir booklet, Los Angeles, Calif., 1970, 77 (in author's possession); "The American Legion Commodore Perry Post 525," Nisei Week souvenir booklet, 1956, n.p. (in author's possession). For the political activism of the American Legion post, see, for example, *Rafu Shimpo*, June 1, 1957 and December 5, 1959.

43. Edwin Hiroto, interview with author, Los Angeles, Calif., February 18, 1993, audiotape (in author's possession).

44. Edwin Hiroto, "Optimist Revue," Nisei Week souvenir booklet (Japanese American National Museum, Los Angeles, Calif., 1955), 35.

45. Montebello Women's Club, meeting minutes, 1953–1955, notes (in author's possession); Yae Aihara, interview with author, Los Angeles, Calif., March 17, 1993, audiotape (in author's possession).

46. Edwin Hiroto, interview with author, February 18, 1993, audiotape (in author's possession).

47. Robert Hayamizu, interview with author, Los Angeles, Calif., March 1, 1993, audiotape (in author's possession).

48. Yae Aihara, interview with author, Los Angeles, Calif., March 17, 1993, audiotape (in author's possession).

49. Gene N. Levine and Colbert Rhodes, *The Japanese American Community: A Three-Generation Study* (New York: Praeger, 1981), 100; *Kashu Mainichi*, July 28, August 17, 1964.

50. Matao Uwate (Nisei Week General Manager), "Report on the Eighteenth Annual Nisei Week Festival," August 28, 1958, n.p. (in author's possession).

51. Ibid.

52. Shohei Ooka, *Rafu Shimpo*, August 26, 1957.

53. George Yoshinaga, *Kashu Mainichi*, July 13 and 15, 1961. For the case of

Iva d'Aquino Toguri, the Nisei known as "Tokyo Rose," see Masayo Duus, *Tokyo Rose: Orphan of the Pacific* (New York: Harper and Row, 1979). The legal and political significance of the case is discussed in Stanley I. Kutler, *The American Inquisition: Justice and Injustice in the Cold War* (New York: Hill and Wang, 1982), 3–32. See also Clifford I. Uyeda, "The Pardoning of 'Tokyo Rose': A Report on the Restoration of American Citizenship to Iva Ikuko Toguri," *Amerasia Journal* 5, no. 2 (fall 1978): 6–94.

54. *Kashu Mainichi*, August 24, 1959; August 18, 12, 1960; June 27, 1961.

55. U.S.-Japan Centennial Celebration Program, Los Angeles, Calif., August 18, 1960 (in author's possession).

56. Fred Taomae, "The Japanese Influence on Southern California," Nisei Week souvenir booklet, 1962, 14, Japanese American National Museum, Los Angeles, Calif.

57. Nisei Week Executive Board, lists of monetary donations to the Nisei Week festival, 1961, 1963–64, 1970, 1975 (in author's possession).

58. *Kashu Mainichi*, July 9, 1959.

59. Yoshinaga, *Kashu Mainichi*, July 30, 1960.

60. Henry Mori, *Rafu Shimpo*, August 18, 1962.

61. Taomae, "Japanese Influence," 14.

62. Saburo Kido, Nisei Week souvenir booklet, 1962, n.p., Japanese American National Museum, Los Angeles, Calif.

63. Mori, *Rafu Shimpo*, July 3, 1965.

64. Kondo, *Rafu Shimpo*, August 24, 1950.

65. Honda, *Rafu Shimpo*, August 10, 1949.

66. Ibid., August 14, 1954.

67. "Mr. and Mrs. Issei, 1956," Nisei Week souvenir booklet, 1956, 7, 46 (in author's possession).

68. *Kashu Mainichi*, August 26, 1959.

69. Yoshinaga, *Kashu Mainichi*, June 7, 1965.

70. Sarah Banet-Weiser, *The Most Beautiful Girl in the World: Beauty Pageants and National Identity* (Berkeley: University of California Press, 1999), 44.

71. Yoshinaga, *Kashu Mainichi*, July 25, August 1, 1959.

72. Mori, *Rafu Shimpo*, June 5, 1965.

73. Yoshinaga, *Kashu Mainichi*, July 14, 1961.

74. Ibid., August 14, 15, 1959.

75. Paul R. Spickard, *Mixed Blood: Intermarriage and Ethnic Identity in Twentieth-Century America* (Madison: University of Wisconsin Press, 1989), 145.

76. "Paradise in Reverse: Ex-Hawaiians Find Opportunity Here," Nisei Week souvenir booklet, 1959 (in author's possession). For the migration of war brides from Japan, see Michael C. Thornton, "The Quiet Immigration: Foreign Spouses of U.S. Citizens, 1945–1985," in *Racially Mixed People in America*, ed. Maria P. P. Root (Newbury Park, Calif.: Sage, 1992), 64–76; Regina Lark, "They Challenged Two Nations: Marriages between Japanese Women and American GIs, 1945 to the Present" (Ph.D. diss., University of Southern California, 1999); and Shizuko Suenaga, "Good-bye to Sayonara: The Reverse Assimilation of Japanese War Brides" (Ph.D. diss., Boston College, 1996).

77. Yosh Akiyama, "When East Meets West," Nisei Week souvenir booklet, 1953, n.p. (in author's possession).

78. See, for example, *Rafu Shimpo*, June 27, 1956; *Kashu Mainichi*, July 5, 1961, July 26, 1958, and August 30, 1962. Also see report on Japanese American gangs in the 1950s and 1960s in *Rafu Shimpo* (special issue), December 18, 1993.

79. "What Is JAY?" Nisei Week souvenir booklet, 1959, 21–22 (in author's possession); *Rafu Shimpo*, July 24, 1958.

80. *Kashu Mainichi*, July 9, 1958.

81. Ibid., May 26, 1961.

82. Ellen Endo, *Rafu Shimpo*, August 21, 1971, August 3, 1973, August 3, 1968.

83. Ibid., June 1, 1968, July 3, 1971, June 1, 1968.

84. Ibid., July 13, 1968, July 23, 1966.

85. Ibid., August 9, 1969.

86. Endo favorably quoted Nisei "integrationist" Mary Oyama's critique of Japanese American parochialism. See Endo, *Rafu Shimpo*, August 9, 1969.

CHAPTER 5. THE NEW COSMOPOLITANISM

1. Mitsuhiko Shimizu, "Message," Nisei Week souvenir booklet, 1965, 5, Japanese American National Museum, Los Angeles, Calif.

2. *Pacific Citizen*, July 29, 1966.

3. Ibid., August 21, 29, 1972; *Kashu Mainichi*, August 28, 1972; Mike Murase, report on Nisei Week parade controversy, *Gidra* 4 (Sept. 1972); Thai Binh Brigade, "Nisei Week—Vietnam," leaflet, 1972, reprinted in *Gidra* 4 (Sept. 1972); *Los Angeles Times*, August 21, 1972. For a discussion of the origins and practice of the Asian American movement newspaper *Gidra*, see William Wei, *The Asian American Movement* (Philadelphia: Temple University Press, 1993), 102–12.

4. *Kashu Mainichi*, August 28, 1972.

5. Ellen Endo, *Rafu Shimpo*, August 26, 1972.

6. Mike Masaoka, *Pacific Citizen*, January 29, 1970.

7. *Pacific Citizen*, March 28, 1968.

8. *Rafu Shimpo*, August 1, 1970.

9. Gene Levine and Colbert Rhodes, *The Japanese American Community: A Three-Generation Study* (New York: Praeger, 1981), 123.

10. Minako K. Maykovich, *Japanese American Identity Dilemma* (Tokyo: Waseda University Press, 1972), 86, and "Political Activation of Japanese American Youth," *Journal of Social Issues* 29, no. 2 (1973): 171.

11. *Pacific Citizen*, July 29, 1966.

12. Jerry Enomoto, *Pacific Citizen*, May 23, 1969.

13. Harry Honda, *Pacific Citizen*, May 24, 1968.

14. *Pacific Citizen*, October 3, 1969, March 21, 1969. For complaints about Sansei apathy, see also May 10, 1968, February 7, 1969.

15. Enomoto, *Pacific Citizen*, May 23, 1969.

16. Roy Nishikawa, *Pacific Citizen*, December 5, 1969.

17. Jeffrey Matsui, *Pacific Citizen*, September 10, 1971.

18. Warren Furutani, interview with author, Los Angeles, Calif., August 9, 1988.

19. Ibid.

20. Steve Tatsukawa, *Gidra* 4 (July 1972).

21. For the early history of the movement for redress, see Yasuko I. Takezawa, *Breaking the Silence: Redress and Japanese American Ethnicity* (Ithaca: Cornell University Press, 1995), 35–42.

22. Matsui, *Pacific Citizen*, July 21, 1972.

23. Ibid., July 14, 1972.

24. Ibid., September 22, 1972.

25. Ron Wakabayashi, interview with author, Los Angeles, Calif., July 25, 1989.

26. Yuji Ichioka, *Pacific Citizen*, June 21, 1968.

27. *Pacific Citizen*, April 23, 1971.

28. Amy Uyematsu, "The Emergence of Yellow Power," in *Roots: An Asian American Reader*, ed. Amy Tachiki et al. (Los Angeles: UCLA Asian American Studies Center, 1971), 10–11.

29. Wei, *Asian American Movement*, 44–45, 70.

30. Daniel Okimoto, "The Intolerance of Success," in Tachiki, *Roots*, 14; "Autobiography of a Sansei Female," in Tachiki, *Roots*, 113.

31. Ron Tanaka, "I hate my wife for her flat yellow face," in Tachiki, *Roots*, 47.

32. Uyematsu, "Yellow Power," 10.

33. *Rafu Shimpo*, August 26, 1972.

34. Uyematsu, "Yellow Power," 10. Uyematsu bases her claims in part on Dinora Gil, "Yellow Prostitution," *Gidra* 1 (Apr. 1969).

35. Thai Binh Brigade, "Nisei Week—Vietnam," leaflet, 1972, reprinted in *Gidra* 4 (Sept. 1972).

36. Quotation is from Wei, *Asian American Movement*, 76.

37. "In the Movement Office," *Gidra* 3 (Jan. 1971).

38. Georgia Lee, on Asian American beauty pageants, *Gidra* 1 (Aug. 1969).

39. "In the Movement Office," *Gidra* 3 (Jan. 1971).

40. Susie Ling, "The Mountain Movers: Asian American Women's Movement in Los Angeles," *Amerasia Journal* 15, no. 1 (1989): 52.

41. *Rafu Shimpo*, August 19, 1980.

42. Ibid., August 12, 1987.

43. James Diego Vigil, *Barrio Gangs: Street Life and Identity in Southern California* (Austin: University of Texas Press, 1988), 121–22. See also Brenda Jo Bright, "Remappings: Los Angeles Low Riders," in *Looking High and Low: Art and Cultural Identity*, ed. Brenda Jo Bright and Liza Bakewell (Tucson: University of Arizona Press, 1995), and Brenda Jo Bright, "Mexican American Low Riders: An Anthropological Approach to Popular Culture" (Ph.D. diss., Rice University, 1994).

44. Kevin Quock, interview with author, Los Angeles, Calif., June 1, 1994; Brian Nakagiri, interview with author, Los Angeles, Calif., August 4, 1994.

45. Tim Mochizuki, interview with author, Torrance, Calif., August 8, 1997.

46. *Jade Magazine* 3 (June 1980): 34.

47. *Rafu Shimpo*, August 25, 1973.

48. Warren Furutani, on car cruising at Nisei Week, *Gidra* (Aug. 23, 1980).

49. Mei Nakano, *Pacific Citizen*, March 29, 1985.

50. Los Angeles *Herald Express* (California Living section), Aug. 19, 1973.

51. Endo, *Rafu Shimpo*, July 6, 1973.

52. Douglas Masuda, *Rafu Shimpo*, March 29, 1985.

53. *Rafu Shimpo*, May 3, 1985.

54. Endo, *Rafu Shimpo*, August 5, 1972.

55. Ibid.

56. Ibid.

57. Theoretically *hapa* could denote a mixture of Japanese and any other racial or ethnic group, but in Nisei society and in this study, *hapa* usually means Eurasian.

58. George Yoshinaga, *Kashu Mainichi*, July 19, August 6, 1976.

59. George Yoshinaga, interview with author, Los Angeles, Calif., August 12, 1994.

60. Interview with Hedy Ann Posey, Nisei Week souvenir booklet, 1981, 5.

61. Nishinaga, letter to editor, *Rafu Shimpo*, August 27, 1982.

62. *Rafu Shimpo*, August 31, 1982.

63. Ibid., September 3, 1982.

64. Ibid., August 31, 1982.

65. Cindy Miller, letter to editor, *Rafu Shimpo*, September 8, 1982.

66. Hedy Ann Posey, letter to editor, *Rafu Shimpo*, September 10, 1982.

67. Cindy Miller, letter to editor, *Rafu Shimpo*, September 8, 1982.

68. Nisei Week souvenir booklet, 1981, 5.

69. *Rafu Shimpo*, September 4, 1982. Paul Spickard reveals that there were at least seven hundred mixed-race internees housed in the WRA camps, some of whom had only a fraction of Japanese blood. For their fascinating story, see Paul Spickard, "Injustice Compounded: Amerasians and Non-Japanese in America's World War II Concentration Camps," *Journal of American Ethnic History* 5 (spring 1986): 5–22.

70. Rebecca Chiyoko King points out that the racial purity rule was instituted in the 1950s, probably in 1954 when the first hapa participated in the beauty contest. This "rule," like many Nisei Week policies, was informal and ad hoc. There was no need to refer again to such a policy until the 1970s; Rebecca Chiyoko King, "The Changing Face of Japanese America: The Making and Remaking of Race in the Japanese American Community" (Ph.D. diss., University of California, Berkeley, 1998), 112.

71. Raymond Okamura, *Pacific Citizen*, April 19, 1985.

72. Mei Nakano, *Pacific Citizen*, April 12, 19, 1985. For scholarly discussions of hapa identities and experiences, see two essays contained in Maria P. P. Root, ed., *Racially Mixed People in America* (Newbury Park, Calif.: Sage, 1992): Amy Iwasaki Mass, "Interracial Japanese Americans: The Best of Both Worlds or the End of the Japanese Community," 265–79; and Theresa Kay Williams, "Prism Lives: Identity of Binational Amerasians," 280–303.

73. Candice Ota, "Radical Awakening, Community Strength," Nisei Week souvenir booklet, 1990, Japanese American National Museum, Los Angeles, Calif., 125.

74. John Higham, "Current Trends in the Study of Ethnicity in the United States," *Journal of American Ethnic History* 2 (fall 1982): 7.

75. Yoshinaga, *Kashu Mainichi*, July 27, 1983, September 4, 1986.

76. Nakayama, *Rafu Shimpo*, August 21, 1986.

CHAPTER 6. NATIONALISM AND INTERNATIONALISM

1. George Yoshinaga, *Kashu Mainichi*, July 3, 1974; August 18, 1975; quotation is from August 21, 1975.

2. *Kashu Mainichi*, August 21, 1963.

3. Kango Kunitsugu, *Little Tokyo Magazine* 1, no. 1 (1969): 65.

4. Ichiro Mike Murase, *Little Tokyo: One Hundred Years in Pictures* (Los Angeles: Visual Communications/Asian American Studies Central, 1983), 20–21.

5. John Modell, *The Economics and Politics of Racial Accommodation: The Japanese of Los Angeles, 1900–1942* (Urbana: University of Illinois Press, 1977), 71–72.

6. *Rafu Shimpo*, June 6, 1947; Murase, *Little Tokyo*, 20.

7. *Little Tokyo Magazine* 2, no. 1 (1970): 14.

8. Little Tokyo Redevelopment Office, memorandum, July 7, 1969, Community Redevelopment Agency of the City of Los Angeles (in author's possession).

9. George Umezawa, *Little Tokyo Magazine* 3, no. 3 (1971).

10. Kango Kunitsugu, interview by Sherry Turner, Japanese American Project, August 6, 1973, O.H. 41334, Oral History Program (Fullerton: California State University).

11. Kunitsugu, *Little Tokyo Magazine* 2, no. 1 (1970): 14.

12. *Little Tokyo Newsletter* 1, no. 3 (Jan. 1970).

13. Little Tokyo Redevelopment Office, memorandum, July 7, 1969, Community Redevelopment Agency of the City of Los Angeles (in author's possession).

14. Kunitsugu, *Little Tokyo Magazine* 2, no. 2 (1970): 66.

15. *Historical Statistics of the United States, Colonial Times to 1970,* Bicentennial Edition, vol. 1 (Washington, D.C.: U.S. Bureau of the Census, Department of Commerce, 1975), 107.

16. *Los Angeles Times,* June 23, 1969.

17. Little Tokyo Redevelopment Office, memorandum, July 7, 1969, Community Redevelopment Agency of the City of Los Angeles (in author's possession).

18. U.S. Immigration and Naturalization Service, *Statistical Yearbook of the Immigration and Naturalization Service,* 1990 (Washington, D.C.: Government Printing Office, 1991), table 40, p. 124, and table H, p. 119; U.S. INS, *Statistical Yearbook of the Immigration and Naturalization Service,* 1982 (Washington, D.C.: Government Printing Office, 1983), 104.

19. Community Redevelopment Agency of the City of Los Angeles, "Fact Book / Little Tokyo," January 1970 (in author's possession).

20. Little Tokyo Redevelopment Office, memorandum, July 7, 1969, Community Redevelopment Agency of the City of Los Angeles (in author's possession).

21. Interview with Kajima International representative, *Gidra* 5 (Aug. 1973). For a critical sketch of Kajima's role in Little Tokyo redevelopment and its use of slave labor during World War II, see Mike Davis, "Kajima's Throne of Blood," *Nation* (Feb. 12, 1996): 18–20.

22. *Rafu Shin.po,* September 29, 1980.

23. Nisei Week Executive Board, press release, March 31, 1976 (in author's possession).

24. *Pacific Citizen,* August 31, 1984.

25. *Rafu Shimpo,* August 22, 1977.

26. Little Tokyo Businessmen's Association, press release, November 18, 1968 (in author's possession).

27. Harry K. Honda to George Yuzawa, October 19, 1978, Los Angeles, Calif. (in author's possession). As the editor of JACL's *Pacific Citizen,* Honda handled press relations for the Nisei Week festival.

28. Nisei Week Executive Board, budgets and financial records for the Nisei Week festival, 1979–92, Nisei Week Japanese Festival office, Japanese American Cultural and Community Center, Los Angeles, Calif. (notes in author's possession).

29. George Yoshinaga, interview with author, August 12, 1994.

30. Yoshinaga, *Kashu Mainichi,* August 26, 1974.

31. Yoshinaga, interview with author, August 12, 1994.

32. While the Los Angeles City Council of Public Works Committee eventually agreed to the Onizuka Street renaming, twenty-two Weller Street foreign businesses opposed the change; see *Kashu Mainichi,* August 27, 1986.

33. Yoshinaga, *Kashu Mainichi,* July 30, 1986.

34. Ibid.

35. Ibid., August 25, 1988.

36. *Kashu Mainichi,* August 4, 1986.

37. The JBA began as the Japan Traders Club in 1961. At that time it was comprised of forty-eight southern California–based Japanese import/export companies. The name changed in 1978 to reflect the organization's expansion beyond trading companies. In 1994 JBA had approximately seven hundred members, including virtually all major Japanese corporations operating in the United States including automobile makers Toyota, Nissan, and Honda.

38. Kenji Ito, *Kashu Mainichi,* April 4, 1986.

39. Katsumi Kunitsugu, *Kashu Mainichi,* July 26, 1972; see also August 16, 1971; *Rafu Shimpo,* August 25, 1970.

40. *Rafu Shimpo,* August 16, 1979.

41. On corporate takeover of Little Tokyo, see *Gidra* 5, no. 8 (Aug. 1973): 7.

42. Anonymous, Little Tokyo People's Rights Organization, newsletter, n.d., c. 1977.

43. Little Tokyo People's Rights Organization, newsletter, n.d., c. 1977.

44. On redevelopment of Japantown, San Francisco, see *Gidra* 5, no. 8 (Aug. 1973): 7.

45. Editorial on redevelopment of San Francisco, *Gidra* 1, no. 6 (Sept. 1969).

46. On redevelopment of Japantown, San Francisco, *Gidra* 5, no. 8 (Aug. 1973): 7.

47. "Who Is Nisei Week For?" Little Tokyo People's Rights Organization, newsletter, Los Angeles, Calif., August 1976.

48. *Sho Tokyo News* (publication of the Little Tokyo Anti-Eviction Task Force) 1, no. 2, Los Angeles, Calif. (Aug. 1974).

49. *Little Tokyo News* (publication of the Little Tokyo People's Rights Organization), Los Angeles, Calif. (May 1979).

50. *Sho Tokyo News*, 1, no. 2 (Aug. 1974).

51. *Little Tokyo News* (Aug. 1978).

52. Little Tokyo People's Rights Organization, newsletter, August 1976.

53. *Little Tokyo News* (Oct. 1977).

54. Ibid., (Aug. 1978).

55. "Who Is Nisei Week For?" Little Tokyo People's Rights Organization, newsletter, August 1976.

56. Little Tokyo Redevelopment Office, "Biennial Report 1988–1990," n.d., Community Redevelopment Agency of the City of Los Angeles.

57. *Downtown News*, Los Angeles, Calif., August 5, 1991.

58. Yoshinaga, *Kashu Mainichi*, August 30, 1984.

59. Ibid., August 26, 1986.

60. *Tozai Times*, Los Angeles, Calif., September 1985. The mayor of Los Angeles in 1969 established LTCDAC as the community liaison to the Community Redevelopment Agency.

61. Kenneth K. Sadanaga, "Redevelopment in Little Tokyo: Amerasia Bookstore," student paper, reading room collections (UCLA Asian American Studies Center, 1981). Other student papers in the reading room collections are also critical of redevelopment: see Joyce Shirado, "Task Force" (1974); Robert Yoshio Mori, "The Dilemma of Small Business in Little Tokyo Redevelopment" (1974); Steven Mori, "Little Tokyo Redevelopment: Who Is It For?" (1977); Minoru David Akiyama, "The Little Tokyo Redevelopment: Housing and the City Plan" (1978).

62. Dwight Chuman, *Rafu Shimpo*, August 10, 1982.

63. Yoshinaga, interview with author, August 12, 1994.

64. Gloria Uchida, *Tozai Times*, September 1985.

65. Ibid.

66. *Rafu Shimpo*, July 22, 1982.

67. See, for instance, Yoshinaga, *Kashu Mainichi*, July 18, 1980.

68. Ibid., July 7, 1982.

69. Christopher Doi, Tom Fujita, Lewis Kawahara, Brian Niiya, and Karen Umemoto, "Little Tokyo Redevelopment: The North Side of First Street," student paper, reading room collection (UCLA Asian American Studies Center, 1986), 41.

Select Bibliography

NEWSPAPERS AND OTHER PERIODICALS

Chamber of Commerce Quarterly (Japanese Chamber of Commerce of Southern California), Los Angeles, vol. 1, nos. 1–2 (Nov. 1, 1991/Apr. 20, 1992)
Doho, Los Angeles, 1938–41
Downtown News, Los Angeles, 1991
Gidra, Los Angeles, 1969–73, 1980
Jade Magazine, Los Angeles, 1980
Kashu Mainichi, Los Angeles, 1934–88
Little Tokyo Magazine, Los Angeles, 1969–71
Little Tokyo News (Little Tokyo People's Rights Organization), Los Angeles, 1978–79
Little Tokyo Newsletter (Little Tokyo Community Development Advisory Committee), Los Angeles, 1969–70
Little Tokyo People's Rights Organization Newsletter, Los Angeles, 1976
Los Angeles Daily News, Los Angeles, 1946–47
Los Angeles Herald Examiner, Los Angeles, 1946, 1973
Los Angeles Times, Los Angeles, 1935–36
Pacific Citizen, San Francisco, Salt Lake City, Los Angeles, 1929–93
Rafu Shimpo, Los Angeles, 1934–87
Sangyo Nippo, Los Angeles, 1940–41
Santa Ana Register, Santa Ana, Calif., 1945
Sho Tokyo News (Little Tokyo Anti-Eviction Task Force), Los Angeles, 1974
Tozai Times, Los Angeles, 1985

ARCHIVAL RECORDS

Japanese American Evacuation and Resettlement Records, BANC MSS 67/14 C, Bancroft Library, University of California, Berkeley
Japanese American Research Project, Special Collections, University of California, Los Angeles
Joseph Kurihara collection, Japanese American National Museum, Los Angeles
War Relocation Authority, Records, National Archive, microfilm, BANC FILM 1932, Bancroft Library, University of California, Berkeley

PERSONAL AND PRIVATE COLLECTIONS

Yae Aihara. Little Tokyo business owner and member, Montebello Women's Club. Montebello Women's Club, meeting minutes, 1953–73 and various Nisei Week souvenir booklets. Los Angeles.
Bob Hayamizu. Member, Veterans of Foreign War, Post 9938. Manuscript about history of Nisei in the VFW. Los Angeles.
Harry Honda. Journalist and editor of *Pacific Citizen*. Various correspondence, official documents, and clippings related to the Nisei Week festival. Los Angeles.
Minoru (Casey) Kasuyama. Member, American Legion, Perry Post 525. Publications of and clippings about the Perry Post. Los Angeles.
Margaret (and Harold) Keimi. Collector. Various Nisei Week souvenir booklets. Monterey Park, Calif.
Little Tokyo Redevelopment Office. Community Redevelopment Agency. Office memoranda and publications. Los Angeles.
Nisei Week Japanese Festival. Correspondence and financial records, 1979–80. Los Angeles.
Dean Toji. Faculty, California State University, Long Beach. Various periodicals and organizational records related to Little Tokyo redevelopment. Culver City, Calif.
Toyo Miyatake Studios. Official Nisei Week photographer. Various photographs, 1949–93. San Gabriel, Calif.

ORAL INTERVIEWS

ARCHIVAL COLLECTIONS

Kango Kunitsugu. Interviewed by Sherry Turner, August 4, 1973. O.H. 1334a, transcript, Japanese American Project, Oral History Program. Fullerton: California State University.
Kango Kunitsugu. Interviewed by David Biniasz, November 28, 1973. O.H. 1334b, transcript, Japanese American Project, Oral History Program. Fullerton: California State University.
Katsuma Mukaeda. Interviewed by David Biniasz, November 28, 1973. O.H. 1341a, transcript, Japanese American Project, Oral History Program. Fullerton: California State University.

Katsuma Mukaeda. Interviewed by Joe Grant Masaoka, April 27, 1966. Japanese American Research Project, Special Collections, UCLA.
Susie Ling. Interviews. Asian American Studies Reading Room Collection, UCLA.

INTERVIEWED BY AUTHOR
(transcript, notes, or audiotape in author's possession)

Yaye Aihara. Los Angeles, March 17, 1993.
Kenji Arai. Los Angeles, May 27, 1994.
Judy Sugita de Querioz. Torrance, Calif. May 31, 1994.
Gerald Fukui. Los Angeles, April 28, 1994.
Warren Furutani. Los Angeles, August 9, 1989.
Frances Hashimoto. Los Angeles, May 12, 1994.
Robert Hayamizu. Los Angeles, March 1, 1993.
Faye Hirata (pseudonym). Gardena, Calif. June 2, 1994.
Edwin Hiroto. Los Angeles, February 18, 1993.
Wimp Hiroto. Gardena, Calif. May 31, 1994.
Harry Honda. Los Angeles, August 5, 1991.
Roy Hoshizaki. Los Angeles, March 6, 1993.
Yuji Ichioka. Los Angeles, July 24, 1989.
Carol Itatani. Long Beach, Calif. May 23, 1994.
Candice Ito. Culver City, Calif. April 22, 1994.
Minoru (Casey) Kasuyama. Los Angeles, March 2, 1993.
Taro Kawa. Pasadena, Calif. March 14, 1994.
Hiromichi Kume. Los Angeles, April 28, 1994.
Katsumi Kunitsugu. Los Angeles, February 23, 1993.
John Maeno. Los Angeles, September 2, 1991.
Archie Miyatake. Los Angeles, April 1, 1993.
Tim Mochizuki, Torrance, Calif. August 8, 1997.
Yoshiko Mori (pseudonym). Gardena, Calif. May 20, 1993.
Katsuma Mukaeda. Van Nuys, Calif. February 3, 1993.
Chiye Naganol (pseudonym). Los Angeles, Calif. April 19, 1993.
Chris Naito. Los Angeles, May 19, 1994.
Brian Nakagiri. Los Angeles, August 4, 1994.
Jane Nakamura (pseudonym). Los Angeles, June 20, 1994.
Mike Nakayama. Culver City, Calif. April 22, 1994.
Sue Okabe. Gardena, Calif. March 23, 1993.
James Okazaki. Los Angeles, May 12, 1994.
Patrick Okura. Phone interview. September 3, 1997.
Kevin Quock. Los Angeles, June 1, 1994.
Sandra Sakai (pseudonym). Los Angeles, January 28, 1993.
Masami Sam Seno. Los Angeles, February 10, 1993.
Victor Shibata. Los Angeles, August 11, 1989.
Louise Suski. Cerritos, Calif. October 5, 1992.
Yo Takagaki. Los Angeles, May 27, 1994.
Arthur Takei. Los Angeles, March 26, 1993.

Togo Tanaka. Los Angeles, October 20, 1992 and February 18, 1999.
Sandra Toshiyuki. Los Angeles, May 24, 1994.
Henry Tsurutani. Santa Monica, Calif. May 18, 1993.
Ron Wakabayashi, Los Angeles, July 25, 1989.
Emiko Yamada. Los Angeles, May 18, 1994.
Harry Yamamoto. Los Angeles, February 12, 1993.
Mike Yamamoto. Los Angeles, August 13, 1989.
Joanne Yamashiro. Phone interview. June 8, 1994.
George Yoshinaga. Los Angeles, August 12, 1994.
Riye Yoshizawa. Los Angeles, March 12, 1993.

ELECTRONIC DATA

Levine, Gene, N. "Japanese-American Research Project (JARP): A Three-
    Generation Study, 1890–1966" (computer file), 2d ed. Los Angeles: UCLA
    Institute for Social Science Research, and Chicago: National Opinion Re-
    search Center [producers], 1985; Ann Arbor, Mich.: Interuniversity Consor-
    tium for Political and Social Research [distributor], 1992.
Ruggles, Steven, et al. Integrated Public Use Microdata Series: Version 2.0. 1950
    and 1970. Minneapolis: Historical Census Projects, University of Minne-
    sota, 1997. [http://www.ipums.umn.edu]
War Relocation Authority. "Form 26: Evacuee Summary Data ('Locator In-
    dex')." Electronic Records. National Archives. Washington, D.C.

OTHER SOURCES

Abrahams, Roger D. "Shouting Match at the Border: The Folklore of Display
    Events." In "And Other Neighborly Names": Social Process and Cultural
    Image in Texas Folklore, edited by Richard Bauman and Roger D. Abrahams.
    Austin: University of Texas Press, 1981.
———. "Toward an Enactment-Centered Theory of Folklore." In Frontiers of
    Folklore, edited by William R. Bascom. Boulder, Colo.: Westview Press,
    1977.
Akiyama, Minoru David. "The Little Tokyo Redevelopment: Housing and the
    City Plan." Student paper, Asian American Studies Reading Room Collec-
    tions, UCLA, 1978.
Archdeacon, Thomas J. Becoming American: An Ethnic History. New York:
    The Free Press, 1983.
Azuma, Eiichiro. "Racial Struggle, Immigrant Nationalism, and Ethnic Identity:
    Japanese and Filipinos in the California Delta." Pacific Historical Review 67
    (May 1998): 163–99.
Bailey, Thomas A. Theodore Roosevelt and the Japanese-American Crisis. Stan-
    ford, Calif.: Stanford University Press, 1934.
Bakhtin, Mikhail M. Rabelais and His World. Trans. Helen Iswolsky. Cam-
    bridge, Mass.: MIT Press, 1968.

Banet-Weiser, Sarah. *The Most Beautiful Girl in the World: Beauty Pageants and National Identity*. Berkeley: University of California Press, 1999.

Banner, Lois W. *American Beauty*. New York: Knopf, 1983.

Bauman, Richard, and Roger D. Abrahams, eds. *"And Other Neighborly Names."* Austin: University of Texas Press, 1981.

Bell, Catherine. *Ritual Theory, Ritual Practice*. New York: Oxford University Press, 1992.

Bender, Thomas. "The Need for Synthesis in American History." *Journal of American History* 73, no. 1 (1986): 120–36.

Bentley, G. Carter. "Ethnicity and Practice." *Comparative Studies in Society and History* 29, no. 1 (Jan. 1987): 24–55.

Bess, Demaree. "California's Amazing Japanese." *Saturday Evening Post*. April 30, 1955: 38–39.

Bodnar, John. *Remaking America: Public Memory, Commemoration, and Patriotism in the Twentieth Century*. Princeton: Princeton University Press, 1992.

Bourdieu, Pierre. *Outline of a Theory of Practice*. Trans. Richard Nice. Cambridge: Cambridge University Press, 1977.

Bourdieu, Pierre, and Loïc J. D. Wacquant. *An Invitation to Reflexive Sociology*. Chicago: University of Chicago Press, 1992.

Bright, Brenda Jo. "Mexican American Low Riders: An Anthropological Approach to Popular Culture." Ph.D. diss., Rice University, 1994.

Bright, Brenda Jo, and Liza Bakewell, eds. *Looking High and Low: Art and Cultural Identity*. Tucson: University of Arizona Press, 1995.

Broom, Leonard, and Ruth Riemer. *Removal and Return: The Socio-Economic Effects of the War on Japanese Americans*. Berkeley: University of California Press, 1949.

Caudill, William. "Japanese-American Personality and Acculturation." *Genetic Psychology Monographs* 1 (1952): 3–102.

Chan, Sucheng. *Asian Americans: An Interpretive History*. Boston: Twayne, 1991.

———, ed. *Entry Denied: Exclusion and the Chinese Community in America, 1882–1943*. Philadelphia: Temple University Press, 1991.

Chaplin, Charles. *My Autobiography*. New York: Simon and Schuster, 1964.

Chow, Rey. *Writing Diaspora: Tactics of Intervention in Contemporary Cultural Studies*. Bloomington: University of Indiana Press, 1993.

Chuman, Frank F. *The Bamboo People: The Law and Japanese-Americans*. Del Mar, Calif.: Publisher's Inc., 1976.

Chun, Ki-Taek. "The Myth of Asian American Success and Its Educational Ramifications," *IRCD Bulletin*, Teacher's College, Columbia University, 15, nos. 1–2 (winter/spring 1980): 1–12.

Clifford, James. *The Predicament of Culture: Twentieth-Century Ethnography, Literature, Art*. Cambridge, Mass.: Harvard University Press, 1988.

Clifford, James, and George E. Marcus, eds. *Writing Culture: The Poetics and Politics of Ethnography*. Berkeley: University of California Press, 1986.

Cohen, Lizabeth. *Making a New Deal: Industrial Workers in Chicago, 1919–1939*. Cambridge: Cambridge University Press, 1990.

Commission of Wartime Relocation and Internment of Civilians. *Personal Justice Denied*. Washington, D.C.: Government Printing Office, 1982. Reprint, Seattle: University of Washington Press, 1997.

Conroy, Hilary, and T. Scott Miyakawa, eds. *East across the Pacific*. Santa Barbara, Calif.: ABC-Clio, 1972.

Conzen, Kathleen Neils. "Ethnicity as Festival Culture: Nineteenth-Century German America on Parade." In *The Invention of Ethnicity*, edited by Werner Sollors, 44–76. New York: Oxford University Press, 1989.

Daniels, Roger. *Asian America: Chinese and Japanese in the United States since 1850*. Seattle: William Morrow, 1988.

———. *Concentration Camps U.S.A.: Japanese Americans and World War II*. New York: Holt, Rinehart and Winston, 1971.

———. *The Decision to Relocate the Japanese Americans*. Malabar, Fla.: Krieger, 1986.

———. "The Japanese." In *Ethnic Leadership in America*, edited by John Higham, 36–63. Baltimore: Johns Hopkins University Press, 1978.

———. "Japanese America, 1930–1941: An Ethnic Community in the Great Depression." *Journal of the West* 24, no. 4 (1985): 35–49.

———. "No Lamps Were Lit for Them: Angel Island and the Historiography of Asian American Immigration." *Journal of American Ethnic History* 17 (fall 1997): 3–18.

———. *The Politics of Prejudice: The Anti-Japanese Movement in California and the Struggle for Japanese Exclusion*. 1962. Reprint, New York: Atheneum, 1968.

———. *Prisoners without a Trial: Japanese Americans in World War II*. New York: Hill and Wang, 1993.

———. "Westerners from the East: Oriental Immigrants Reappraised." *Pacific Historical Review* 35, no. 4 (1966): 373–84.

———, ed. *American Concentration Camps*. Vol. 2. New York: Garland Publishing, 1989.

Davis, Mike. "Kajima's Throne of Blood." *Nation* (Feb. 12, 1996): 18–20.

Davis, Susan G. *Parades and Power: Street Theatre in Nineteenth-Century Philadelphia*. Berkeley: University of California Press, 1986.

De Certeau, Michel. *The Practice of Everyday Life*. Trans. Steven Rendall. Berkeley: University of California Press, 1984.

Desan, Suzanne. "Crowds, Community, and Ritual in the Work of E. P. Thompson and Natalie Davis." In *The New Cultural History*, edited by Lynn Hunt, 47–71. Berkeley: University of California Press, 1989.

DeVos, George. "A Quantitative Rorschach Assessment of Maladjustment and Rigidity in Acculturation of Japanese Americans." *Genetic Psychology Monographs* 52 (1955): 51–87.

Doi, Christopher, Tom Fujita, Lewis Kawahara, Brian Niiya, and Karen Umemoto. "Little Tokyo Redevelopment: The North Side of First Street." Student paper, Asian American Studies Reading Room Collections, UCLA, 1986.

Dorson, Richard M., ed. *Handbook of American Folklore*. Bloomington: Indiana University Press, 1983.

Dower, John W. *War without Mercy: Race and Power in the Pacific War.* New York: Pantheon Books, 1986.

Drinnon, Richard. *Keeper of Concentration Camps: Dillion S. Meyer and American Racism.* Berkeley: University of California Press, 1987.

Duus, Masayo. *Tokyo Rose: Orphan of the Pacific.* New York: Harper and Row, 1979.

Embrey, Sue Kunitomi, et al., eds. *Manzanar Martyr: An Interview with Harry Y. Ueno.* Fullerton: California State University, 1986.

Espiritu, Yen Le. *Asian American Panethnicity: Bridging Institutions and Identities.* Philadelphia: Temple University Press, 1992.

Fass, Paula. *The Damned and the Beautiful: American Youth in the 1920s.* New York: Oxford University Press, 1977.

Ferenczi, Imre. *International Migrations.* Vol. 1, *Statistics.* New York: National Bureau of Economic Research, 1929.

Fiske, John. *Understanding Popular Culture.* Boston: Unwin Hyman, 1989.

Flacks, Richard. "The Liberated Generation: An Exploration of the Roots of Student Protest." *Journal of Social Issues* 23, no. 3 (1967): 52–75.

Foucault, Michel. *Discipline and Punish: The Birth of the Prison.* Trans. Alan Sheridan. New York: Vintage Books, 1979.

———. *Power/Knowledge: Selected Interviews and Other Writings, 1972–1977.* Edited by Colin Gordon. New York: Pantheon Books, 1980.

Fujita, Stephan S., and David J. O'Brien. *Japanese American Ethnicity: The Persistence of Community.* Seattle: University of Washington Press, 1991.

Fujitani, Takashi. "Inventing, Forgetting, Remembering: Toward a Historical Ethnography of the Nation State." In *Cultural Nationalism in East Asia: Representation and Identity,* edited by Harumi Befu. Berkeley: Institute of East Asian Studies, University of California Berkeley, 1993.

———. *Splendid Monarchy: Power and Pageantry in Modern Japan.* Berkeley: University of California Press, 1996.

Gaines, Kevin K. *Uplifting the Race: Black Leadership, Politics, and Culture in the Twentieth Century.* Chapel Hill: University of North Carolina Press, 1996.

Geertz, Clifford. *The Interpretation of Cultures.* New York: Basic Books, 1973.

Genovese, Eugene D. *Roll, Jordan, Roll: The World the Slaves Made.* New York: Vintage Books, 1972.

Girdner, Audrie, and Anne Loftis. *The Great Betrayal: The Evacuation of the Japanese-Americans during World War II.* London: Macmillan, 1969.

Gitlin, Todd. *The Sixties: Years of Hope, Days of Rage.* Toronto: Bantam Books, 1987.

Glazer, Nathan. *Ethnic Dilemmas, 1964–1982.* Cambridge, Mass.: Harvard University Press, 1983.

Gleason, Philip. "Identifying Identity: A Semantic History." *Journal of American History* 69, no. 4 (1983): 910–31.

Glenn, Evelyn Nakano. *Issei, Nisei, War Bride: Three Generations of Japanese American Women in Domestic Service.* Philadelphia: Temple University Press, 1986.

Goldberg, Janet. "The Manzanar 'Incident': December 5 to December 19, 1942."

N.d., miscellaneous documents on Manzanar Riot, 1942–43, O 7.00, p. 2, JAERR.

Gordon, Milton M. *Assimilation in American Life: The Role of Race, Religion, and National Origins.* New York: Oxford University Press, 1964.

Grenfell, Michael, and David James, eds. *Bourdieu and Education: Acts of Practical Theory.* London: Falmer Press, 1998.

Gyory, Andrew. *Closing the Gate: Race, Politics, and the Chinese Exclusion Act.* Chapel Hill: University of North Carolina Press, 1998.

Hansen, Arthur A., and David A. Hacker. "The Manzanar Riot: An Ethnic Perspective." *Amerasia Journal* 2, no. 2 (1974): 112–57.

Hansen, Arthur A., and Betty Mitson, eds. *Voices Long Silent: An Oral Inquiry into the Japanese American Evacuation.* Oral History Program. Fullerton: California State University, 1974.

Hatamiya, Leslie T. *Righting a Wrong: Japanese Americans and the Passage of the Civil Liberties Act of 1988.* Stanford, Calif.: Stanford University Press, 1993.

Hayashi, Brian Masaru. *"For the Sake of Our Japanese Brethren": Assimilation, Nationalism, and Protestantism among the Japanese of Los Angeles, 1895–1942.* Stanford, Calif.: Stanford University Press, 1995.

———. *Governing Japanese: Internees, Social Scientists, and Administrators in the Making of America's Concentration Camps.* Princeton: Princeton University Press, forthcoming.

Henry, Sheila E. *Cultural Persistence and Socio Economic Mobility: A Comparative Study of Assimilation among Armenians and Japanese in Los Angeles.* San Francisco: R & E Research Associates, 1978.

Higginbotham, Evelyn Brooks. "African-American Women's History and the Metalanguage of Race." *Signs* 17 (winter 1992): 251–74.

Higgs, Robert. "Landless by Law: Japanese Immigrants in California Agriculture to 1941." *Journal of Economic History* 38 (Mar. 1978): 205–25.

Higham, John. "Current Trends in the Study of Ethnicity in the United States." *Journal of American Ethnic History* 2 (1982): 5–15.

———, ed. *Ethnic Leadership in America.* Baltimore: Johns Hopkins University Press, 1978.

———. *Send These to Me: Immigrants in Urban America.* Rev. ed. Baltimore: Johns Hopkins University Press, 1984.

———. *Strangers in the Land: Problems of American Nativism.* New Brunswick, N.J.: Rutgers University Press, 1955.

Hobsbawm, Eric, and Terence Ranger, eds. *The Invention of Tradition.* Cambridge: Cambridge University Press, 1983.

Hohri, William Minoru. *Repairing America: An Account of the Movement for Japanese-American Redress.* Pullman: Washington State University Press, 1988.

Hosokawa, Bill. *JACL in Quest of Justice: The History of the Japanese American Citizens League.* New York: William Morrow, 1982.

———. *Nisei: The Quiet Americans.* New York: William Morrow, 1969.

Hosokawa, Fumiko. *The Sansei: Social Interaction and Ethnic Identification among the Third-Generation Japanese.* San Francisco: R & E Research Associates, 1978.

Houston, Jeanne Wakatsuki, and James D. Houston. *Farewell to Manzanar: A True Story of Japanese American Experience during and after the World War II Internment.* Boston: Houghton-Mifflin, 1973.

Ichihashi, Yamato. *Japanese in the United States.* Stanford, Calif.: Stanford University Press, 1932.

Ichioka, Yuji. *The Issei: The World of the First Generation Japanese Immigrants, 1885–1924.* New York: The Free Press, 1988.

———. "Japanese Associations and the Japanese Government: A Special Relationship, 1909–1926." *Pacific Historical Review* 46 (1977): 409–37.

———. "Japanese Immigrant Nationalism: The Issei and the Sino-Japanese War, 1937–1941." *California History* 69, no. 3 (1990): 260–75, 310–11.

———. "A Study of Dualism: James Yoshinori Sakamoto and the Japanese American Courier, 1928–1942." *Amerasia Journal* 13, no. 2 (1987): 49–81.

———, ed. *Views from Within: The Japanese American Evacuation and Resettlement Study.* Los Angeles: UCLA Asian American Studies Center, 1989.

Ignacio, Lemel. *Asian Americans and Pacific Islanders.* San Jose, Calif.: Filipino Development and Associates, 1976.

Iriye, Akira. *After Imperialism: The Search for a New Order in the Far East, 1921–1931.* Cambridge, Mass.: Harvard University Press, 1965.

———. *Pacific Estrangement: Japanese and American Expansion, 1897–1911.* Cambridge, Mass.: Harvard University Press, 1972.

Irons, Peter. *Justice at War: The Story of the Japanese American Internment Cases.* New York: Oxford University Press, 1983.

Israely, Hilla Kuttenplan. "An Exploration into Ethnic Identity: The Case of Third-Generation Japanese Americans." Ph.D. diss., University of California, Los Angeles, 1976.

Iwata, Masakazu. "The Japanese Immigrants in California Agriculture." *Agricultural History* 36 (1962): 25–37.

———. *Planted in Good Soil: A History of the Issei in the United States Agriculture.* American University Studies, ser. 9, *History,* vol. 1. New York: Peter Lang, 1992.

Jackman, Norman R. "Collective Protest in Relocation Centers." *American Journal of Sociology* 63, no. 3 (1957): 264–72.

———. "Collective Protest in Relocation Centers." Ph.D. diss., University of California, Berkeley, 1955.

Jacobson, Matthew Frye. *Special Sorrows: The Diasporic Imagination of Irish, Polish, and Jewish Immigrants in the United States.* Cambridge, Mass.: Harvard University Press, 1995.

Jensen, Richard C., and Cara J. Abeyta. "The Minority in the Middle: Asian-American Dissent in the 1960s and 1970s." *Western Journal of Speech Communication* 51, no. 4 (1987): 402–16.

Kagiwada, George. "Ethnic Identification and Socio-Economic Status: The Case of the Japanese-Americans in Los Angeles." Ph.D. diss., University of California, Los Angeles, 1969.

Kelley, Robin D. G. "'We Are Not What We Seem': Rethinking Black Working-class Opposition in the Jim Crow South." *Journal of American History* 80, no. 1 (1993): 75–112.

Kendis, Kaoru Oguri. *A Matter of Comfort: Ethnic Maintenance and Ethnic Style among Third-Generation Japanese Americans.* New York: AMS Press, 1989.

King, Rebecca Chiyoko. "The Changing Face of Japanese America: The Making and Remaking of Race in the Japanese American Community." Ph.D. diss., University of California, Berkeley, 1998.

Kitano, Harry H. L. *Japanese Americans: Evolution of a Subculture.* Englewood Cliffs, N.J.: Prentice-Hall, 1969.

Kiyota, Minoru. *Beyond Loyalty: The Story of a Kibei.* Trans. Linda Keplinger Keenan. Honolulu: University of Hawaii Press, 1997.

Kumamoto, Bob. "The Search for Spies: American Counterintelligence and the Japanese American Community, 1931–1942." *Amerasia Journal* 6, no. 2 (1979): 45–75.

Kung, S. W. *Chinese in American Life: Some Aspects of Their History, Status, Problems, and Contributions.* Seattle: University of Washington Press, 1962.

Kutler, Stanley I. *The American Inquisition: Justice and Injustice in the Cold War.* New York: Hill and Wang, 1982.

Kwong, Peter. *The New Chinatown.* New York: Noonday Press, 1987.

Ladurie, Emmanuel Leroy. *Carnival in Romans.* New York: George Braziller, 1979.

Lark, Regina. "They Challenged Two Nations: Marriages between Japanese Women and American GIs, 1945 to the Present." Ph.D. diss., University of Southern California, 1999.

Leonard, Karen Isaksen. *Making Ethnic Choices: California's Punjabi Mexican Americans.* Philadelphia: Temple University Press, 1992.

Levine, Gene N., and Colbert Rhodes. *The Japanese American Community: A Three-Generation Study.* New York: Praeger, 1981.

Levine, Lawrence W. *Black Culture and Black Consciousness: Afro-American Folk Thought from Slavery to Freedom.* New York: Oxford University Press, 1977.

Lewin, Kurt. "The Problem of Minority Leadership." In *Studies in Leadership: Leadership and Democratic Action,* edited by Alvin W. Gouldner, 192–94. New York: Russell and Russell, 1965.

Light, Ivan H. *Ethnic Enterprise in America: Business and Welfare among Chinese, Japanese, and Blacks.* Berkeley: University of California Press, 1972.

Ling, Susie. "The Mountain Movers: Asian American Women's Movement in Los Angeles." *Amerasia Journal* 15, no. 1 (1989): 51–67.

Lipsitz, George. *Time Passages: Collective Memory and American Popular Culture.* Minneapolis: University of Minnesota Press, 1990.

Lourerio, Pedro. "Japanese Espionage and American Countermeasures in Pre-Pearl Harbor California." *Journal of American-East Asian Relations* 3 (fall 1994): 197–210.

———. "The Imperial Japanese Navy and Espionage: The Itaru Tachibana Case." *International Journal of Intelligence and Counterintelligence* 3 (spring 1989): 105–21.

Lowe, Lisa. *Immigrant Acts: On Asian American Cultural Politics.* Durham, N.C.: Duke University Press, 1998.

Lyman, Stanford M. *The Asian in North America*. Santa Barbara, Calif.: ABC-Clio, 1977.

MacAloon, John J. "Introduction: Cultural Performances, Cultural Theory." In *Rite, Drama, Festival, Spectacle: Rehearsal toward a Theory of Cultural Performance*, edited by John J. MacAloon. Philadelphia: Institute for the Study of Human Issues, 1984.

——, ed. *Rite, Drama, Festival, Spectacle: Rehearsal toward a Theory of Cultural Performance*. Philadelphia: Institute for the Study of Human Issues, 1984.

Marchetti, Gina. *Romance and the "Yellow Peril": Race, Sex, and Discursive Strategies in Hollywood Fiction*. Berkeley: University of California Press, 1993.

Mass, Amy Iwasaki. "Interracial Japanese Americans: The Best of Both Worlds or the End of the Japanese Community." In *Racially Mixed People in America*, edited by Maria P. P. Root. Newbury Park, Calif.: Sage, 1992.

Matsumoto, Valerie. "Desperately Seeking 'Dierdre': Gender Roles, Multicultural Relations, and Nisei Women Writers of the 1930s." *Frontiers* 12, no. 1: 19–32.

——. *Farming the Home Place: A Japanese American Community in California, 1919–1928*. Ithaca, N.Y.: Cornell University Press, 1993.

——. "Japanese American Women during World War II." In *Unequal Sisters: A Multicultural Reader in U.S. Women's History*, edited by Ellen Carol Dubois and Vicki L. Ruiz. New York: Routledge, 1990.

Maykovich, Minako K. *Japanese American Identity Dilemma*. Tokyo: Waseda University Press, 1972.

——. "Political Activation of Japanese American Youth." *Journal of Social Issues* 29, no. 2 (1973): 167–85.

Misaki, H. K. "Delinquency and Crime." In *Vocational Aptitudes of Second-Generation Japanese in the United States*, edited by Edward K. Strong Jr. et al. Stanford, Calif.: Stanford University Publications, Educational Psychology, no. 1, 1933.

Miyamoto, S. Frank. *Social Solidarity among the Japanese in Seattle*. Seattle: University of Washington Press in cooperation with the Asian American Studies Program, University of Washington, 1984.

Modell, John. "Class or Ethnic Solidarity: The Japanese American Company Union." *Pacific Historical Review* 38 (1969): 192–206.

——. *The Economics and Politics of Racial Accommodation: The Japanese of Los Angeles, 1900–1942*. Urbana: University of Illinois Press, 1977.

Modell, John, and Edna Bonacich. *The Economic Basis of Ethnic Solidarity: A Study of Japanese Americans*. Berkeley: University of California Press, 1981.

Montero, Darrel. *Japanese Americans: Changing Patterns of Ethnic Affiliation over Three Generations*. Boulder, Colo.: Westview Press, 1980.

Mori, Robert Yoshio. "The Dilemma of Small Business in Little Tokyo Redevelopment." Student paper, Asian American Studies Reading Room Collections, UCLA, 1974.

Mori, Steven. "Little Tokyo Redevelopment: Who Is It For?" Student paper, Asian American Studies Reading Room Collections, UCLA, 1977.

Moriyama, Alan Takeo. *Imingaisha: Japanese Emigration Companies and Hawaii, 1894–1908.* Honolulu: University of Hawaii Press, 1985.

Murase, Ichiro Mike. *Little Tokyo: One Hundred Years in Pictures.* Los Angeles: Visual Communications/Asian American Studies Central, 1983.

Myer, Dillon S. *Uprooted Americans: The Japanese Americans and the War Relocation Authority during World War II.* Tucson: University of Arizona Press, 1971.

Nakayama, Thomas K. "'Model Minority' and the Media: Discourse on Asian America." *Journal of Communication Inquiry* 12, no. 1 (1988): 65–73.

Neu, Charles E. *An Uncertain Friendship: Theodore Roosevelt and Japan, 1906–1909.* Cambridge, Mass.: Harvard University Press, 1967.

Ngai, Mae M. "The Architecture of Race in American Immigration Law: A Reexamination of the Immigration Act of 1924." *Journal of American History* 86 (June 1999): 67–92.

———. "Illegal Aliens and Alien Citizens: United States Immigration Policy and Racial Formation, 1924–1945." Ph.D. diss., Columbia University, 1998.

Nishi, Midori. "Changing Occupance of Japanese in Los Angeles County, 1940–1950." Ph.D. diss., University of Washington, 1955.

———. "Japanese Settlement in the Los Angeles Area." *Association of Pacific Coast Geographers Yearbook* 20 (1958): 35–48.

Nishi, Midori, and Young Il Kim. "Recent Japanese Settlement Changes in the Los Angeles Area." *Association of Pacific Coast Geographers Yearbook* 26 (1964): 24–32.

Nishimoto, Richard. "Japanese in Personal Services and Urban Trade." Manuscript, n.d. Folder W 1.90 Japanese American Evacuation and Resettlement Records, BANC MSS 67/14 C. Bancroft Library, University of California, Berkeley.

Notoji, Masako. "The Effect of Ethnicity on Work Attitudes: A Study of Japanese American Employees of Japanese Multinational Corporations in Southern California." Master's thesis, UCLA, 1980.

Okihiro, Gary Y. "African and Asian American Studies: A Comparative Analysis and Commentary." In *Asian Americans: Comparative and Global Perspectives,* edited by Shirley Hune et al. Pullman: Washington State University Press, 1991.

———. *Cane Fires: The Anti-Japanese Movement in Hawaii.* Philadelphia: Temple University Press, 1991.

———. "Japanese Resistance in America's Concentration Camps: A Reevaluation." *Amerasia Journal* 1, no. 2 (1973): 20–34.

———. *Margins and Mainstreams: Asians in American History and Culture.* Seattle: University of Washington Press, 1994.

Okimoto, Daniel. "Autobiography of a Sansei Female." In *Roots: An Asian American Reader,* edited by AmyTachiki, Eddie Wong, Franklin Odo, and Buck Wong. Los Angeles: UCLA Asian American Studies Center, 1971.

———. "The Intolerence of Success." In *Roots: An Asian American Reader,* edited by AmyTachiki, Eddie Wong, Franklin Odo, and Buck Wong. Los Angeles: UCLA Asian American Studies Center, 1971.

Omatsu, Glenn. "The 'Four Prisons' and the Movements for Liberation." *Amerasia Journal* 15, no. 1 (1989): xv–xxx.

Omi, Michael, and Howard Winant. *Racial Formation in the United States: From the 1960s to the 1980s.* New York: Routledge and Kegan Paul, 1986.

Opler, Morris Edward. "A History of Internal Government at Manzanar, March 1942 to December 6, 1942." July 15, 1944, O 3.02, pp. 84–85, JAERR.

Orsi, Robert Anthony. *The Madonna on 115th Street: Faith and Community in Italian Harlem, 1880–1950.* New Haven: Yale University Press, 1985.

Osajima, Keith. "Asian Americans as the Model Minority: An Analysis of the Popular Press Image in the 1960s and 1980s." In *Reflections on Shattered Windows: Promises and Prospectus for Asian American Studies,* edited by Gary Okihiro et al. Pullman: Washington State University Press, 1988.

Ozouf, Mona. *Festivals and the French Revolution.* Cambridge, Mass.: Harvard University Press, 1988.

Park, Robert E. "Human Migration and the Marginal Man." *American Journal of Sociology* 33 (May 1928): 881–93.

Peffer, George Anthony. *If They Don't Bring Their Women Here: Chinese Female Immigration Before Exclusion.* Urbana: University of Illinois Press, 1999.

Petersen, William. *Japanese Americans: Oppression and Success.* New York: Random House, 1971.

———. "Success Story: Japanese American Style." *New York Times Magazine* (Jan. 9, 1966): 22–26.

Polenberg, Richard. *One Nation Divisible: Class, Race, and Ethnicity in the United States since 1938.* New York: Viking Press, 1980.

Pyle, Kenneth. *The New Generation in Meiji Japan: Problems of Cultural Identity, 1885–1895.* Stanford, Calif.: Stanford University Press, 1969.

Robinson, David. *Chaplin: His Life and Art.* New York: McGraw-Hill, 1985.

Root, Maria P. P., ed. *Racially Mixed People in America.* Newbury Park, Calif.: Sage, 1992.

Rosaldo, Renato. *Culture and Truth: The Remaking of Social Analysis.* Boston: Beacon Press, 1989.

———. "Others of Invention: Ethnicity and Its Discontents." *Voice Literary Supplement* (Feb. 1990): 27–29.

Rosenstone, Robert A. *Mirror in the Shrine: American Encounters with Meiji Japan.* Cambridge, Mass.: Harvard University Press, 1988.

Ryan, Mary P. *Women in Public: Between Banners and Ballots, 1825–1880.* Baltimore: Johns Hopkins University Press, 1990.

Sakoda, James. "Personal Adjustment." Unpublished manuscript, January 12, 1943, pp. 17–18, folder 11, "James Sakoda Reports on Tule Lake." R 20.86, JAERR.

Sadanaga, Kenneth K. "Redevelopment in Little Tokyo: Amerasia Bookstore." Student paper, Asian American Studies Reading Room Collections, UCLA, 1981.

Said, Edward. *Orientalism.* New York: Vintage Books, 1978.

Sánchez, George J. *Becoming Mexican American: Ethnicity, Culture, and Identity in Chicano Los Angeles.* New York: Oxford University Press, 1993.

Sawada, Mitziko. "Culprits and Gentlemen: Meiji Japan's Restrictions of Emigrants to the United States, 1891–1909." *Pacific Historical Review* 60, no. 3 (1991): 339–59.

Schultz, April. "'The Pride of the Race Has Been Touched': The 1925 Norse-American Immigration Centennial and Ethnic Identity." *Journal of American History* 77, no. 4 (Mar. 1991): 1265–95.

Scott, James C. *Domination and the Arts of Resistance: Hidden Transcripts*. New Haven, Conn.: Yale University Press, 1990.

———. *Weapons of the Weak: Everyday Forms of Peasant Resistance*. New Haven, Conn.: Yale University Press, 1985.

Scott, Joan Wallach. *Gender and the Politics of History*. New York: Columbia University Press, 1988.

Shirado, Joyce. "Task Force." Student paper, Asian American Studies Reading Room Collections, UCLA, 1974.

Shirota, Jon. *Pineapple White*. Los Angeles: Ohara Publications, 1972.

Smith, Anthony D. *The Ethnic Origins of Nations*. Oxford: Basil Blackwell, 1986.

———. "The Nation: Invented, Imagined, Reconstructed?" In *Reimagining the Nation*, edited by Marjorie Ringrose and Adam J. Lerner, 9–28. Buckingham: Open University Press in association with *Millennium: Journal of International Studies*, 1993.

Spickard, Paul R. *Mixed Blood: Intermarriage and Ethnic Identity in Twentieth-Century America*. Madison: University of Wisconsin Press, 1989.

———. "Injustice Compounded: Amerasians and Non-Japanese in America's World War II Concentration Camps." *Journal of American Ethnic History* 5 (spring 1986): 5–22.

———. *Japanese Americans: The Formation and Transformations of an Ethnic Group*. New York: Twayne, 1996.

———. "*Nisei* Assume Power: The Japanese Citizens League, 1941–1942." *Pacific Historical Review* 52, no. 2 (1983): 147–74.

Stephan, John J. *Hawaii under the Rising Sun: Japan's Plans for Conquest after Pearl Harbor*. Honolulu: University of Hawaii Press, 1984.

Stonequist, Everett V. *The Marginal Man: A Study in Personality and Culture Conflict*. 1937. Reprint, New York: Russell and Russell, 1961.

Strong, Edward K., Jr. *The Second Generation Japanese Problem*. Stanford, Calif.: Stanford University Press, 1934.

Suenaga, Shizuko. "Good-bye to Sayonara: The Reverse Assimilation of Japanese War Brides." Ph.D. diss., Boston College, 1996.

Suzuki, Bob H. "Education and the Socialization of Asian Americans: A Revisionist Analysis of the 'Model Minority' Thesis." *Amerasia Journal* 4, no. 2 (1977): 23–51.

Suzuki, Masao. "Success Story? Japanese Immigrant Economic Achievement and Return Migration, 1920–1930." *Journal of Economic History* 55 (Dec. 1995): 889–901.

Tachiki, Amy, Eddie Wong, Franklin Odo, Buck Wong, eds. *Roots: An Asian American Reader*. Los Angeles: UCLA Asian American Studies Center, 1971.

Takagi, Dana Y. "Maiden Voyage: Excursion into Sexuality and Identity Poli-
tics in Asian America." *Amerasia Journal* 20, no. 1 (1994): 1–17.
———. *The Retreat from Race: Asian American Admissions and Racial Politics.*
New Brunswick, N.J.: Rutgers University Press, 1992.
Takagi, Paul. "The Myth of Assimilation in American Life." *Amerasia Journal*
1, no. 2 (fall 1973): 149–57.
Takahashi, Jere. "Japanese American Responses to Race Relations: The Forma-
tion of *Nisei* Perspectives." *Amerasia Journal* 9, no. 1 (June 1982): 29–57.
———. Nisei /Sansei: *Shifting Japanese American Identities and Politics.* Phila-
delphia: Temple University Press, 1997.
Takaki, Ronald T. *Iron Cages: Race and Culture in Nineteenth-Century Amer-
ica.* New York: Knopf, 1979.
———. *Pau Hana: Plantation Life and Labor in Hawaii, 1835–1920.* Hono-
lulu: University of Hawaii Press, 1983.
———. *Strangers from a Different Shore: A History of Asian Americans.* Bos-
ton: Little, Brown, 1989.
Takezawa, Yasuko I. *Breaking the Silence: Redress and Japanese American Eth-
nicity.* Ithaca, N.Y.: Cornell University Press, 1995.
Tamura, Eileen. *Americanization, Acculturation, and Ethnic Identity: The* Nisei
Generation in Hawaii. Urbana: University of Illinois Press, 1994.
Tanaka, Ron. "I hate my wife for her flat yellow face." In *Roots: An Asian
American Reader,* edited by AmyTachiki, Eddie Wong, Franklin Odo, and
Buck Wong. Los Angeles: UCLA Asian American Studies Center, 1971.
TenBroek, Jacobus, Edward N. Barnhard, and Floyd W. Matson. *Prejudice, War,
and the Constitution.* Berkeley: University of California Press, 1954.
Thomas, Dorothy Swaine, with Charles Kikuchi and James Sakoda. *The Sal-
vage.* Berkeley: University of California Press, 1952.
Thomas, Dorothy Swaine, and Richard Nishimoto. *The Spoilage.* Berkeley: Uni-
versity of California Press, 1946.
Thompson, E. P. *The Making of the English Working Class.* New York: Vintage
Books, 1966.
Thornton, Michael C. "The Quiet Immigration: Foreign Spouses of U.S. Citi-
zens, 1945–1985." In *Racially Mixed People in America,* edited by Maria
P. P. Root. Newbury Park, Calif.: Sage, 1992.
Turner, Victor, ed. *Celebration: Studies in Festivity and Ritual.* Washington,
D.C.: Smithsonian Institution Press, 1982.
Ulm, Gerith von. *Charlie Chaplin: King of Tragedy.* Caldwell, Idaho: Caxton
Printers, 1940.
U.S. Bureau of the Census. Characteristics of the Population, 1920.
———. 1930.
———. 1940.
———. 1950.
———. 1960
———. 1970
———. 1980.
———. *Historical Statistics of the United States, Colonial Times to 1970,* Bi-

centennial Edition, vol. 1. Washington, D.C.: U.S. Bureau of the Census, Department of Commerce, 1975, 107.

U.S. Immigration and Naturalization Service. *Statistical Yearbook of the INS.* 1990.

Uono, Kiyoshi. "The Factors Affecting the Geographical Aggregation and Dispersion of the Japanese Residences in the City of Los Angeles." Master's thesis, UCLA, 1927.

Uyeda, Clifford I. "The Pardoning of 'Tokyo Rose': A Report on the Restoration of American Citizenship to Iva Ikuko Toguri." *Amerasia Journal* 5, no. 2 (fall 1978): 6–94.

Uyematsu, Amy. "The Emergence of Yellow Power in America." In *Roots: An Asian American Reader,* edited by Amy Tachiki, Eddie Wong, Franklin Odo, with Buck Wong, 9–13. Los Angeles: UCLA Asian American Studies Center, 1971.

Varon, Barbara F. "The Japanese Americans: Comparative Occupational Status, 1960 and 1950." *Demography* 4 (1967): 809–19.

Vecoli, Rudolf. "Contadini in Chicago: A Critique of the Uprooted." *Journal of American History* 51 (Dec. 1964): 404–17.

Vigil, James Diego. *Barrio Gangs: Street Life and Identity in Southern California.* Austin: University of Texas Press, 1988.

Wacker, R. Fred. *Ethnicity, Pluralism, and Race: Race Relations Theory in America before Myrdal.* Westport, Conn.: Greenwood Press, 1983.

Wakatsuki, Yasuo. "Japanese Emigration to the United States, 1866–1924." *Perspectives in American History* 12 (1979): 389–516.

Warren, William Halford. "Asian Populations in Los Angeles County: A Focus on the Development of Japanese Communities from a Cartographic and Landscape Perspective." Master's thesis, UCLA, 1985.

Waugh, Isami Arufuku. "Hidden Crime and Deviance in the Japanese-American Community." Ph.D. diss., University of California, Berkeley, 1978.

Weglyn, Michi. *Years of Infamy: The Untold Story of America's Concentration Camps.* New York: Morrow Quill, 1976.

Wei, William. *The Asian American Movement.* Philadelphia: Temple University Press, 1993.

Williams, Theresa Kay. "Prism Lives: Identity of Binational Amerasians." In *Racially Mixed People in America,* edited by Maria P. P. Root. Newbury Park, Calif.: Sage, 1992.

Wilson, Robert A., and Bill Hosokawa. *East to America: The History of Japanese in the United States.* New York: William Morrow, 1980.

Wilson, William Julius. *The Declining Significance of Race: Blacks and Changing American Institutions.* Chicago: University of Chicago Press, 1980.

———. *The Truly Disadvantaged: The Inner City, the Underclass, and Public Policy.* Chicago: University of Chicago Press, 1987.

Wong, K. Scott. "Liang Qichao and the Chinese of America: A Re-evaluation of His *Selected Memoir of Travels in the New World.*" *Journal of American Ethnic History* 11, no. 4 (summer 1992): 3–24.

Yanagisako, Sylvia Junko. *Transforming the Past: Tradition and Kinship among Japanese Americans.* Stanford, Calif.: Stanford University Press, 1985.

Yanagita, Kunio. *About Our Ancestors—The Japanese Family System*. Trans. Fanny Hagin Mayer and Ishiwara Yasuyo. Tokyo: Mombusho, 1970. Reprint, New York: Greenwood Press, 1988.

Yatsuhiro, Toshio, Iwao Ishino, and Yoshiharu Matsumoto. "The Japanese American Looks at Resettlement." *The Public Opinion Quarterly* 8 (summer 1944): 188–201.

Yoo, David K. *Growing Up Nisei: Race, Generation, and Culture among Japanese Americans of California, 1924–49*. Urbana: University of Illinois Press, 2000.

———. "'Read All about It': Race, Generation, and the Japanese American Ethnic Press, 1925–41." *Amerasia Journal* 19, no.1 (1993): 69–92.

Zunz, Olivier. "American History and the Changing Meaning of Assimilation." *Journal of American Ethnic History* 4 (spring 1985): 53–84.

———. *The Changing Face of Inequality: Urbanization, Industrial Development, and Immigrants in Detroit, 1880–1920*. Chicago: University of Chicago Press, 1982.

Index

Abiko, Kyutaro, 25–26, 35
Abrahams, Roger, 60
advertising campaigns (Nisei Week), 43–48
African Americans. *See* black Americans
agriculture: and Alien Land Act, 110, 236n86; during the depression, 23; Issei success in, 18–19, 22; Nisei Week role of, 54, 55 fig.; postwar losses in, 127–28
Aihara, Yae, 135–36, 137
Alien Land Act (1913), 17, 18–19, 110, 123, 134, 236n86
Americanism: citizenship theme of, 29–30, 63–65; class-based response to, 37–38, 91–95; *Doho* on, 69; Issei's lack of, 34–36; as JACL priority, 3, 58–59, 67–69, 77, 79–80, 115–16; of Manzanar fair, 76; Nisei's lack of, 36–37; of Nisei Week events, 55 fig., 145–47; radicals' rearticulation of, 152–53; retreat from, in Pacific Rim era, 138–43; "white identities" of, 163–65. *See also* cosmopolitan identity
American Legion, 59, 66, 109, 134
anti-Axis committee (JACL), 79
Archdeacon, Thomas J., 222n5
Ariyoshi, Koji, 90
Asian American movement. *See* radical youth movement
assimilation: ethnic identity's compromise with, xiii–xiv, 163–65; of in-

ternee resettlers, 104–6; of "marginal men," 2–3, 218n5; in mid-1960s, 137; retentionist debate with, 3–6, 220n11. *See also* Americanism; integration

baby contest (Nisei Week), 56, 146–47
Bakhtin, Mikhail, 41
Barnes, Janet, 179
beauty pageant (Nisei Week): and American standards, 55 fig., 145–47; and biculturalism, 54, 56, 64, 64 fig., 173; ethnic pride's centrality to, 173–75, 184; female leadership of, 176–77; hapa controversy of, 178–81, 182–83, 185; Japan's connection to, 142, 194–95, 197; kimonos in, 57; mixed-Asian contestants in, 183; and queens' reunion, 177–78; radicals' condemnation of, 165, 166–67; voting for contestants in, 44, 129, 130 fig.; WCC's attack on, 171–73
biculturalism: beauty pageant's expression of, 54, 56, 64, 64 fig., 173; of Issei leadership, 25–26; JACL's retreat from, 67–69, 77, 79; of Nisei, 25, 138–39; Nisei Week's vision of, 42–43, 48, 48 fig., 59–60; postwar collapse of, 120–21; and U.S.-Japan trade, 139–43, 195–96
Biddle, Francis, 82
Biltmore Hotel (Los Angeles), 54, 55 fig.

CPSIA information can be obtained
at www.ICGtesting.com
Printed in the USA
FSOW02n0759181016
26274FS